T0301347

Rigour and Relevance in Entrepreneurship
Research, Resources and Outcomes

# Rigour and Relevance in Entrepreneurship Research, Resources and Outcomes

Frontiers in European Entrepreneurship Research

*Edited by*

Eddy Laveren

*Professor, University of Antwerp and Antwerp Management School, Belgium*

Robert Blackburn

*Professor, Small Business Research Centre, Kingston University, UK*

Ulla Hytti

*Research Director, University of Turku, Finland*

Hans Landström

*Professor, Sten K. Johnson Centre for Entrepreneurship, Lund University, Sweden*

IN ASSOCIATION WITH THE ECSB

Cheltenham, UK • Northampton, MA, USA

Published by
Edward Elgar Publishing Limited
The Lypiatts
15 Lansdown Road
Cheltenham
Glos GL50 2JA
UK

Edward Elgar Publishing, Inc.
William Pratt House
9 Dewey Court
Northampton
Massachusetts 01060
USA

A catalogue record for this book
is available from the British Library

Library of Congress Control Number: 2019947919

This book is available electronically in the **Elgar**online
Business subject collection
DOI 10.4337/9781789903980

ISBN 978 1 78990 397 3 (cased)
ISBN 978 1 78990 398 0 (eBook)

Printed and bound in Great Britain by TJ International Ltd, Padstow, Cornwall

# Contents

# Contributors

| | |
|---|---|
| **Maria Aggestam** | Sten K. Johnson Centre for Entrepreneurship, Lund University, Sweden |
| **Robert Blackburn** | Small Business Research Centre, Kingston University, UK |
| **Christine Blanka** | Institute for Entrepreneurship and Organizational Development, Johannes Kepler University Linz, Austria |
| **Ethel Brundin** | Jönköping International Business School, Jönköping University, Sweden |
| **Francesca Maria Cesaroni** | Department of Economics, Society and Politics, University of Urbino Carlo Bo, Italy |
| **Immanuel Commarmond** | Mindstate Set for Growth (PTY) Ltd, Cape Town, South Africa |
| **Serena Cubico** | Department of Business Administration, University of Verona, Italy |
| **Karin Hellerstedt** | Jönköping International Business School, Jönköping University, Sweden |
| **Ulla Hytti** | University of Turku, Finland |
| **Anders Isaksson** | Chalmers University of Technology, Sweden |
| **Marfuga Iskandarova** | Small Business Research Centre, Kingston University, UK |
| **Amélie Jacquemin** | Louvain Research Institute in Management and Organizations, Université Catholique de Louvain, Mons, Belgium |
| **Frank Janssen** | Louvain Research Institute in Management and Organizations, Université Catholique de Louvain, Louvain-La-Neuve, Belgium |
| **Norbert Kailer** | Institute for Entrepreneurship and Organizational Development, Johannes Kepler University Linz, Austria |

| | |
|---|---|
| **John Kitching** | Small Business Research Centre, Kingston University, UK |
| **Stefan Koch** | Institute for Business Informatics – Information Engineering, Johannes Kepler University Linz, Austria |
| **Hans Landström** | Sten K. Johnson Centre for Entrepreneurship, Lund University, Sweden |
| **Eddy Laveren** | University of Antwerp and Antwerp Management School, Belgium |
| **Hans Löfsten** | Chalmers University of Technology, Sweden |
| **Piritta Parkkari** | University of Lapland, Finland |
| **David Rückel** | Institute for Business Informatics – Information Engineering, Johannes Kepler University Linz, Austria |
| **Hanna Rydehell** | Chalmers University of Technology, Sweden |
| **Annalisa Sentuti** | Department of Economics, Society and Politics, University of Urbino Carlo Bo, Italy |
| **Kelly G. Shaver** | College of Charleston and MindCette, Charleston, USA |
| **Anna Stevenson** | Sten K. Johnson Centre for Entrepreneurship, Lund University, Sweden |
| **Karen Verduijn** | VU University Amsterdam, the Netherlands |
| **Caroline Wigren-Kristoferson** | Sten K. Johnson Centre for Entrepreneurship, Lund University, Sweden |
| **Johan Wiklund** | Whitman School of Management, Syracuse University, USA |
| **Amélie Wuillaume** | Louvain Research Institute in Management and Organizations, Université Catholique de Louvain, Mons, Belgium |

# Acknowledgements

We would like to thank Edward Elgar Publishing for their encouragement and support in the development of this book. We are also grateful for the reviewers listed below who helped in the selection and development of the chapters:

Gry Agnete Alsos, Nord University, Norway
Martina Battisti, Portsmouth University, UK
Robert Blackburn, Kingston University, UK
Richard Blundel, Open University, UK
Tiago Botelho, Norwich Business School, UK
Malin Brännback, Åbo Akademi, Finland
Servane Delanoe Gueguen, Toulouse Business School, France
Dimo Dimov, University of Bath, UK
Ziad El-Awad, Lund University, Sweden
Kerstin Ettl, University of Siegen, Siegen, Germany
Maribel Guerrero, Northumbria University, UK
Gustav Hägg, Lund University, Sweden
Jarna Heinonen, University of Turku, Finland
Julie Hermans, Université de Louvain – Mons, Belgium
Ulla Hytti, University of Turku, Finland
Frank Janssen, Université Catholique de Louvain, Belgium
Inna Kozlinska, University of Groeningen, the Netherlands
Hans Landström, Lund University, Sweden
Eddy Laveren, University of Antwerp and Antwerp Management School,
    Belgium
Agnieszka Kurczewska, University of Lodz, Poland
Elisabet Ljunggren, Nord University, Norway
Colm O'Gorman, Dublin City University, Ireland
Annaleena Parhankangas, South Dakota State University, USA
Tobias Pret, Pace University, USA
Elena Ruskovaara, Lappeenranta University of Technology, Finland
Silke Tegtmeier, University of Southern Denmark
Richard Tunstall, Leeds University, UK
Lex Van Teeffelen, HU Business School Utrecht, the Netherlands
Edwin Weesie, HU Business School Utrecht, the Netherlands
Mirela Xheneti, University of Sussex, Brighton, UK

# 1. Introduction: rigour and relevance in European entrepreneurship research

**Eddy Laveren, Robert Blackburn, Ulla Hytti and Hans Landström**

## INTRODUCING THE CHAPTERS

Although entrepreneurship research has progressed significantly in the past 40 years or so, a possible gap between the relevance and rigour in our research has emerged. This issue has exercised researchers in business and management for some time (e.g. Hodgkinson and Rousseau, 2009) and has also been identified as an issue in the field of entrepreneurship (Frank and Landström, 2016). Given the applied nature of the field of entrepreneurship, it is important that researchers understand and realize the benefits of connectivity with practitioners, consultants and policy makers, ultimately to have an impact on real-world activities. Whilst this is happening and there are exemplary cases of such engagement (see Ram et al., 2017), more is needed if we are to see entrepreneurship research help shape the economy and society. Organizations, such as the European Council for Small Business and Entrepreneurship (ECSB) and the International Council for Small Business (ICSB), its global equivalent, provide a forum in which this kind of dialogue can be initiated and take place.

This volume presents chapters that demonstrate contemporary examples of excellent research in the field and their relevance to policy and practice, directly or indirectly. The chapters are organized in three parts. In Part I, four chapters are presented regarding rigour and relevance in entrepreneurship research. In Part II, two chapters are presented about the entrepreneurial mindset and intrapreneurial orientation as factors of entrepreneurial behaviour. In Part III, attention is given to four chapters regarding entrepreneurial behaviour, resources and outcomes.

PART I:        RIGOUR AND RELEVANCE IN
                     ENTREPRENEURSHIP RESEARCH

In Chapter 2, Johan Wiklund starts with some references stating that tenure
track faculty are spending too much time and effort on research that is only
of interest and value to them and their peers, while the bill for the research is
being paid by those who receive little or nothing in return. However, Wiklund
argues that relevance in research is not merely an option, but a matter of survival. Wiklund believes that the outlook for entrepreneurship research might
be more positive and likely to have a great societal impact. His text suggests
that entrepreneurship is well equipped for relevant research. He presents a different model for generating interest in research. In this model a distinction is
made between the number of people that care versus how much people care
about the research. Wiklund advocates an approach to relevance that starts
with researchers asking themselves what they really care about themselves and
try to find other people that care about this research.

In Chapter 3, Hans Landström argues that one requirement of good research
is that our knowledge should not only attract interest among our peers, but
also be useful for external stakeholders such as entrepreneurs, investors,
policy makers and politicians, the media and our students. Traditionally,
entrepreneurship and small business research has been regarded as a practical
and relevant research field, providing knowledge to be used to solve various
societal problems. As the field is becoming more and more institutionalized in
the academic system, scientific rigour in research has been emphasized at the
expense of relevance, triggering frustration among many entrepreneurship and
small business scholars.

Bridging the gap between scientific rigour and practical relevance is a task
not only to be accomplished by senior scholars, but also by young scholars.
Therefore, the issue needs to be addressed in the infrastructure of universities and business schools, for example, by adapting the incentive criteria for
promotion, or encouraging PhD students with practical experience who can
serve as role models. Landström strives to show, in Chapter 3, that producing research with practical relevance does not conflict with the production
of scientifically rigorous research. On the contrary, it is important that the
implications formulated for external stakeholders are well-rooted in rigorous
scientific research. The conclusion to be drawn is that we need research that is
scientifically rigorous, practically relevant and actionable.

Entrepreneurship as a field of research has expanded in a number of directions, with a wide range of ontological, epistemological, methodological,
theoretical and empirical variations existing alongside one another. In Chapter
4, Parkkari and Verduijn provide an introduction to three recent conversations

within the entrepreneurship research domain: (1) Critical Entrepreneurship Studies (CES), which has emerged to question and challenge mainstream, taken-for-granted understandings and ways of researching entrepreneurship; (2) Entrepreneurship as Practice (EaP), which incorporates an interest in doing entrepreneurship as an everyday practice by utilizing social practice theories; and (3) a Radical Processual Approach (RPA) towards entrepreneurship, which incorporates process philosophical premises to studying entrepreneuring as flux, as constant becoming. These conversations offer radical, complex and nuanced ways of understanding the entrepreneurship phenomena, to open it up so that novel possibilities, practical or conceptual, can materialize. An appreciation of the specific value each conversation might bring to entrepreneurship research is also discussed.

In many European countries family firms play an important role. In recent decades, one of the main changes occurring in family firms has been the increasing involvement of women in their ownership, leadership and management. In Chapter 5, Sentuti, Cesaroni and Cubico aim to contribute to the ongoing debate through a structured literature review of studies in the business and management literature, by exploring and outlining the state of the art of relevant research topics concerning women's involvement in family firms. Sentuti et al. include author affiliation as well as the location of research. The country of research is particularly relevant for analysing women in family firms because cultural models, traditional values and rules embedded in social behaviours may differ among countries. Three important tendencies were identified. First, there is a significant increase in the number of publications over the period 2000–2017. Second, this field of research is no longer North American scholar dominated, as a growing contribution is now coming from European researchers. Third, the geographical context of research has progressively expanded from North America and the UK towards other countries such as those in Northern and Southern Europe, Asia and Africa. With regard to the focus of literature concerning women's involvement in family firms, four main themes are identified and discussed: women in family firms, succession, women-owned family firms and female entrepreneurship, and a new theme, copreneurial ventures.

## PART II: ENTREPRENEURIAL MINDSET AND INTRAPRENEURIAL ORIENTATION

In Part II, two chapters are presented that examine entrepreneurial attitudes and factors predicting entrepreneurial activity or behaviour. In Chapter 6, Shaver and Commarmond present a model for developing a scale regarding measuring the entrepreneurial mindset. The authors believe that none of the previous existing measures capture the full breadth of individual differences that can be said to constitute the entrepreneurial mindset as explanations for entrepreneurial behaviour. A comprehensive approach to measuring the entrepreneurial mindset must, according to Shaver and Commarmond, (1) assess cognitive processes and behavioural tendencies as well as traditional personality traits, and (2) do so while paying attention to the varied roles that an entrepreneur might play. Based on a literature review and further quantitative analysis, the authors identified 37 separate constructs from the 76 conceptual statements found in the literature. They create a list of 116 items to assess these constructs. These items will be subsequently tested in a national study of 3661 individuals.

In Chapter 7, Blanka, Rückel, Koch and Kailer present a quantitative study that analyses the importance of intrapreneurial orientation within the context of technology firms and discuss future opportunities for IT students. Intrapreneurship is a subfield of entrepreneurship. Intrapreneurs, as entrepreneurial-thinking employees, are considered key to companies' growth and innovativeness. The topic of intrapreneurship in the technological context will gain in importance in research and practice, as so-called technology interpreneurs combine business and technological skills. Based on the entrepreneurial orientation dimensions of innovativeness, proactiveness and risk taking, the authors develop a scale that captures the individual-level orientation. Five items were developed for each dimension, leading to a scale of 15 items measuring individual intrapreneurial orientation. Based on an online questionnaire answered by 106 students in business informatics, the students' entrepreneurial and intrapreneurial potential was measured. The majority of the intrapreneurial orientation items based on the dimensions innovativeness and proactiveness are correlated to personal initiative, supporting the hypothesis that individual initiative is an important key to activating intrapreneurial potential. Students with considerable work experience as well as being in a late stage of the studies, show higher levels of intrapreneurial orientations than students with no work experience respectively being at the beginning of their studies. The dimension of risk-taking offered non-significant results. The results of the empirical investigation also show that IT students have high levels of intrapreneurial orientation and possible future careers as technology entrepreneurs.

## PART III:   ENTREPRENEURIAL BEHAVIOUR, RESOURCES AND OUTCOMES

In Part III, four chapters pay attention to entrepreneurial behaviour and discuss the relationship between resources and outcomes. Technology-based firms have an important impact on an economy's long-term development and can be seen as drivers of economic growth and innovation. Technology-based start-ups need to utilize existing internal resources and acquire external resources to be able to grow. In Chapter 8, Rydehell, Isaksson and Löfsten study the effects of two kinds of resources on early firm performance. They found empirical evidence, based on a sample of 401 young technology-based Swedish firms, that human capital and external relations are important drivers for good firm perfomance during the start-up phases of technology-based firms. In terms of resources at founding, founders' business experiences enhance early firm performance. Contrary to expectations, founders' attitudes regarding growth orientation had no significant effect on early firm performance and were seen as an initial obstacle rather than a competitive advantage. Growth orientation as an internal resource dimension, seems less important in the early stages.

In entrepreneurship research, there has been a strong focus on the importance of being in control of resources and being embedded in networks and industries. The role of prior industry experience has attracted attention from entrepreneurship scholars for decades. In particular, if has been argued that industry experience can be beneficial because it provides access to customer and supplier networks as well as important rules and norms. Yet this may also represent a limitation when lock-in effects impose limits on the innovation activities. The opportunity creation process is complex and contingent on factors ranging from individual personality traits, prior knowledge and social networks to favourable circumstances in the environment and personal interest in the topic. In Chapter 9, Hellerstedt, Wigren-Kristoferson, Aggestam, Stevenson and Brundin investigate how entrepreneurs handle a lack of industry embeddedness in their venturing process. The authors address this by building on the literature on prior knowledge and embeddedness phenomena to advance our understanding of the entrepreneurial process. They also conduct three exploratory case studies with entrepreneurs to illustrate how they manage to change their position from disembedded to embedded in their venturing process. The study by Hellerstedt et al. challenges the assumption that prior industry experience is decisive for the success of entrepreneurs, by showing how disembeddedness in an industry can contribute to radical innovations. Entrepreneurs who lack particular experiences perceive challenges but are also able to adopt an open view in the opportunity creation process. The ability to compensate for the lack of knowledge at a certain level, by drawing on resources that are disembedded at another level, appears to be important for the opportunity creation process. The authors conclude that depending on their previous experiences, entrepreneurs adopt different approaches when entering a new industry. They rely on storytelling to build a strong brand and acceptance in the market or use prior knowledge and experiences from other industries (or a combination of both approaches) to build a convincing venturing process.

Acquiring funds constitutes an important and challenging activity for an entrepreneur. In this activity, scholars consider 'narrative' as an effective mechanism because of its capability to shape investors' decision making. In Chapter 10, Wuillaume, Jacquemin and Janssen develop and test a set of hypotheses concerning how the tone of entrepreneurial narratives affects funding success of different crowdfunding operations. The propositions are tested on a sample of projects seeking resources on a donation and reward-based crowdfunding platform (Ulule) as well as on a lending- and equity-based crowdfunding platform (MyMicroInvest). The results concerning the use of non-financial crowdfunding platforms suggest that money providers on such a platform prefer narratives characterized by a relatively high emotional language. The results also indicate that the community (social) sense displayed has a particularly high influence and even dominates the influence of the emotional tone while both aspects are present in the entrepreneurial narrative. The results concerning the use of financial crowdfunding platforms indicate that funding success is enhanced by a cognitive tone and that the sense of community stays an indicator of success. Funders on donation and reward-based platforms seem to be motivated by the emotional dimension while funders on lending- and equity-based platforms seem to be guided by cognitive considerations to a greater extent. The study shows that the crowdfunder, as a resource provider, must be distinguished from the traditional investor, and that emotions may affect an entrepreneur's ability in resources acquisition.

The final chapter, by Kitching and Iskandarova, provides a different focus from the other chapters in Part III. Their study investigates the extent to which freelancers or independent own-account workers are able to control their working time. Control over working time is one important dimension of freelancer autonomy and a source of greater meaningfulness in work. But freelancers must also contribute the labour time necessary to satisfy a portfolio of fee-paying clients to generate sufficient work income. Using qualitative data from interviews with 25 skilled freelance workers in two professional sectors, the authors present two contributions to the literature. First, freelance workers vary in their capacity to control work-time, conditional upon parties' relative bargaining power towards type of clients. Second, freelance workers engage in a variety of practices to preserve and extend control of work-time scheduling and duration. The research of Kitching and Iskandarova recognize the occupational heterogeneity of freelance work and its impact on struggles for work-time control.

## OUTLOOK

Overall, this anthology demonstrates the breadth and scientific quality of European entrepreneurship research, adding to the accumulated body of knowledge published in previous anthologies. Specifically the book highlights the importance of both rigour and relevance in the field: research that is scientifically and theoretically sound but also of utility outside the academic arena. Certainly, this book demonstrates that both rigour and relevance is alive in this field of study. Many of the chapters in this book have agendas that are influenced by pragmatic questions as much as theoretical insights, showing that engaged research begins at the agenda-setting phase rather than an add-on at the end of a study. Additionally, the volume showcases interesting new work in the area of entrepreneurial behaviour and mindsets, intrapreneurship, family businesses, the role of prior experience or absence of it as a resource, funding and time allocation amongst freelances. Whilst the chapters are focused on specific issues, they all illustrate that excellent research can have implications for practice and policy.

## REFERENCES

Frank, H. and H. Landström (2016), 'What makes entrepreneurship research interesting? Reflections on strategies to overcome the rigour–relevance gap', *Entrepreneurship & Regional Development*, **28**(1–2), 51–75.

Hodgkinson, G.P. and D.M. Rousseau (2009), 'Bridging the rigour–relevance gap in management research: It's already happening!', *Journal of Management Studies*, **46**(3), 534–546.

Ram, M., T. Jones and M. Villares-Varela (2017), 'Migrant entrepreneurship: Reflections on research and practice', *International Small Business Journal*, **35**(1), 3–18.

PART I

Rigour and relevance in entrepreneurship research

# 2. Relevance in entrepreneurship research[1]

## Johan Wiklund

## THE NEED FOR RELEVANCE

The business school as an academic institution is under threat. To an increasing extent, business schools are becoming focused on teaching, with tenure track positions being converted to full-time teaching positions, or replaced by adjuncts. At the same time, research once conducted by business schools is increasingly undertaken by more or less politicized think tanks or consultants. The movement from tenure track to teaching positions is part of a general trend, starting in humanities almost 50 years ago. Today, the majority of faculty positions at US universities and colleges have been moved off tenure track. Almost 70 percent of all faculty members are now non-tenure track. And the trend continues. Among new hires, 75 percent are non-tenure track (Kezar and Gehrke, 2014). The situation, however, may be particularly difficult for business schools where faculty members earn high salaries and have lighter teaching loads. In a 2015 interview with *Fortune Magazine*, former Dean of University of Toronto's Rotman School of Management, Roger Martin, lamented that tenure track faculty members earn $300,000 per year, while teaching fewer than three courses, doing research that had very little relevance to real businesses. He predicted a dramatic change with 90 percent cuts in tenure track faculty positions (Byrne, 2015).

Similar complaints have been raised elsewhere. For example, Bennis and O'Toole (2005) note that business schools have lost their way, generating research that is less and less relevant to practitioners of management. Ghoshal (2005) suggests that not only is business school research irrelevant, but it can even be harmful when taught in the classroom. Specifically, he points to assumptions inherent in agency theory about people's drive to maximize individual (economic) utility, and act opportunistically at the expense of others being depicted as the most relevant representations of reality, and even propagated as appropriate. Of course, many others disagree with these views.

These views of business school research are not only presented by business school deans and professors, but also by those responsible for the nature and funding of higher education. In 2011, David Willetts, the universities minister of the UK at the time, suggested that business schools research was too academic in nature and that business school professors should focus more on helping businesses (Willetts, 2011; Bounds, 2011).

In essence, the criticism leveled against business school research boils down to tenure track faculty spending too much time and effort on research that is only of interest and value to them and their peers, while the bill for the research is being paid by those who get little or nothing in return. As a consequence, the number of individuals engaged in research and the time they have available to do research are both shrinking.

The above observations paint a rather bleak picture of business school research both in terms of its relevance and its future outlook. Fortunately, I believe that the outlook for entrepreneurship research might be more positive and likely to have a great societal impact. Interestingly, this impact is likely to emerge for reasons that are often used by scholars in other fields as signs of illegitimacy within the academy (see e.g. Wiklund et al., 2011). Thus, our field's potential weaknesses may also be its potential strengths. First, entrepreneurship is a young discipline rooted in practice. It was the downfall of the largest Fortune 500 firms, and the rise of new entrepreneurial firms that led to the initial systematic academic interest in entrepreneurship during the 1980s (Landström and Harirchi, 2018). Scholarship at the time was phenomenon-driven with limited attention to theory, and there was a genuine interest in understanding entrepreneurs and entrepreneurship in order to help entrepreneurs and to take entrepreneurship into the classroom. To some extent, entrepreneurship research has remained this way. Most often, this phenomenon-driven, rather than theory-driven, research has been lamented, seen as a legitimacy problem among the broader field of management (e.g. Wiklund et al., 2011). At the same time, however, it can be an advantage when it comes to thoroughly understanding the phenomenon under study, researching relevant issues, and communicating results. A second strength of entrepreneurship research is that it is not firmly rooted in any particular discipline. Rather, it draws on a kaleidoscope of theories and perspectives (e.g. Shepherd, 2015). This allows entrepreneurship scholars to explore a wide range of issues, applying diverse theoretical and empirical approaches. As a result, entrepreneurship research thrives in many different environments, including those located outside of the business school. For example, there are professorships in entrepreneurship in art schools, engineering schools, and science departments. As such, if business schools see dramatic cuts in tenure track positions along the lines sketched by Roger Martin above, entrepreneurship research can still flourish within other schools and departments that are facing a more promising future provided that entrepreneurship scholars conduct relevant research.

Third and relatedly, there is no commonly accepted unifying definition of entrepreneurship, and scholars use the term flexibly for their own purposes. While this is often seen as a curse (Shepherd, 2015), it is also a blessing in terms of entrepreneurship remaining relevant. The entrepreneurship landscape is ever changing. For example, with the rise of the 'gig' economy, the creation and management of new organizations seems to be less of a necessity for exercising entrepreneurship than it was just a few years ago. This might create problems for organization scholars accustomed to studying long-standing traditional organizational forms! Not so for entrepreneurship scholars defining entrepreneurship in terms of the pursuit of opportunity regardless of resources controlled and regardless of the organizational form involved.

These forces suggest that relevance in entrepreneurship research is not an option. It is a matter of survival. At the same time, the opportunity of conducting relevant research that really matters is better than for many other fields of research carried out at the business school.

## HOW TO ENSURE RELEVANCE IN OUR RESEARCH

Much entrepreneurship scholarship implicitly assumes entrepreneurs and policymakers to be the primary audiences for our research. That is evident, among other things, from the discussion sections of typical entrepreneurship papers. Apart for stating implications for future scholarship, often they include subsections with titles such as "implications for entrepreneurs" and "implications for policymakers." While I don't believe that many expect entrepreneurs or policymakers read academic journals, I also question if and how they can inspire research relevance.

First and most important, there is a large difference between doing research that is relevant, that is, research that is potentially important for stakeholders, and research that these same stakeholders care about. That something is potentially important (e.g. exercise) does not necessarily imply that people care about it, and the things that people care about (e.g. the Kardashians) are not necessarily important. As entrepreneurship scholars we can't 'force' our insights onto entrepreneurs and policymakers, but have to appeal to the things that they care deeply about, and this is typically difficult. Research takes time. The time from hatching an interesting research idea, through securing the necessary resources, collecting and analyzing data, and drawing appropriate conclusions is usually several years. At the same time, entrepreneurs are attuned to the latest trends in their fields. One year something is in vogue, and the next, it is something different. Consequently, a research idea that seems of great interest to entrepreneurs when conceived might be far less appealing to this audience once the project is finished. Thus, selecting research topics based on what is currently regarded a hot topic by entrepreneurs may not lead to relevant research because of the rapid changes of entrepreneurs' preferences, and the slow process of research.

Doing research that policymakers care about is associated with similar problems—they are also sensitive to trends and change their opinions regarding what's important. To further complicate things, it's hard to understand what drives policymakers. It is logical to believe that policymakers should be interested in devising entrepreneurship policies that provide the most 'bang for the bucks.' If that were the case, policymakers should be interested in designing policy evaluation schemes that could appropriately evaluate policies, and then weed out those that seem less effective, while retaining the most effective. In fact, policymakers appear prone to well-known agency problems. It seems that policymakers are driven by other incentives, including staying in office, and promoting personal hobby horses. Following elections, and associated changes in key offices, policies often change. In essence, I propose that building research around the issues that entrepreneurs and/or policymakers care the most about does not guarantee relevant outcomes once the and, conversely, conducting research that should be highly relevant to entrepreneurs and policymakers does not guarantee that they care about it.

I propose a different model for generating interest in research and contrast it with the typical approach. Figure 2.1 illustrates the two approaches. The horizontal line displays the number of people that care and the vertical line illustrates how much people care. The 'X' in the upper right corner illustrates the ideal position where lots of people care a great deal. This is a difficult position to reach. Most entrepreneurship scholarships try to move as far as possible along the horizontal axis. Target audiences are typically not very well identified, and the kinds of messages they care about are usually not very well known. The hope is that the power of the research findings themselves are so powerful that I will convince the audience—whether entrepreneurs or policymakers—to care. As an alternative, I propose to instead move along the vertical axis. The first step is to ensure that one single person cares deeply about the research. That person should be you. It is impossible to get other people to care about a topic, a finding, or an implication, unless you as the scholar generating the research care deeply about it yourself. If you are deeply emotionally involved in your research, it is easier to make other people involved. Once you have ensured that you conduct research that you care deeply about, the next step is to test the ideas on others that you have frequent and recurrent interactions with, and that will honestly let you know if they share your enthusiasm or not. I refer to these people as 'students broadly defined.' The three central dimensions of academic work are teaching, research, and service. Taking the research to the classroom is an excellent idea of testing if there is broader interest for your research. Whether undergraduates, MBAs, or executives, it is likely that if they understand, can relate to, and appreciate your research, entrepreneurs and policymakers will as well. But this group also includes family members, and entrepreneurial friends. If your research is truly relevant to people outside the academy, you should be able to articulate it over a dinner table or a round of golf in such a way that those who care about you also care about your research, show interest and listen. Added benefits of taking this approach to relevance is that it is much easier for you to maintain your motivation to carry out the actual research when you're working on something that you care deeply about, and it is also much more enjoyable to communicate it to various groups of stakeholders.

| | | | |
|---|---|---|---|
| **A lot** | | | |
| **Quite a bit** | | | |
| **A little bit** | | | |
| | **Few** | **Quite a few** | **Many** |

*Figure 2.1      Relevance in entrepreneurship research*

## MY OWN EXPERIENCE OF RELEVANCE IN RESEARCH

I first put this approach into practice a few years ago. I had reason to seek out mental health professionals, which was a new experience. As an academic, I immediately started consulting the literature on the topic. As I did, I soon came across books published on the fringes of research with titles such as *The Dyslexic Advantage, The ADHD Advantage, Neurodiversity: Discovering the Extraordinary Gifts of Autism, ADHD, Dyslexia, and Other Brain Differences.* These books were written by people with medical and/or research degrees and seemed credible. The essence of all these books is the idea that conditions that we normally consider as mental disorders can actually convey certain advantages. For example, people with ADHD and dyslexia have been credited for high creativity. I found these ideas fascinating and they also resonated with my own experiences. Therefore, I confronted these books with clinical psychologists and medical doctors that I know who have extensive experiences of these mental disorders. I simply asked them if these books made any sense. They responded that based on their own personal experiences, the ideas indeed seem plausible, but there has been limited research focusing on possible advantages of mental disorders. Given the many thousands of articles on all sorts of negative consequences of mental disorders generated by scholars in medicine, sociality, education, economics, neuroscience and so on, at first, I was very surprised by this. I later understood that the very fact that they are mental disorders, as defined by the medical profession, leads to the focus on the negative consequences as opposed to possible strengths and advantages. As I read more about the disorders, I started making connections to entrepreneurship. It seemed that certain aspects of the actual psychiatric diagnosis (e.g. sensation-seeking among people with ADHD) or 'side effects' like the creativity of dyslexics, could be advantageous in entrepreneurship. As I conducted more systematic searches, looking for research connecting mental disorders to entrepreneurship, I found that there were very few papers. Probably less than a handful. Was there a good reason for this? Maybe it is simply not a very interesting or promising line of research. As I thought more about it, I became more and more convinced that research on the link between entrepreneurship and mental disorders would meet several of the criteria that makes research interesting to me. First, I have a personal relationship to the topic. From first-hand experience, I can see that what we usually regard as deficits associated with mental disorders can actually be strengths in the appropriate contexts. Second, the topic itself and theorizing around it runs counter to the received wisdom in mental health research. In his famous article "That's interesting," Murray Davis (1971) notes that the counterintuitive is innately interesting.

Third, this research could have extensive real-world implications. The negative personal, social, and economic implications of mental health problems are very far reaching. Research that focuses on strengths and possibilities as opposed to deficits and problems has the potential of changing the conversation and providing productive avenues for people who suffer. It is certainly possible to do meaningful and impactful research in other areas. For example, I have done and continue to do research on university spinoffs and incubators and have also engaged with policymakers regarding these and other issues. While such research can be potentially influential, it certainly does not have the same potential at the individual level. People who start university spinoffs, or start their businesses in incubators usually belong to the more fortunate in life. In my encounters with entrepreneurs diagnosed with mental disorders, it is clear that they immediately connect with the essential message and are genuinely thankful that I carry out this research. That is greatly and immediately rewarding in a way than none of my previous research has been.

Fourth, it is a new and novel research field. Only a small group of scholars is starting to get interested in this line of research. When a research field is new, there is greater opportunity to make a substantial contribution. There are also fewer established rules and standards, which makes it feasible to seek out new research questions, research designs, and theoretical approaches, something which I find very stimulating.

Looking back, I am very happy that I started with this kind of research. I did not know how mental health symptoms would pan out in entrepreneurship and neither did other scholars. The case studies gave me broad insights into and intuitive understanding of how mental health symptoms and entrepreneurship can be entwined.

The case studies made me realize that ADHD was potentially the most interesting mental diagnosis to study. Being a neurodevelopment disorder, it is pervasive. It is also very common, and the number of diagnoses are increasing worldwide. Today, no less than 11 percent of all American children have a formal ADHD diagnosis. Most importantly in this context, however, it seems that the actual symptoms of the condition were directly associated with entrepreneurial behavior. In particular, it seemed that impulsivity manifested in risk taking, innovativeness, and proactiveness within their businesses (see Wiklund et al., 2016). Put simply it seems that impulsivity drives EO. Much more research is needed to establish if this is the case. However, if it is, with the knowledge we have about EO and performance, it would provide for an important mechanism related to how ADHD potentially translates into positive entrepreneurial outcomes. Being able to establish such a mechanism can potentially have vast implications for research on entrepreneurship in mental health (see also Wiklund et al., 2017). It would also be an interesting and surprising way of tying together two streams of research that caught my interest for completely different reasons. I guess that it is a consequence of conducting research that I find deeply meaningful. We only have a limited repertoire of issues that we find truly interesting and these things tend to remain relatively stable over time.

At the current time, I have conducted many related studies on the topic of mental health and entrepreneurship. This research has been noticed by entrepreneurs and media alike. I often receive appreciating emails from entrepreneurs who identify with the overall message of the research. There is no doubt that the research I consider relevant and important is also considered highly relevant by entrepreneurs and other stakeholders.

## NOTE

1. This text builds on my keynote at the RENT 2017 Conference in Lund, Sweden. Part of the text coincides with text in Wiklund et al. (2018). and in Wiklund (2016).

## REFERENCES

Bennis, W.G. and J. O'Toole (2005), 'How business schools lost their way', *Harvard Business Review*, **83**(5), 96–104.

Bounds, A. (2011), 'Business schools urged to do more teaching and less research', *Financial Times*, April 1, https://www.ft.com/content/4eaa5bd6 -6146-11e0-ab25-00144feab49a (accessed May 5, 2019).

Byrne, J.A. (2015), 'Are American business schools headed for a GM like catastrophe?', *Fortune*, August 17, http://fortune.com/2015/08/17//business -schools-future (accessed May 14, 2019).

Davis, M.S. (1971), 'That's interesting: Towards a phenomenology of sociology and a sociology of phenomenology', *Philosophy of the Social Sciences*, **1**(4), 309.

Ghoshal, S. (2005), 'Bad management theories are destroying good management practices', *Academy of Management Learning & Education*, **4**(1), 75–91.

Kezar, A. and S. Gehrke (2014), 'Why are we hiring so many non-tenure-track faculty?', *Liberal Education*, **100**(1), 1.

Landström, H. and G. Harichi (2018), 'The social structure of entrepreneurship as a scientific field', *Research Policy*, **47**(3), 650–662.

Shepherd, D. (2015), 'Party on! A call for entrepreneurship research that is more interactive, activity based, cognitively hot, compassionate, and prosocial', *Journal of Business Venturing*, **30**, 489–507.

Wiklund, J. (2016), '*Re-search = me-search*', in Audretsch, D. and Lehmann, E. (eds), *The Routledge Companion to the Makers of Modern Entrepreneurship*, London: Routledge, 233–255.

Wiklund, J., H. Patzelt and D. Dimov (2016), 'Entrepreneurship and psychological disorders: How ADHD can be productively harnessed', *Journal of Business Venturing Insights*, **6**, 14–20.

Wiklund, J., M. Wright and S.A. Zahra (2018), 'Conquering relevance: Entrepreneurship research's grand challenge', *Entrepreneurship Theory and Practice*, **43**(3), 419–436.

Wiklund, J., P. Davidsson, D.B. Audretsch and C. Karlsson (2011), 'The future of entrepreneurship research', *Entrepreneurship Theory and Practice*, **35**(1), 1–9.

Wiklund, J., W. Yu, R. Tucker and L. Marino (2017), 'ADHD, impulsivity and entrepreneurship', *Journal of Business Venturing*, **32**(6), 627–656.

Willetts, D. (2011), 'Business schools urged to do more teaching and less research', *Financial Times*, April 7, https://www.ft.com/content/4eaa5bd6 -6146-11e0-ab25-00144feab49a (accessed May 14, 2019).

# 3. The rigour–relevance debate: strategies to avoid creating an ivory tower in entrepreneurship research[1]

**Hans Landström**

## INTRODUCTION

If our research fails to address relevant issues and lacks contributions that capture the interest of external stakeholders, it can be argued that we have failed in our social responsibility as researchers to stimulate societal progress. Thus, one requirement of good research is that our knowledge should not only attract interest among our peers, but also be useful for external stakeholders such as entrepreneurs, investors, policy-makers and politicians, the media and our students.

Traditionally, entrepreneurship and small business research has been regarded as a practical and relevant research field, providing knowledge to be used to solve various societal problems, for example, by helping entrepreneurs to build better businesses and stimulating policy-makers to implement measures to improve entrepreneurship in society. As the field is becoming more and more institutionalized in the academic system, scientific rigour in research has been emphasized at the expense of relevance, triggering frustration among many entrepreneurship and small business scholars. The gap between practical relevance and scientific rigour in our research was the theme of the XXXI RENT Conference in Lund, Sweden on the 15–17 November 2017.

## CHANGE OF THE LEGITIMACY BASIS IN ENTREPRENEURSHIP RESEARCH

Since the emergence of entrepreneurship research in the 1980s, a basic assumption has been underlying the field: that a better understanding of entrepreneurship and small businesses can help solve various societal problems and advance entrepreneurial practice (Frank and Landström, 2016). During the emergence of entrepreneurship as a research field, a large number of scholars rushed into this promising field, many of whom had a background as practicing entrepreneurs. They sometimes kept one foot in practice and felt comfortable in this dual role (Baker and Welter, 2015). As a consequence, in the early stages of the development of the field, the field was mainly legitimized by external stakeholders. For example, entrepreneurship was perceived as important knowledge by policy-makers, students and the media, while external stakeholders contributed significantly to the growth of the field, particularly as a lot of research funding came from different policy organizations, not least in Europe.

These characteristics created strong imprinting elements (Marquis and Tilcsik, 2013) among entrepreneurship scholars over a long period of time and many scholars are firmly convinced that entrepreneurship knowledge should support policy and practice by helping to solve societal problems and assisting entrepreneurs to ensure the success of their ventures. Thus, for a long time, practical relevance has been the focus of entrepreneurship research!

However, in recent decades entrepreneurship as an academic field has grown significantly and become more and more institutionalized in the academic arena (Landström et al., 2017; Wiklund et al., 2019). The institutionalization of the field is reflected by, among other things, the number of entrepreneurship chairs, highly ranked journals and a reasonably coherent set of research questions and methodologies (Welter and Lasch, 2008; Landström et al., 2017). Today, scholars in entrepreneurship seldom have any practical experience as entrepreneurs, which can sometimes create a split between scholars with and without entrepreneurial experience within the faculty at many universities (Baker and Welter, 2015). Instead, research has been more and more devoted to solving academic puzzles and less to addressing problems that are important for society and for individual entrepreneurs. The institutionalization of entrepreneurship as a scientific field has been reinforced by the prevailing development of the business schools around the world – moving towards marketization and managerialism, including stronger performance indicators for judging quality, for example, a stronger focus on university rankings, accreditations and individual scholarly rankings based on top journal publications (Harley et al., 2004; Pearce II, 2012).

The institutionalization of research tends to favour scientific rigour at the cost of practical relevance, while at the same time it can be argued that rigour promotes the institutionalization of the research field (Frank and Landström, 2016). In this respect we have seen that legitimacy is increasingly anchored in academia and to a lesser extent among external stakeholders, thus scientific rigour has been in focus in entrepreneurship research!

## THE CONSEQUENCES OF INCREASED RIGOUR AND A DECREASED FOCUS ON RELEVANCE

The change of the basis for legitimacy and in the focus of research – from external stakeholders to academia – has created a rigour–relevance frustration among many entrepreneurship scholars. In the study by Frank and Landström (2016), several scholars expressed this frustration. For example, one entrepreneurship scholar described it in the following way: 'We are not 2–3 years behind reality, but probably almost 10 years behind …. Mainstream entrepreneurship research is the result of the past … but it provides a better chance of being published', while another scholar stated: 'When you read articles in top-ranked journals and come to the last pages where the implications are presented, you find some implications are really stupid. If you know anything about the real world, they are really stupid' (Frank and Landström, 2016, p. 63). This frustration among many entrepreneurship scholars has triggered a debate about the gap between scientific rigour and practical relevance within entrepreneurship research.

The stronger focus on rigour in entrepreneurship research (and lack of relevance) will have several consequences for the field. First, there is a risk that our research on entrepreneurship will become less interesting. In order to become a legitimate academic field, entrepreneurship research has in many ways begun to conform to the norms and standards of more established fields by adapting a 'normal science' approach. For example, entrepreneurship research is more and more characterized by a focus on hypothetico-deductive testing, the use of large samples, pre-tested variables, sophisticated statistical analysis, and so on. Thus, in these kind of institutionalization processes there is always a risk that individual scholars become embedded in a culture and incentive system that places greater emphasis on the more incremental research questions addressed, where studies contribute less and less, merely creating nuances of what we already know and not stimulating individual scholars to conduct challenging and novel research – making entrepreneurship research less and less interesting (Landström, 2016).

Second, in becoming an inward-looking academic research field, there is a risk that entrepreneurship scholars will not contribute to the main challenges in society today (Landström et al., 2017). In a changing and often turbulent world characterized by great challenges of rapid political changes, climate change, water constraints, digitalization of the economy, industry and technological changes, the development of the 'gig' economy, and so on, the landscape of entrepreneurship is changing continuously. In order to remain relevant, entrepreneurship scholars need be part of this development and entrepreneurship as a scholarly field has great potential to make valuable contributions to societal development.

Third, there is a risk of losing connection to and funding from external stakeholders. Following the argumentation by Rosa (2013), the research funding from policy sources has been of significant importance for the development of the field. The competition for such funding is high and the allocation of funding is often based on publication in leading international journals. However, very little of this policy-funded research focusing on policy and practical problems is actually published in top-ranked journals. Instead, these journals have been dominated by theory-driven publications and it is problematic to convert research that is funded by and tied up in policy projects into 'theory-driven' international research that might promote the scholars' careers.

However, it is important to emphasize that practical relevance and high scientific standards are not conflicting goals (Hodgkinson and Rosseau, 2009; Wiklund et al., 2019). On the contrary, it is necessary to conduct basic research that might not be relevant for external stakeholders today, but that builds knowledge for the future, and it is also important that our advice to policy-makers and practitioners is based on rigorous research, or as Lumpkin (2011) argued, too many pieces of bad advice have been given to policy-makers and practitioners due to bad research forming the basis for the advice, and Ghoshal (2005) further states that this can be even more problematic when such knowledge is taught in the classroom.

The conclusion to be drawn is that we need research that is both scientifically rigorous *and* practically relevant! Thus, this discussion leads to the questions: Is it possible to bridge the gap between 'rigour' and 'relevance'? and if so, how can we make our research both 'relevant' and 'actionable' as well as rigorously developed, that is, how can we conduct research that is both rigorous and relevant?

## THE POSSIBILITY OF BRIDGING THE RIGOUR–RELEVANCE GAP

The possibility of bridging the gap between scientific rigour and practical relevance has been debated for a long time in many academic disciplines (see summary in Frank and Landström, 2016). In this debate, some scholars are fairly pessimistic about the possibility of bridging the rigour–relevance gap and argue that it is unbridgeable (Keiser and Leiner, 2009). Practitioners and researchers belong to different 'systems' that are largely self-referential and focus on their own logic. The difficulty of bridging the two systems is caused by different goal criteria, and the systems are stabilized by peer reviews and reputational mechanisms, which leads to a disconnection with other social structures and a social community that adheres to its own logic, including its own time frames, that is, researchers and practitioners act on different time horizons, which creates an additional asynchrony between theory and practice (Flickinger et al., 2014). Scholars (e.g. Alvesson, 2012) even argue that scholars do not have anything to say to practitioners as much has already been said and the vast majority of articles are incremental, narrowly defined and based on the same assumptions, thus most ideas are taken-for-granted and reproduced.

On the other hand, some scholars argue that management studies as well as entrepreneurship are strongly 'reality-oriented' academic fields that aim to support external stakeholders (Wolf and Rosenberg, 2012) and these scholars also consider it necessary and possible to bridge the rigour–relevance gap. The bridging of the rigour–relevance gap is not only about improving the dissemination of research results, that is, bridging the 'dissemination gap' through adequate translation and communication of our research findings to external stakeholders. The bridging of the gap requires something more than improved dissemination (Frank and Landström, 2016). It also includes the possibility to bridge the 'problem formulation gap', which implies that researchers and external stakeholders perceive different kinds of problems and formulate questions in different ways and that we need to research issues that are of interest to external stakeholders. In addition, we need to bridge the 'research process gap', which concerns the involvement and dialogue between researchers and external stakeholders throughout the knowledge production process. The efforts to bridge different parts of the rigour–relevance gap have been scarce with a few exceptions that follow methodological approaches that, for example, are labelled engaged scholarship (e.g. Van de Ven, 2007; Van de Ven and Johnson, 2006), interactive approaches (e.g. Aagaard-Nielsen and Svensson, 2006) and enactive research (e.g. Johannisson, 2018).

## STRATEGIES TO BRIDGE THE GAP BETWEEN RIGOUR AND RELEVANCE IN ENTREPRENEURSHIP RESEARCH

The attempts to bridge the gap between research and practice need to be significantly intensified. We must increase the level of beneficial exchange between the two systems and create a closer connection between the 'real world', which would be valuable in entrepreneurship research. Below, I will present some strategies that may contribute to narrowing the gap between scientific rigour and practical relevance in entrepreneurship research. It is far from a comprehensive list of strategies and even though connectivity is a challenge for both sides – academia and external stakeholders – the discussion below only takes strategies from 'one side of the coin' into consideration, but the proposals could be a starting point for further discussion.

## Who Should Be Practically Relevant?

We cannot assess practical relevancy by only looking at individual scholars and individual studies. Basic research that is not immediately relevant for policy-makers and practitioners is nevertheless important for advancing our knowledge, and in order to say something of practical relevance, we need a larger number of rigorously conducted studies that can reveal a coherent pattern of results. In addition, we have to be aware that scholars may be more or less experienced with regard to their interaction with external stakeholders – many scholars seldom engage in interactions with entrepreneurs and policy-makers and do not have the language to communicate with external stakeholders, which means that they feel less confident and comfortable in the dialogue with external stakeholders.

A reflection that can be made is that not all research within entrepreneurship needs to be relevant to external stakeholders. And not all entrepreneurship scholars have something to say to policy-makers and practitioners. In many cases the 'practical implications' in their articles are rather vague and obvious for external stakeholders and will probably have little impact on their behaviour. However, those entrepreneurship scholars who feel confident in their interaction with external stakeholders and who can make insightful and useful contributions should be encouraged to further improve their skills to become the 'bridge makers' between academic scholars and stakeholders, as well as role models for how to overcome the 'ivory divide' in our research.

## What Kind of Knowledge are We Creating?

An issue that has been almost forgotten in the rigour–relevance debate is the types of knowledge that we develop in entrepreneurship research. As researchers we can develop different kinds of knowledge – from more technical knowledge to more theoretical knowledge – and different kinds of knowledge could be more or less useful for external stakeholders. Policy-makers and practitioners often search for knowledge that can help them solve rather specific problems, as well as for knowledge that is action-oriented, what we might call 'applicative' knowledge (Hirschheim and Klein, 2003).

Applicative knowledge cannot always be acquired by 'traditional' scientific methodologies, but requires close connection and exchange with practice, that is, a more holistic and hermeneutical approach that goes beyond pure cognitive knowledge. It is based on a co-created exchange between the researcher and practitioner and is not always explicit but tacit, that is, the result of personal experience and learning processes from successes and failures, which often create a special know-how. Practitioners' knowledge may be such tacit knowledge. While tacit knowledge is an important part of many entrepreneurial activities, entrepreneurship researchers have rarely dealt with it.

In order to bridge the rigour–relevance gap we need different kinds of researcher producing different kinds of knowledge and in order to reach out to practitioners we particularly need researchers who produce applicative knowledge.

## How to Create an Institutional Context that Stimulates a Connection to External Stakeholders?

Of course our academic incentive systems – for tenure, salary and recognition – greatly affect our behaviour and in order to have more practical relevance, the incentives systems at universities and business schools require reappraisal. Current systems, with focus on measures of impact on our peers, favour rigorous research published in top journals, and the measures are often based on easily quantifiable measures that lack a pluralistic conceptualization of the incentive systems (Aguinis et al., 2014). The effects on behaviour hold particularly true for many young scholars who usually have temporary positions and as a consequence, feel unsure in their positions and experience a pressure to follow the 'rules of the game' more strictly in order to obtain permanent positions. Thus, the existing incentive system has become a powerful tool in shaping employees' behaviour and also the research conducted, but as expressed by Anne Tsui in her Academy of Management 2012 Presidential Address: 'When we are judged only in how many papers we publish in certain journals and not whether our research is important to society, we lose meaning in our work. With these problems, how can we feel good about ourselves?' (Tsui, 2013, p. 176). In order to stimulate practically relevant and meaningful research, the incentives and measures should not only focus on the requirement to publish studies in high-ranked journals – as practically relevant research should be anchored in research with high scientific rigour, these measures are important – but we also need to find incentives and measures for scholars who demonstrate a capacity to interact with external stakeholders.

## How Can the Research Process Stimulate the Relevance of Our Research?

Entrepreneurship researchers can reduce the gap between scientific rigour and practical relevance by modifying how they identify and construct research questions, conduct their research and disseminate their results (Wolf and Rosenberg, 2012).

We have to acknowledge the fact that external stakeholders are a very heterogeneous group with different ideas about what makes research results useful and applicative. When researchers do not differentiate among external stakeholders, their knowledge can be too vague and limited. Thus, a fruitful starting point in bridging the rigour–relevance gap might be to gain a better understanding of the different groups of external stakeholders and greater knowledge about their different realities. As expressed by Silvia (2005), we need to understand the 'copying potential' of the audience. This knowledge often takes a long time to build, thus we need scholars who are faithful to their research subjects over a longer period, but we must also find arenas for a dialogue with practitioners and/or policy-makers that includes the entire research process, that is, problem formulation, the research process itself, and the dissemination of our results, which will help to ensure a better understanding of results and 'practical' interpretations of the research findings.

In addition, we need to broaden the methodological arsenal used in research. Today, the quantitative hypothetico-deductive methodology is dominant in entrepreneurship research. This approach tends to lead to the creation of a closed academic arena that is more or less sealed from the concerns of practitioners (Binks et al., 2007). However, entrepreneurship as a phenomenon is characterized by high diversity, non-linear behaviour and sometimes non-rational thinking, where 'luck' may have a significant impact on the outcome. Thus, the phenomenon cannot be adequately explained by calculating the 'average' and we therefore need methodologies and methods that have the potential to capture the specifics of entrepreneurship (Landström et al., 2017). Consequently, more methodological open-mindedness is required to capture the essence of entrepreneurship, which will improve the possibility of conducting research of practical relevance.

Of course when discussing practically relevant knowledge, we tend to focus on research that is applicative and conducted in close dialogue with external stakeholders. However, we have to be aware that this is not the only kind of research that can be regarded as having a practical relevance. For example, in order to increase the external validity of studies, literature reviews and replication studies are potentially useful tools for establishing the practical relevance of previous research. Too many findings in entrepreneurship research are only developed and/or tested in one study. Thus, we need a stock of robust entrepreneurship knowledge that practitioners and policy-makers can use, which puts an emphasis on replication studies (Hubbard and Vetter, 1996; Tsang and Kwan, 1999) and on the importance of evidence-based research (Frese et al., 2014).

## CONCLUDING REMARKS

So far, bridging the gap between scientific rigour and practical relevance seems essentially to be a task that is accomplished by senior scholars – with permanent positions and experienced enough to communicate with external stakeholders. It is not easy for young scholars who are under pressure in terms of their positions and the many early career requirements to become involved in time-consuming external stakeholder relationships, not least because many of their colleagues perceive such involvement as foolish and career-limiting. But bridging the gap needs to be part of young scholarly careers. In many cases, young scholars are the ones who identify new problems, provide us with new ideas, challenge old truths, and so on, and have the potential not only to contribute to academia, but also to external stakeholders. Thus, as I have tried to show in this chapter, producing research with practical relevance does not conflict with the production of scientifically rigorous research – on the contrary, it is important that our implications for external stakeholders are well rooted in rigorous scientific research.

In order to encourage more young scholars to become involved in a dialogue with external stakeholders and to bridge the gap between scientific rigour and practical relevance, the issue needs to be addressed in the infrastructure of universities and business schools. For example, the traditional incentive criteria should be supplemented by measures that give young scholars the incentive to engage in external stakeholder relationships. In addition, senior scholars need to improve the research environment for young scholars by giving them opportunities to follow their interests and hearts, and enable the creation of an environment that involves not only other academics but also a dynamic inflow of different kinds of external stakeholder. Discussions of how to bridge the rigour–relevance gap must also be included in the doctoral programmes in entrepreneurship, for example by offering courses on researcher–practitioner collaboration and encouraging PhD students with practical experience who can serve as role models.

## NOTE

1. The argumentation in this chapter is based on the article by Frank and Landström (2016).

## REFERENCES

Aagaard-Nielsen, K. and L. Svensson (2006), *Action and Interactive Research. Beyond Practice and Theory*, Maastricht: Shaker Publishing.
Aguinis, H., D.L. Shapiro, E.P. Antonacopoulou and T.G. Cummings (2014), 'Scholarly impact: A pluralist conceptualization', *Academy of Management Learning and Education*, **13**(4), 623–639.
Alvesson, M. (2012), 'Do we have something to say? From re-search to roi-search and back again', *Organization*, **20**(1), 79–90.

Baker, T. and F. Welter (2015), 'Bridges to the future: Challenging the nature of entrepreneurship scholarship', in: T. Baker and F. Welter (eds), *The Routledge Companion to Entrepreneurship*, London: Routledge, pp. 3–17.

Binks, M., K. Starkey and C.L. Mahon (2007), 'Entrepreneurship education and the business school', *Technology Analysis and Strategic Management*, **18**(1), 1–18.

Flickinger, M., A. Tuschke, T. Gruber-Muecke and M. Fiedler (2014), 'In search of rigor, relevance, and legitimacy: What drives the impact of publications', *Journal of Business Economics*, **84**(1), 99–128.

Frank, H. and H. Landström (2016), 'What makes entrepreneurship research interesting? Reflections on strategies to overcome the rigour–relevance gap', *Entrepreneurship and Regional Development*, **28**(1–2), 51–75.

Frese, M., D.M. Rousseau and J. Wiklund (2014), 'The emergence of evidence-based entrepreneurship', *Entrepreneurship Theory and Practice*, **38**(2), 209–216.

Ghoshal, S. (2005), 'Bad management theories are destroying good management practices', *Academy of Management Learning and Education*, **4**(1), 75–91.

Harley, S., M. Muller-Camen and A. Collin (2004), 'From academic communities to managed organisations', *Journal of Vocational Behavior*, **64**, 329–345.

Hirschheim, R. and H.K. Klein (2003), 'Crisis in the IS field. A critical reflection on the state of the discipline', *Journal of the Association of Information Systems*, **4**(1), 237–293.

Hodgkinson, G.P. and D.M. Rosseau (2009), 'Bridging the rigour–relevance gap in management research: It's already happening!', *Journal of Management Studies*, **46**(3), 534–546.

Hubbard, R. and D.E. Vetter (1996), 'An empirical comparison of published replication research in accounting, economics, finance, management, and marketing', *Journal of Business Research*, **35**(2), 153–164.

Johannisson, B. (2018), *Disclosing Entrepreneurship as Practice. The Enactive Approach*, Cheltenham, UK and Northampton, MA, USA: Edward Elgar Publishing.

Keiser, A. and L. Leiner (2009), 'Why the rigour–relevance gap in management research is unbridgeable', *Journal of Management Studies*, **46**(3), 516–533.

Landström, H. (2016), 'What makes scholars "interesting" in entrepreneurship research', in: A. Fayolle and P. Riot (eds), *Rethinking Entrepreneurship*, London: Routledge, pp. 147–170.

Landström, H., A. Parhankangas, A. Fayolle and P. Riot (2017), 'Institutionalization of entrepreneurship as a scholarly field', in: H.

Landström, A. Parhankangas, A. Fayolle and P. Riot (eds), *Challenging Entrepreneurship Research*, London: Routledge, pp. 1–17.

Lumpkin, G.T. (2011), 'From legitimacy to impact: Moving the field forward by asking how entrepreneurship informs life', *Strategic Entrepreneurship Journal*, **5**, 3–9.

Marquis, C. and A. Tilcsik (2013), 'Imprinting: Toward a multilevel theory', *Academy of Management Annals*, **7**(1), 195–245.

Pearce II, J.A. (2012), 'Revising manuscripts for premier entrepreneurship journals', *Entrepreneurship Theory and Practice*, **36**(2), 193–203.

Rosa, P.J. (2013), 'Recent trends in leading entrepreneurship research: The challenge for European researchers', *Entrepreneurship Research Journal*, **3**(1), 35–43.

Silvia, P.J. (2005), 'What is interesting? Exploring the appraisal structure of interest', *Emotion*, **5**, 89–102.

Tsang, E.W.K. and K.M. Kwan (1999), 'Replication and theory development in organizational science', *Academy of Management Review*, **24**(4), 759–780.

Tsui, A.S. (2013), 'On compassion in scholarship: Why should we care?', *Academy of Management Review*, **38**(2), 167–180.

Van de Ven, A.H. (2007), *Engaged Scholarship: A Guide for Organizational Social Research*, Oxford: Oxford University Press.

Van de Ven, A.H. and P.E. Johnson (2006), 'Knowledge for theory and practice', *Academy of Management Review*, **31**(4), 802–821.

Welter, F. and F. Lasch (2008), 'Entrepreneurship research in Europe: Taking stock and looking forward', *Entrepreneurship Theory and Practice*, **32**(2), 241–248.

Wiklund, J., M. Wright and S.A. Zahra (2019), 'Conquering relevance: Entrepreneurship research's grand challenge', *Entrepreneurship Theory and Practice*, **43**(3), 419–436.

Wolf, J. and T. Rosenberg (2012), 'How individual scholars can reduce the rigor–relevance gap in management research', *BuR-Business Research*, **5**(2), 178–196.

# 4. Introducing three academic conversations: Critical Entrepreneurship Studies, Entrepreneurship as Practice and a Radical Processual Approach to entrepreneurship

**Piritta Parkkari and Karen Verduijn**

## INTRODUCTION

Entrepreneurship as a field of research has expanded in a number of directions, with a wide range of ontological, epistemological, methodological, theoretical and empirical variations existing alongside one another. This chapter provides an introduction to three recent conversations within the entrepreneurship research domain: (1) Critical Entrepreneurship Studies (CES), which seeks to question and challenge mainstream, taken-for-granted understandings and ways of researching entrepreneurship; (2) Entrepreneurship as Practice (EaP), which incorporates an interest in doing entrepreneurship as an everyday practice by utilizing social practice theories; and (3) a Radical Processual Approach (RPA) towards entrepreneurship (entrepreneur*ing*, Steyaert 2007; Johannisson, 2011), which incorporates process philosophical premises to studying entrepreneuring as flux, as constant becoming.

As conversations diverging from 'mainstream', functionalist entrepreneurship research, these conversations offer novel, radical, complex and nuanced ways of understanding and researching entrepreneurship phenomena. Although at times used interchangeably, there is a need to gauge what specifically is addressed within each of them, to evaluate what sets them apart and what is their common ground. This will allow an appreciation of the specific value each conversation might bring to entrepreneurship research, together and separately – an effort that may offer guidance for any 'newcomers' to these emerging conversations within entrepreneurship research.

In order to go beyond simply 'mapping' the three conversations, we utilize a classic (Baron, 2004) question in entrepreneurship research: 'Why do some people become entrepreneurs, and others don't?' We fabulate (Hjorth, 2013a) how studies within each of the three conversations would deal with this question. That is, based on our introduction to each of the conversations we use the question as an illustrative tool for bringing out the idiosyncratic foci and ways of asking questions within the conversations – we do not look into the conversations for answers per se.

## CRITICAL ENTREPRENEURSHIP STUDIES

Critical Entrepreneurship Studies (CES) is a conversation that seeks to question and challenge the taken-for-granted norms and assumptions of 'mainstream' entrepreneurship research (for overviews see Tedmanson et al., 2012; Rehn et al., 2013; Verduijn et al., 2014; Verduyn et al., 2017; Essers et al., 2017). This includes the self-evidence and paradigmatic roots of entrepreneurship scholarship as a whole, including its (neo-liberal) ideologies and grand narratives (e.g. Martin, 1990; Ogbor, 2000; Ahl, 2004; Armstrong, 2005; Jones and Murtola, 2012b; Rehn et al., 2013). Critical studies tend to argue that the study of entrepreneurship promotes entrepreneurship as something positive and desirable in economies and societies (Rehn and Taalas, 2004; Calás et al., 2009; Jones and Murtola, 2012b; Rehn et al., 2013; Farny et al., 2016). Critical scholars consider this focus, on entrepreneurship as a desirable activity, obscures important questions such as those relating to the messy, heterogeneous and problematic nature of entrepreneurship (Tedmanson et al., 2012); and the hegemonic ideological underpinnings and effects of entrepreneurship discourse (cf. Costa and Saraiva, 2012; Kenny and Scriver, 2012).

For CES, the 'entrepreneur' is sooner a target of critique than the 'epitome of the autonomous [freely acting] individual' (Weiskopf and Steyaert, 2009, p. 188). Hence, studies have raised provocative questions that challenge pre-conceived notions of the 'entrepreneur' and 'entrepreneurship', such as 'Is the Marquis de Sade an entrepreneur' (Jones and Spicer, 2009, p. 70), in their attempt at 'uncovering' entrepreneurship as an 'empty signifier' (also see Jones and Spicer, 2005). CE studies have also illustrated and challenged the (re-)production of the archetype of a white, masculine, individualistic and heroic entrepreneur (e.g. Ogbor, 2000; Nicholson and Anderson, 2005; Hytti and Heinonen, 2013). For example, Essers and Benschop (2007) have investigated how the social categories of entrepreneurship, gender and ethnicity are negotiated in the construction of professional identities and how these identities are embedded in power relations.

There is a vein of critical entrepreneurship research aiming at rearticulating entrepreneurship in light of issues related to freedom and emancipation, and societal production (Verduijn et al., 2014). Such contributions posit entrepreneurship as a 'society-creating force' (cf. Spinosa et al.,1997; Steyaert and Hjorth, 2006; Calás et al., 2009; Al-Dajani and Marlow, 2013; Hjorth, 2013b; Daskalaki et al., 2015), challenging and destabilizing existing knowledge in order to open up new and different understandings that may change society for the better, thus seeking to critique in order to create (Weiskopf and Steyaert, 2009). Studies have asked us to reframe entrepreneurship as social change instead of entrepreneurship as (positive) economic activity (Calás et al., 2009). Hence, they have offered views of how entrepreneurial initiatives can be (re) aligned to (matters of) the common good (as a way out of neoliberalist capitalist economic systems), and how this productive potential results in social realities that are less distorted by oppressive, asymmetrical relations of power.

Put like this, CES can be thought of as a promising, double movement: one that critically engages with the mainstream understanding of entrepreneurship to open it up so that novel possibilities, be they practical or conceptual, can materialize.

## Exploring the Illustrative Question: A Critical Entrepreneurship Studies Approach

A Critical Entrepreneurship Studies take on the question of 'Why do some people become entrepreneurs whereas others don't?' would probably start by a critical scrutiny of the question itself, rather than taking it at face value and looking for ways to answer it. It would look at what assumptions the question entails, on what premises it builds. For example, one might ask what valuations are placed upon entrepreneurship by posing such a question, what is meant by 'an (non-)entrepreneur', what is accepted as entrepreneurship and who as a (legitimate) entrepreneur. From this, one might problematize such valuations and start to ask further questions regarding whether becoming or not becoming an entrepreneurship is a 'good thing' – individually, socially, societally, culturally, politically and economically. Critical studies are not interested in finding a definite answer to the question of who the entrepreneur is, but they do take issue with the way for example the stereotypical, excluding images of entrepreneurs are reproduced in doing research. In doing so, the questions push and probe the limits of what and who we accept as legitimate entrepreneurship and entrepreneurs, and what dynamics of inclusion and exclusion are at play as some people might be encouraged, forced to, discouraged, or even prevented from becoming entrepreneurs.

We now turn to the second conversation: Entrepreneurship as Practice (EaP). We start with a general introduction, and then move on to how we think this approach would deal with our illustrative question.

## ENTREPRENEURSHIP AS PRACTICE

Recently, entrepreneurship scholars have started to respond to pleas (Steyaert, 2007; Johannisson, 2011) for bringing the general social scientific 'practice turn' (Schatzki et al., 2001; Feldman and Orlikowski 2011; Nicolini, 2012) into entrepreneurship research. For Entrepreneurship as Practice, as the name suggests, the interest is in *practices*, as organized constellations of collaborative activities (De Clercq and Voronov, 2009; Anderson et al., 2010; Johannisson, 2011), and in understanding the constitution and consequences of specific entrepreneurial practices in specific settings.

Whilst Entrepreneurship as Practice is united by a theoretical interest in practice theories, there is no unitary 'practice theory'. Interest in 'practice(s)' can be traced back to the legacy of such thinkers as Wittgenstein, Derrida, Heidegger, Lyotard, Giddens, Bourdieu and Foucault and it is fair to say that there is a variety of theoretical positions gathering in the practice turn (Nicolini, 2012). Different practice theories can be seen to unite in their interest in the activity patterns that constitute daily life (Schatzki et al., 2001). That is, relational, material accomplishments of everyday life (Nicolini, 2012) are objects of interest.

EaP scholars share an agreement about the primacy of a relational and dynamic understanding of entrepreneurship, such that the unit of analysis is not the organization (venture, business, start-up), nor the individual entrepreneur, but real-time, jointly performed practices (Fletcher, 2006). EaP shifts the focus from individual entrepreneurial action (Gartner, 1988), towards wanting to understand the joint activities that constitute entrepreneurial activity (Anderson and Ronteau, 2017; McKeever et al., 2015).

Entrepreneurship as Practice adopts multiple practice theories, with Giddens (e.g. Jack and Anderson, 2002; Chiasson and Saunders, 2005; Sarason et al., 2006) and Bourdieu (e.g. De Clercq and Voronov; 2009; Terjesen and Elam, 2009; Anderson et al., 2010; Spigel, 2013) being among the first and most prominent ones to have been taken up. Other contributions take their inspiration from such practice theorists as Schatzki (e.g. Keating et al., 2014), and Engeström (activity theory, cf. Holt, 2008; Jones and Holt, 2008). There are also studies interested in entrepreneurial practices without explicit reference to certain practice theories or to a certain ontological position (e.g. Drakopoulou Dodd, 2014; Engstrom, 2012; Fletcher, 2006; Goss et al., 2011; Imas et al., 2012; Tobias et al., 2013).

Studies have, for example, investigated how early venture entrepreneurs engage in socially embedded practices to resource their firm (Keating et al., 2014); how transnational entrepreneurs navigate multiple institutional environments (Terjesen and Elam, 2009) and how networking practices of growing entrepreneurial firms are deployed and with whom (Anderson et al., 2010). They have also asked how newcomers entering a field gain legitimacy (De Clercq and Voronov, 2009). Other studies have wondered how gender and entrepreneurship are enacted as situated practices (Bruni et al., 2004) and how insights from the 'practice turn' can be brought together with ethnomethodology and conversation analysis to offer new perspectives on the situated nature of entrepreneurial practices (Chalmers and Shaw, 2017). Goss et al. (2011) even combine a practice theory perspective with a reflexive and critical outlook on entrepreneurial practice, in providing a detailed understanding of the complex dynamics involved in the 'doing' of power and resistance in entrepreneurship.

**Exploring the Illustrative Question: An Entrepreneurship as Practice Approach**

For the practice approach, interest is in the social and material accomplishment of practices (Nicolini, 2012), which means that Entrepreneurship as Practice would think of ways to reframe the question of 'Why do some people become entrepreneurs and others don't?' so that it could be re-thought in terms of practices. This approach implies stepping away from asking questions about what individuals *as such* are or do and away from looking for explanations resulting from reified entities.

At the simplest, EaP would ask questions about 'becoming an entrepreneur' as a practice: what routinized ways of doing, talking and feeling (Reckwitz, 2002) are involved; how does one (not) accomplish becoming an entrepreneur materially and discursively; what shared understandings, rules, norms and meanings, and various artefacts and (bodily) competences are involved; how does someone become seen as a competent practitioner (entrepreneur) within a certain field; how are 'entrepreneurs' constructed in and through practices and practicing? Asking these questions would imply that such practices cannot be studied in isolation though, since practices are always interconnected (Gherardi, 2012; Nicolini, 2012).

Practice theories see motivations, wants, needs, and feelings not as individual property, but as part of practices (Reckwitz, 2002). This means that 'mental' activities such as (not) desiring to be an entrepreneur should be considered as elements and qualities of a constellation of practices, not as qualities of the individual (Reckwitz, 2002). This is important if studies were to approach 'becoming an entrepreneur' as a matter of identity and 'wanting to become one'. Adopting a practice approach entails reframing the example question by asking how practices recruit practitioners (Shove et al., 2012). Practices might 'produce' entrepreneurial practitioners, where it can be viewed upon as an empirical task to consider what are the practices within which it even makes sense to understand be(com)ing an entrepreneur. From this angle, it might be that studies in other fields, such as consumption or volunteering, may produce compelling insights into when, where and how practices instilling 'becoming an entrepreneur' emerge as something that makes sense. Furthermore, to understand if and how entrepreneurship emerges from and affects social relations and arrangements would mean to study how bundles and complexes of practices form, persist, and disappear (Shove et al., 2012), thus exceeding such 'immediate acts' as registering a venture or writing a business plan.

In moving on to the third conversation in this chapter, we once again start by a general introduction, followed by offering ideas on how this approach would tackle the illustrative question.

## RADICAL PROCESSUAL ENTREPRENEURSHIP STUDIES

'Traditional' attempts at theorizing entrepreneurial processes present 'the' entrepreneurial process predominantly as one that involves starting up a (new) venture as an intentionally planned activity, a linear trajectory (Steyaert, 2007). Most such conceptualizations assume that the development of a new venture proceeds through (identifiable) sequences of stages or steps – a road towards a pre-defined goal (Churchill and Lewis, 1983; Carter et al., 1996). The Radical Processual Approach to entrepreneurship diverges from this understanding of process. The conversation claims that entrepreneuring cannot 'be captured in plain predictions, complete deterministic schemes or pre-existing patterns' (Steyaert, 2004, p. 19).

This conversation sees that, traditionally, ontological assumptions are predicated on the premise of there being a 'world' consisting of fixed things (rather than processes), with an inclination to 'treat' 'an abstraction as if it were real' (Demir and Lychnell, 2015, p. 87). A processual approach implies 'a major shift in one's perception of the world' (Demir and Lychnell, 2015, p. 87). Indeed, the *radical* processual approach is a conversation interested in a shift in ontology. Such a processual approach (also: process metaphysics (Chia, 1999)) finds its roots in the works of philosophers such as Whitehead (1929), and Heidegger (1971). It entails abandoning linear conceptualizations of process, rather viewing upon 'the world' as being in continuous flux, with change being the standard, and not the exception (Tsoukas and Chia, 2002). For radical processual theorists, movement becomes the primordial quality (Nayak, 2008) in theory development. Radical processual theorists thus criticize 'thingification', or reification (cf. Rescher, 1996), the thinking about phenomena in terms of things and (stable) entities.

As said, there is a budding conversation taking up radical processual insights in understanding entrepreneurship (or in the conversation's words, *entrepreneuring*), incorporating a process view that is predicated on an ontology of becoming. Instead of conceptualizing the entrepreneurial process in terms of stages, and (sequential) steps, this conversation would view any emergent ordering – 'fixity' (Hjorth, 2017) – as a social achievement, precariously achieved, indeterminate, always remaining open to further becoming (Verduyn, 2015). The radical approach sees entrepreneurial activity as organization-creation, a creative mode of becoming that intervenes with well-instituted organizational settings (Hjorth et al., 2015). As Hjorth et al. (2015) assert, from a radical processual point of view, entrepreneuring is to be seen as an act of 'disclosing that which is not yet fully known' (p. 600).

The Radical Processual Approach has been taken up in various (but limited) contributions (e.g. Steyaert, 1997; Hjorth, 2003; 2013a; 2014; 2017; Chia, 2008; Styhre, 2008; Hjorth et al., 2015; Verduyn, 2015). Processual entrepreneurship studies form an attempt at moving beyond a reductionist understanding of the entrepreneurship phenomenon. This understanding appeals to how entrepreneurship inadvertently varyingly provokes and appropriates existing 'orders' (cf. Steyaert, 2007; Nayak and Chia, 2011). Scholars have been asking questions such as how processual thinking of subjectivity could be applied to study of 'becoming entrepreneur' (Hjorth, 2013a) and how the 'hesitant entrepreneur' could be used as an exemplar of radical processual thinking (Nayak and Chia, 2011). They have also sought to understand spatio-temporal rhythm of the creation of organization that makes the entrepreneurial venture emerge (Verduyn, 2015) and to adopt process metaphysics to generate a view on the nature of entrepreneurship and entrepreneurial learning that requires 'peripheral vision' rather than focal awareness (Chia, 2008).

We feel that we need to stipulate that even if the radical processual promise has been taken up in various (but, as said (still) limited) contributions, the focus in them is predominantly conceptual. For example, calling for how such an approach has merit in offering *deeper* processual analyses (Nayak and Chia, 2011), or in offering an attempt at taking it up to offer a further conceptualization of how this might play out.

**Exploring the Illustrative Question: A Radical Processual Approach**

A processual approach to understanding the question of 'Why do some people become entrepreneurs whereas others don't?' would evidently take the *becoming* in the question seriously. In the process approach that is based on ontology of becoming, 'to be' becomes 'to become' (Cloots, 1968 in Steyaert, 1997). This means that any act, event or 'decision' is seen as temporary, prone to further becoming. On rejecting the way 'becoming' is implied in the illustrative question, the radical processual approach would move on to reframe the question to emphasize the provisional of/in entrepreneurship: the 'entre', the in-between, where actually anyone always already 'is' and 'is not' (to be seen as) an entrepreneur. The approach would start to ask novel questions regarding the nature of the processes in and through which such (relational) events come about, where they stem from, and how they are interwoven with 'what is already there', changing directions, eroding 'fixities' (Hjorth, 2017), finding ways to establishing temporary 'new' arrangements. Questions would be geared towards entrepreneuring as world-making (Spinosa et al., 1997), and the consequences and impact(s) this may or may not create (Verduyn, 2015).

The radical processual approach would object to the (reified) use of 'entrepreneur' in the illustrative question. The ontological position of becoming rejects 'becoming or not becoming an entrepreneur' as a matter of some *final* entity or identity. According to the radical processual approach, entrepreneuring cannot be reduced 'to a quality of a mind … a quality of human beings … or a skill' (Hjorth et al., 2015, p. 607). From a processual approach, questions would not be asked in a way that makes a divide, whereby 'to be an entrepreneur' is a different category from 'not being one'.

## DISCUSSION

In this chapter, we have presented three conversations: Critical Entrepreneurship Studies, Entrepreneurship as Practice and the Radical Processual Approach (for a summary, see Table 4.1).

Although at times used interchangeably, we have signalled a need to gauge what specifically is addressed within each conversation, so as to be able to evaluate what sets them apart and to comprehend what is their common ground. All three share an interest in stepping away from individualized, overtly economized, deterministic accounts of entrepreneurship and advocating an interest in the mundane, the everydayness of entrepreneurship. The practice approach shares with the radical processual approach the interest in how certain practices change the order of things just going as they go, invading everyday life. Furthermore, they share a non-entitative stance, where entrepreneur*ing* is posited as unfinalized/open-ended and scholars are wary of such words as 'essentially' and 'really'. EaP and RPA are both processual in their outlook, albeit EaP not being a 'radical' processual approach. To understand the intricacies of each conversation, and to work towards appreciating each of them, we now postulate tentative ideas on how insights from each conversation could inform future research.

First, Entrepreneurship as Practice studies could benefit from a critical 'attitude' in not losing sight of the politicality in and of the intricate practice constellations being materialized in doing entrepreneurship and in order to avoid entrepreneurship research's general 'hegemony of the positive' (Farny et al., 2016). In other fields, the practice approach has been mobilized explicitly

*Table 4.1*    Summary of the three conversations

| Conversation | Understanding of entrepreneurship | What the conversation focuses on | Example research questions/aims |
|---|---|---|---|
| **Critical Entrepreneurship Studies** | - Entrepreneurship as an (ideological) discourse. | - Social and political connotations of entrepreneurship. | - How does the signifier 'entrepreneurship' function within the social context of economic crisis and with what consequences? (Kenny and Scriver, 2012). |
| | - 'Entrepreneurship is simultaneously both a political and economic category and one that rests on symbolic and ideological fantasies' (Jones and Murtola, 2012a, p. 636). | - Being wary of capitalist system. | - How are the social categories of entrepreneurship, gender and ethnicity negotiated in the construction of professional identities and how are these identities embedded in power relations? (Essers and Benschop, 2007). |
| | - Entrepreneurship is an empty signifier and as such it can be almost whatever one desires it to be, which makes it perennially attractive (Jones and Spicer, 2005, 2009). | - No a priori positive view of entrepreneurship. | - Entrepreneur[ial] stories of 'barefoot' entrepreneurs operating in marginal, poor and excluded places and contexts (Imas et al., 2012). |
| | - All entrepreneurship activity can be seen as a process of social change (Calás et al., 2009). | - Interest in the 'dark side' of entrepreneurship, but also the affirmative side (means of emancipating, changing (society). | - How can we develop critique of entrepreneuring? (Jones and Murtola, 2012b). |
| | | - Questioning who and what are represented within 'mainstream' research and who and what is left out; voicing 'alternative' subjectivities. | - How does entrepreneuring release emancipatory possibilities by changing extant relations of power? (Goss et al., 2011). |

| Conversation | Understanding of entrepreneurship | What the conversation focuses on | Example research questions/aims |
| --- | --- | --- | --- |
| **Entrepreneurship as Practice** | - Entrepreneurship as an assemblage, an everyday hands-on practice and creative organizing (Johannisson, 2011). | - Interest in *practices*, unit of analysis is practices. | - 'How are gender and entrepreneurship enacted as situated practices?' (Bruni et al., 2004). |
| | - Entrepreneurship as a set of practices intrinsically intertwined with the very fabric of contemporary society; as an unfolding of everyday practices (De Clercq and Voronov, 2009). | - Understanding the constitution and consequences of specific entrepreneurial practices in specific settings. | - 'How do early venture entrepreneurs engage in socially embedded practices to resource their firm?' (Keating et al., 2014). |
| | | - Understanding the joint activities that constitute entrepreneurial activity. | - 'How do newcomers entering a field gain legitimacy?' (De Clercq and Voronov, 2009). |
| | | - Applying practice theories to the study of entrepreneurship. | - 'How can the situated nature of entrepreneurial practices be understood?' (Chalmers and Shaw, 2017). |

| Conversation | Understanding of entrepreneurship | What the conversation focuses on | Example research questions/aims |
|---|---|---|---|
| **Radical Processual Approach** | - Entrepreneurial activity as organization-creation, a creative mode of becoming that intervenes with well-instituted organizational settings (Hjorth et al., 2015). | - Taking an alternative ontological stance. | - To adopt process metaphysics to generate a view on the nature of entrepreneurship and entrepreneurial learning that requires 'peripheral vision' rather than focal awareness (Chia, 2008). |
| | - *Entrepreneuring* is to be seen as 'the appearing and re-appearing of events', as an act of 'disclosing that which is not yet fully known' (Hjorth et al., 2015, p. 600). | - Incorporating a process view that is predicated on an ontology of becoming into the study of entrepreneurship. | - To apply processual thinking of subjectivity in the study of 'becoming entrepreneur' (Hjorth, 2013a). |
| | | | - Exploring the 'hesitant entrepreneur' as an exemplar of radical processual thinking (Nayak and Chia, 2011). |
| | | | - Positing entrepreneuring as a form of 'history-making', opening up well-instituted organization settings, and appreciating entrepreneurial activity as the becoming of organization-creation (Hjorth et al., 2015). |
| | | | - How to understand the spatio-temporal rhythm of the creation of organization? (Verduyn, 2015). |

from a critical position (for example Gherardi, 2009; Geiger, 2009; Corradi et al., 2010) and EaP could follow such examples.

On the other hand, the practice approach could provide additional theoretical resources for CES that could be utilized to ask, for example, how both problematic and emancipatory aspects of entrepreneurship are being materialized and kept in existence in and through constant repetition of (mundane) practices. Furthermore, EaP could be insightful for CES studies engaging in *affirmative* critique (e.g. Weiskopf and Steyaert, 2009; Hjorth, 2013a; Tobias et al., 2013; Dey and Steyaert, 2018). The guiding idea of critique as affirmation (Braidotti, 2011, 2013; MacLure, 2015; Raffnsøe, 2016) is that critique should transform the object of critique. EaP theorizing can help in making oppressive practices *visible* in order to *change* them. That is, the practice approach can assist in arriving at a nuanced understanding of 'how things are done' (before rushing to change them).

Through its emphasis on sociomateriality, the practice approach could also be a further source of inspiration in moving from human-centric critique in entrepreneurship, at the favour of moving towards acknowledging the challenges we are faced with today (Braidotti, 2013; Gherardi, 2017; Ergene et al., 2017). Combining practice theoretical insights with the alternative-seeking, affirmative critique type of CES research could guide interest towards new ways of organizing that are called for to enable living on our finite planet (cf. Houtbeckers (2018), who calls for research that would focus on everyday practices perceived as 'post-growth organizing').

The radical processual approach can provide insights for CES relating to *how* theorizing is done. Some CES research seems to be postulated on universal principles ('we should reduce oppression', 'we should reduce inequality', 'emancipation is possible'). The radical processual approach reminds us to avoid moulding insights into (fixed) categories. Thus, it can help let go of the notion of there being universal principles and instead stipulate the inherent movement in and of understanding (social) phenomena. Process studies remind us that when theorizing things, we should not 'stop' phenomena to comprehend them, thus losing sight of their processual dynamics. Likewise, RPA could urge critical research to reconsider the 'duality' found in many critical contributions (cf. 'male–female', 'oppression–emancipation').

The same applies to what RPA may remind EaP of: that when we theorize, we try to fix and 'hold' things. It might critique practice studies for 'showing' (understanding of) certain practices, and then pausing the analysis, resulting in a 'fixing' of understanding the world which in fact is actually (still) constantly going on. The radical processual approach may act as a reminder for practice theories to embrace processual understandings of the world and not to present practices as some deterministic external entities that 'float above people'.

Given that the radical processual approach apparently faces challenges in operationalizing its ontological ideas in empirical work, it may mean that EaP's 'toolset vocabulary' (Nicolini, 2012) can further the radical processual conversation in making the radical processual promises more 'concrete'.

This chapter has provided a brief overview of three conversations in entrepreneurship research, a mere thought exercise to learn more about the idiosyncrasies and interrelations between these discussions. As a conclusion, we would like to acknowledge that contemporary entrepreneurship research hosts a wonderful array of 'different' approaches in terms of meta-theoretical assumptions, theories and methods. The three conversations covered here offer just a minor glimpse into what is going on in the field. Generally, we call for continuing to embrace conversations going on in the humanities and social sciences to help understand the entrepreneurship phenomenon. A fruitful task for future research would be to continue to add conversations, to be looked at side-by-side without the intention of arguing for the superiority of one approach over another. A trap that may occur with having these conversations is that they may tend to start producing boundaries (deciding what is 'in', and what is 'out'), and thus run the risk of becoming encapsulating, rather than opening up. We call for fluidity of current and future conversations, thus keeping them 'alive'.

## REFERENCES

Ahl, H. (2004), *The Scientific Reproduction of Gender Inequality: A Discourse Analysis of Research Texts upon Women's Entrepreneurship*, Copenhagen: CBS Press.

Al-Dajani, H. and S. Marlow (2013), 'Empowerment and entrepreneurship: A theoretical framework', *International Journal of Entrepreneurial Behaviour & Research*, **19**, 503–524.

Anderson, A.R. and S. Ronteau (2017), 'Towards an entrepreneurial theory of practice: Emerging ideas for emerging economies', *Journal of Entrepreneurship in Emerging Economies*, **9** (2), 110–120.

Anderson, A.R., S. Drakopoulou Dodd and S. Jack (2010), 'Network practices and entrepreneurial growth', *Scandinavian Journal of Management*, **26** (2), 121–133.

Armstrong, Peter (2005), *Critique of Entrepreneurship: People and Policy*, Basingstoke, UK: Palgrave Macmillan.

Baron, R.A. (2004), 'The cognitive perspective: A valuable tool for answering entrepreneurship's basic "why" questions', *Journal of Business Venturing*, **19**, 221–239.

Braidotti, R. (2011), *Nomadic Theory: The Portable Rosi Braidotti*, New York, NY: Columbia University Press.

Braidotti, R. (2013), *The Posthuman*, Cambridge, UK: Polity Press.

Bruni, A., S. Gherardi and B. Poggio (2004), 'Doing gender, doing entrepreneurship: An ethnographic account of intertwined practices', *Gender, Work and Organization*, **11** (4), 406–429.

Calás, M.B., L. Smircich and K.A. Bourne (2009), 'Extending the boundaries: Reframing "entrepreneurship as social change" through feminist perspectives', *Academy of Management Review*, **34** (3), 552–569.

Carter, N., W.B. Gartner and P. Reynolds (1996), 'Exploring start-up event sequences', *Journal of Business Venturing*, **11**, 151–166.

Chalmers, D.M. and E. Shaw (2017), 'The endogenous construction of entrepreneurial contexts: A practice-based perspective', *International Small Business Journal*, September, **35** (1), 19–39.

Chia, R. (1999), 'A 'rhizomic' model of organizational change and transformation. Perspective from a metaphysics of change', *British Journal of Management*, **10**, 209–227.

Chia, R. (2008), 'Enhancing entrepreneurial learning through peripheral vision', in Richard T. Harrison and Claire Leitch (eds), *Entrepreneurial Learning. Conceptual Frameworks and Applications*, London, UK: Routledge, pp. 27–43.

Chiasson, M., and C. Saunders (2005), 'Reconciling diverse approaches to opportunity research using the structuration theory', *Journal of Business Venturing*, **20** (6), 747–767.

Churchill, N. and V. Lewis (1983), 'The five stages of small business growth', *Harvard Business Review*, **61**, 30–50.

Corradi, G., S. Gherardi and L. Verzelloni (2010), 'Through the practice lens: Where is the bandwagon of practice-based studies heading?', *Management Learning*, **4** (3), 265–283.

Costa, A.S.M. and L.A.S. Saraiva (2012), 'Hegemonic discourses on entrepreneurship as an ideological mechanism for the reproduction of capital', *Organization*, **19** (5), 587–614.

Daskalaki, D., D. Hjorth and J. Mair (2015), 'Are entrepreneurship, communities, and social transformation related?', *Journal of Management Inquiry*, **24**, 419–423.

De Clercq, D. and M. Voronov (2009), 'Toward a practice perspective of entrepreneurship: Entrepreneurial legitimacy as habitus', *International Small Business Journal*, **27** (4), 395–419.

Demir, R., and L.O. Lychnell (2015), 'Mangling the process: A meta-theoretical account of process theorizing', *Qualitative Research*, **15** (1), 85–104.

Dey, P. and C. Steyaert (eds) (2018), *Social Entrepreneurship: An Affirmative Critique*, Cheltenham, UK and Northampton, MA, USA: Edward Elgar Publishing.

Drakopoulou Dodd, S.L. (2014), 'Roots radical – place, power and practice in punk entrepreneurship', *Entrepreneurship & Regional Development*, **26** (1–2), 165–205.

Engstrom, C. (2012), 'An autoethnographic account of prosaic entrepreneurship', *Tamara: Journal for Critical Organization Inquiry*, **10**, 41–54.

Ergene, S., M.B. Calás and L. Smircich (2017), 'Ecologies of sustainable concerns: Organization theorizing for the Anthropocene', *Gender, Work & Organization*, **25** (3), 222–245.

Essers, C. and Y. Benschop (2007), 'Enterprising identities: Female entrepreneurs of Moroccan or Turkish origin in the Netherlands', *Organization Studies*, **28** (1), 49–69.

Essers, C., P. Dey, D. Tedmanson and K. Verduyn (2017), *Critical Perspectives on Entrepreneurship: Challenging Dominant Discourses*, Abingdon, Oxon, New York, NY: Routledge.

Farny, S., S. Hedeboe Frederiksen, M. Hannibal and S. Jones (2016), 'A CULTure of entrepreneurship education', *Entrepreneurship & Regional Development*, **28** (7–8), 514–535.

Feldman, M.S. and W.J. Orlikowski (2011), 'Theorizing practice and practicing theory', *Organization Science*, **22** (5), 1240–1253.

Fletcher, D.E. (2006), 'Entrepreneurial processes and the social construction of opportunity', *Entrepreneurship & Regional Development*, **18** (5), 421–440.

Gartner, W.B. (1988), '"Who is an entrepreneur?" Is the wrong question', *American Journal of Small Business*, **12** (4), 11–32.

Geiger, D. (2009), 'Revisiting the concept of practice: Toward argumentative understanding of practicing', *Management Learning*, **40** (2), 129–144.

Gherardi, S. (2009), 'Introduction: The critical power of the "practice lens"', *Management Learning*, **40** (2), 115–128.

Gherardi, S. (2012), *How to Conduct a Practice-Based Study. Problems and Methods,* Cheltenham, UK and Northampton, MA, USA: Edward Elgar Publishing.

Gherardi, S. (2017), 'Sociomateriality in posthuman practice theory', in A. Hui, T. Schatzki and E. Shove (eds), *The Nexus of Practices*, London, UK: Routledge, pp. 50–63.

Goss, D., R. Jones, M. Betta and J. Latham (2011), 'Power as practice: A micro-sociological analysis of the dynamics of emancipatory entrepreneurship', *Organization Studies*, **32** (2), 211–229.

Heidegger, M. (1971), 'The nature of language', in Peter D. Hertz (ed.), *On the Way to Language*, New York: Harper & Row, pp. 57–110.

Hjorth, D. (2003), *Rewriting Entrepreneurship: For a New Perspective on Organisational Creativity*, Malmö/Copenhagen/Oslo: Liber/CBS Press/Abstrakt.

Hjorth, D. (2013a), 'Absolutely fabulous! Fabulation and organization-creation in processes of becoming-entrepreneur', *Society and Business Review*, **8**, 205–224.

Hjorth, D. (2013b), 'Public entrepreneurship: Desiring social change, creating sociality', *Entrepreneurship & Regional Development*, **25**, (1–2), 34–51.

Hjorth, D. (2014), 'Sketching a philosophy of entrepreneurship', in Ted Baker and Friederike Welter (eds), *The Routledge Companion to Entrepreneurship*, London, UK: Routledge, pp. 41–58.

Hjorth, D. (2017), 'Critique nouvelle – an essay on affirmative-performative entrepreneurship research', *Revue de l'Entrepreneuriat*, **16** (1), 47–54.

Hjorth, D., R. Holt and C. Steyaert (2015), 'Entrepreneurship and process studies', *International Small Business Journal*, **33** (6), 599–611.

Holt, R. (2008), 'Using activity theory to understand entrepreneurial opportunity', *Mind, Culture, and Activity*, **15** (1), 52–70.

Houtbeckers, E. (2018), 'Framing social enterprise as post-growth organising in the diverse economy', *Management Revue. Socio-Economic Studies*, **29** (3), 257–280.

Hytti, U. and J. Heinonen (2013), 'Heroic and humane entrepreneurs: Identity work in entrepreneurship education', *Education + Training*, **55** (8/9), 886–898.

Imas, J.M., N. Wilson and A. Weston (2012), 'Barefoot entrepreneurs', *Organization*, **19** (5), 563–585.

Jack, S. L. and A.R. Anderson (2002), 'The effects of embeddedness on the entrepreneurial process', *Journal of Business Venturing*, **17** (5), 467–487.

Johannisson, B. (2011), 'Towards a practice theory of entrepreneuring', *Small Business Economics*, **36**, 135–150.

Jones, C. and A.-M. Murtola (2012a), 'Entrepreneurship and expropriation', *Organization,* **19** (5), 635–655.

Jones, C. and A.-M. Murtola (2012b), 'Entrepreneurship, crisis, critique', in Daniel Hjorth (ed.), *Handbook of Organizational Entrepreneurship*, Cheltenham, UK and Northampton, MA, USA: Edward Elgar Publishing, pp. 116–133.

Jones, C. and A. Spicer (2005), 'The sublime object of entrepreneurship', *Organization*, **12** (2), 223–246.

Jones, C. and A. Spicer (2009), *Unmasking the Entrepreneur*, Cheltenham, UK and Northampton, MA, USA: Edward Elgar Publishing.

Jones, O. and R. Holt (2008), 'The creation and evolution of new business ventures: An activity theory perspective', *Journal of Small Business and Enterprise Development*, **15** (1), 51–73.

Keating, A., S. Geiger and D. McLoughlin (2014), 'Riding the practice waves: Social resourcing practices during new venture development', *Entrepreneurship Theory and Practice*, **38** (5), 1207–1235.

Kenny, K. and S. Scriver (2012), 'Dangerously empty? Hegemony and the construction of the Irish entrepreneur', *Organization*, **19** (5), 615–633.

Maclure, M. (2015), 'The 'new materialisms': A thorn in the flesh of critical qualitative inquiry?', in Gaile S. Cannella, Michelle Salazar Pérez and Penny A. Pasque (eds), *Critical Qualitative Inquiry: Foundations and Futures*, California: Left Coast Press, pp. 93–112.

Martin, J. (1990), 'Organizational taboos: The suppression of gender conflict in organizations', *Organization Science*, **1** (4), 339–359.

McKeever, E., S. Jack and A. Anderson (2015), 'Embedded entrepreneurship in the creative *re*-construction of place', *Journal of Business Venturing*, **30**, 50–65.

Nayak, A. (2008), 'On the way to theory: A processual approach', *Organization Studies*, **29** (2), 173–190.

Nayak, A. and R. Chia (2011), 'Thinking becoming. Process philosophy and organization studies', *Philosophy and Organization Theory Research in the Sociology of Organizations*, **32**, 281–309.

Nicholson, L. and A.R. Anderson (2005), 'News and nuances of the entrepreneurial myth and metaphor: Linguistic games in entrepreneurial sense-making and sense-giving', *Entrepreneurship Theory and Practice*, **29** (2), 153–172.

Nicolini, D. (2012), *Practice Theory, Work, and Organization*, Oxford, UK: Oxford University Press.

Ogbor, J. (2000), 'Mythicizing and reification in entrepreneurial discourse: Ideology-critique of entrepreneurial studies', *Journal of Management Studies*, **37** (5), 605–635.

Raffnsøe, S. (2016), *Philosophy of the Anthropocene: The Human Turn*, London, UK: Palgrave Pivot.

Reckwitz, A. (2002), 'Toward a theory of social practices. A development in culturalist theorizing', *European Journal of Social Theory*, **5** (2), 243–263.

Rehn, A. and S. Taalas (2004), '"Znakomstva I Svyazi" (Acquaintances and connections) – Blat, the Soviet Union, and mundane entrepreneurship', *Entrepreneurship & Regional Development*, **16**, 235–250.

Rehn, A., M. Brännback, A. Carsruda and M. Lindahl (2013), 'Editorial. Challenging the myths of entrepreneurship?', *Entrepreneurship & Regional Development*, **25** (7–8), 543–551.

Rescher, N. (1996), *Process Metaphysics*, New York: State University of New York Press.

Sarason, Y., T. Dean and F.J. Dillard (2006), 'Entrepreneurship as the nexus of individual and opportunity: A structuration view', *Journal of Business Venturing*, **21**, 286–305.

Schatzki, T.R., K. Knorr-Cetina and E. von Savigny (eds) (2001), *The Practice Turn in Contemporary Theory*, London, UK: Psychology Press.

Shove, E., M. Pantzar and M. Watson (2012), *The Dynamics of Social Practice: Everyday Life and How it Changes*, Los Angeles, London, New Delhi, Singapore, Washington DC: Sage.

Spigel, B. (2013), 'Bourdieuian approaches to the geography of entrepreneurial cultures, *Entrepreneurship & Regional Development*, **25** (9–10), 804–818.

Spinosa, C., F. Flores and H.L. Dreyfus (1997), *Disclosing New Worlds. Entrepreneurship, Democratic Action and the Cultivation of Solidarity*, Cambridge, MA: MIT Press.

Steyaert, C. (1997), 'A qualitative methodology for process studies of entrepreneurship: Creating local knowledge through stories', *International Studies of Management & Organization*, **27**, 13–33.

Steyaert, C. (2004), 'The prosaics of entrepreneurship', in Daniel Hjorth and Chris Steyaert (eds), *Narrative and Discursive Approaches in Entrepreneurship Studies*, Cheltenham, UK and Northampton, MA, USA: Edward Elgar Publishing, pp. 8–21.

Steyaert, C. (2007), '"Entrepreneuring" as a conceptual attractor. A review of process theories in 20 years of entrepreneurship studies', *Entrepreneurship & Regional Development*, **19**, 453–477.

Steyaert, C. and D. Hjorth (2006), *Entrepreneurship as Social Change*, Cheltenham, UK and Northampton, MA, USA: Edward Elgar Publishing.

Styhre, A. (2008), 'Transduction and entrepreneurship: A biophilosophical image of the entrepreneur', *Scandinavian Journal of Management*, **24** (2), 103–112.

Tedmanson, D., K. Verduyn, C. Essers and W.B. Gartner (2012), 'Critical perspectives in entrepreneurship research', *Organization*, **19** (5), 531–541.

Terjesen, S. and A. Elam (2009), 'Transnational entrepreneurs' venture internationalization strategies: A practice theory approach', *Entrepreneurship Theory and Practice*, **33** (5), 1093–1120.

Tobias, J.M., J. Mair and C. Barbosa-Leiker (2013), 'Toward a theory of transformative entrepreneuring: Poverty reduction and conflict resolution in Rwanda's entrepreneurial coffee sector', *Journal of Business Venturing*, **28** (6), 728–742.

Tsoukas, H. and R. Chia (2002), 'On organizational becoming: Rethinking organizational change', *Organization Science*, **13** (5), 567–582.

Verduyn, K. (2015), 'Entrepreneuring and process. A Lefebvrian perspective', *International Small Business Journal*, **33** (6), 638–648.

Verduyn, K., P. Dey and D. Tedmanson (2017), 'A critical understanding of entrepreneurship', *Revue de l'Entrepreneuriat*, **16**, (1), 37–45.

Verduijn, K., P. Dey, D. Tedmanson and C. Essers (2014), 'Emancipation and/or oppression? Conceptualizing dimensions of criticality in entrepreneurship studies', *International Journal of Entrepreneurial Behaviour & Research*, **20** (2), 98–107.

Weiskopf, R. and C. Steyaert (2009), 'Metamorphoses in entrepreneurship studies: Towards affirmative politics of entrepreneuring', in Daniel Hjorth and Chris Steyaert (eds), *The Politics and Aesthetics of Entrepreneurship. A Fourth Movements in Entrepreneurship Book*, Cheltenham, UK and Northampton, MA, USA: Edward Elgar Publishing, pp. 183–201.

Whitehead, Alfred North (1929), *Process and Reality*, New York: Free Press.

# 5. Women and family firms: a state of the art literature review

**Annalisa Sentuti, Francesca Maria Cesaroni and Serena Cubico**

## INTRODUCTION

One of the main changes occurring in family firms (FFs) in recent decades has been the increasing involvement of women in the ownership, leadership and management of such businesses (Ernst & Young, 2015). Family business studies have been dealing with this topic since the mid-1980s, and scholars have produced significant findings regarding the varied, complex and multifaceted universe of women within FFs. A number of literature reviews (Jimenez, 2009; Wang, 2010; Heinonen and Hytti, 2011; Gupta and Levenburg, 2013; Campopiano et al., 2017; Gnan et al., 2017; Nelson and Constantinidis, 2017; Kubíček and Machek, 2018) have discussed the state of this field of research and its possible future directions. Jimenez (2009) identified both obstacles and positive aspects related to the participation of women in FFs. Wang (2010) focused on daughters' exclusion from FF succession and analysed barriers and pathways to leadership. Gupta and Levenburg (2013) identified an evolutionary trend in this field of research, from the concept of invisibility, to the different women's roles, and finally to their characters in different cultural contexts. Heinonen and Hytti (2011) explored and outlined how gender issues are tackled in family business research while Nelson and Constantinidis (2017) and Kubíček and Machek (2018) respectively analysed the effects on family business succession of sex, gender, and gender-related factors mentioned in the literature. Gnan et al. (2017) paid particular attention to women's representation in ownership and governance bodies and their key role in the succession process. Finally, Campopiano et al. (2017) proposed a broad and comprehensive systematic literature review on women's involvement in FFs, identifying four topics (entrepreneurial entry, succession, career dynamics, and presence), research gaps and research opportunities.

Adopting diverse methodological approaches, these articles have made an impressive contribution to mapping research on women in FFs, focusing on a range of topics and offering various perspectives on analysis. However, when the current study was undertaken, only the literature reviews of Jimenez (2009), Wang (2010), and Heinonen and Hytti (2011) had been published and were available to the authors. Since Heinonen and Hytti (2011) focused on gender in family business research and the main interest of the authors in the current study was to undertake a literature review on women in FFs, we decided to focus on the contributions of Jimenez (2009) and Wang (2010) to establish what was already known about this topic before beginning our literature review.

Taking into account these premises, this chapter aims to contribute to the ongoing debate by conducting a structured review (Massaro et al., 2016) of FF studies in the business and management literature, by exploring and outlining the state of the art with regards to women's involvement in FFs. For this purpose, the following research questions were defined: RQ1, What are the evolutionary trends in the field?; and RQ2, What is the focus of literature concerning women's involvement in FFs?

The structured literature review (SLR) method is considered particularly rigorous and has been recently suggested as an approach to analysing the business and management literature (Massaro et al., 2016). Although traditional literature reviews are 'the most common technique in management research' (Denyer and Tranfield, 2006), they are criticized as too subjective (Petticrew and Roberts, 2008) because they are conducted without predefined rules that are followed to search and analyse contributions (Massaro et al., 2016). In contrast, a SLR is guided by a rigid set of rules aiming to reduce subjectivity in selection, evaluation and analysis of data, producing transparent and comprehensive results (Massaro et al., 2016).

Analysing contributions published in 2000–2017 (June 30), 81 academic studies were selected from the Scopus database. These were categorized and examined based on year, journal of publication, impact, country of research, authors' affiliation and methodological approach. Contributions were also analysed to identify the research focus/topic and define the themes and issues addressed.

The remainder of the chapter is structured as follows. First, we provide an overview on previous selected literature reviews. We then present our methodology, describe and summarize the main findings, and finally outline concluding remarks.

## WOMEN IN FAMILY FIRMS: WHAT WE ALREADY KNOW AND WHAT WE NEED TO KNOW

Over the last three decades, several significant studies have examined women's involvement in FFs. Some topics of interest have received particular attention, including succession (Dumas, 1992, 1998; Vera and Dean, 2005; Haberman and Danes, 2007), obstacles (Cole, 1997), roles (Curimbaba, 2002; Barrett and Moores, 2009b; Cesaroni and Sentuti, 2014), and motivations (Salganicoff, 1990).

As stated by Cesaroni and Sentuti (2018) an evolutionary trend in this field of research is evident, and according to Gupta and Levenburg (2013) and Campopiano et al. (2017), there are three generations of studies on the topic. The first generation, published up to the end of the 1990s, focused on the obstacles and difficulties women encountered when joining their FFs. These women's presence within FFs has been described as 'invisible' (Cole, 1997; Dumas, 1989, 1992; Gillis-Donovan and Moynihan-Bradt, 1990; Hollander and Bukovitz, 1990; Salganicoff, 1990); they had no influence in decision-making processes (Cole, 1997; Dumas, 1989, 1992; Salganicoff, 1990), and no proper recognition and reward for their efforts (Gillis-Donovan and Moynihan-Bradt, 1990; Rowe and Hong, 2000). In the second generation of contributions during the first decade of the new millennium, scholars' interest moved to women's roles (Curimbaba, 2002) and careers (Vera and Dean, 2005) within FFs. Researchers reported a more optimistic view of women's involvement in FFs (Campopiano et al., 2017), finding that they often play a crucial role (especially in succession processes) and are 'on the stage' of the FF (Barrett and Moores, 2009b). The third generation of studies, from the end of 2010, has confirmed the optimistic view of women's involvement in FFs by investigating the role of conditions and cultural context in exploiting their potential within the business (Gupta and Levenburg, 2013; Campopiano et al., 2017).

Jimenez (2009) and Wang (2010) offer an important overview of the main research contributions on the topic of women in FFs with regards to the first and second generations of publications. Jimenez (2009) reviewed 48 articles, 23 books and three doctoral dissertations published between 1985 and 2008. She discussed the issue of obstacles and positive aspects related to the involvement of women in FFs and identified three obstacles that needed to be overcome for women to achieve leadership positions: invisibility, emotional leadership, and succession primogeniture. Women's invisibility was mainly related to gender stereotypes that existed in society, and cultural traditions that discriminated against women and prevented them from reaching positions of responsibility, or at least slowed their progress. Women also experienced problems related to the specific context of a FF, such as conflict over roles and loyalties, relationships with parents, siblings and nonfamily members, and struggles for power and authority. However, women assumed a crucial role in emotional leadership within the family and the business. They aimed to maintain peace and harmony in the family and in the firm by mediating and avoiding conflicts 'between the relatives who work together in the firm—particularly, the founder and his son'. Nevertheless, the latter remained the main actors of the business. Finally, women's invisibility and gender stereotypes were evident in leadership succession processes, in which women were rarely considered serious candidates, and the primogeniture criterion was largely followed by FFs. In terms of positive aspects, Jimenez highlighted women's professional pathways and careers within FFs, how they reached leadership positions, and which kind of leadership style they adopted. However, she concluded that the question of how women enter and run FFs remained unclear and suggested several research questions to address.

Wang (2010)—using university academic journal databases (EBSCO, Wiley Inter-Science, ABI/Inform, Science Direct, Emerald)—focused on daughters' exclusion from FF succession and analysed barriers and pathways to leadership. As noted by Kubíček and Machek (2018, p. 4), 'Wang is noticeably more pessimistic as he argues that the succession process is heavily biased by gender and that the underestimation of daughters in the succession process results from both macro- and micro factors which render their capabilities almost invisible.' According to Wang (2010), daughters can assume leadership of the FF only in 'special circumstances', such as when all siblings are female and the family has no male; no male family members are interested in running the business; or the family or business is experiencing a crucial transition or crisis event.

These authors provide a first overview of the literature beginning with the pioneering studies of the 1980s and including investigations carried out in the first years of the new millennium. However, some concerns arise and several issues remain to be addressed, both from the methodological and conceptual points of view. Both Jimenez (2009) and Wang (2010) adopted a descriptive approach and no specific methods or protocols for review were mentioned. Several quality criteria for the studies reviewed (such as authors' affiliations, country of research, and methodological approach employed) were not considered and contributions were not systematically clustered. Consequently, there remains a lack of sufficient information gathered in a well-structured way; thus an updated and SLR may be necessary. Although these gaps were partially filled by more recent literature reviews (especially Campopiano et al., 2017), some important issues remain to be tackled. More effort is necessary to analyse the complexity of women's experiences within FFs and understand how female participation may vary. Further, we consider author affiliation is relevant because analysis of women in FFs was initiated by North American scholars (e.g. Cole, Dumas, Salganicoff) with European scholars taking the backstage. Thus the author affiliation element is included here with the aim of identifying possible changes in perspective. Finally, the location of research allows scholars 'to understand what are the geographic areas that are more investigated and if there are other countries/regions that require attention' (Massaro et al., 2016, p. 783). We consider the country of research particularly relevant for analysing women in FFs because cultural models, traditional values, and rules embedded in social behaviors may have a strong influence and may differ among countries.

## METHODOLOGY

To review and organize the existing findings on women in FFs, the SLR approach based on the guidelines of Massaro et al. (2016) was used, with some customization. Following the authors, the following steps were adopted. First, the research questions (see *Introduction*) intended to be addressed in the literature review were defined (step 1). The literature search and selection of contributions was then undertaken based on a set of explicit rules (step 2). Finally, the analytical framework for the analysis, criteria for the classification of studies, and a taxonomy of research themes and issues were identified (step 3).

With regards to step 2, contributions were selected from Scopus (limited to the business, management and accounting area as our main expertise is in business and management), published between 2000 and 2017 (June 30). Keyword searches were performed within titles, abstracts, and keywords of the studies using various combinations of the following terms (including plurals): woman, daughter, wife, mother, and family business/firm/enterprise/company. The term 'gender' was not considered because the main focus of the study was women's participation and involvement in FFs and not how gender being studied within the family business literature.

Following removal of duplicates from the search results, this process yielded a sample of 126 studies. The sample was further revised to eliminate introductions to special issues, interviews, company case histories, book reviews, and contributions that did not provide insights related to women's participation and inclusion in FFs. Finally, contributions in which the author's name and/or the abstract were not available in the Scopus database were excluded. This resulted in a sample of 81 contributions: 68 articles, 10 book chapters, and three books. Because of space restrictions, only some contributions are described in detail and the reference list includes only studies explicitly mentioned in the text. The complete list of the titles is available on request from the authors.

With respect to the analytical framework (step 3), selected studies were classified considering the following criteria: year of publication, journal in which the study was published (only for articles), authors' affiliation country (authors' location), country in which the research was carried out (research location), methodological approach, and impact. Contributions were also analysed to identify the research focus/topic and define themes and issues addressed by different studies.

In terms of location (of both the authors' affiliation and the research), the following categories were established: Northern Europe (Austria, Belgium, Denmark, Finland, France, Germany, Iceland, Ireland, the Netherlands, Norway, Poland, Romania, Russia, Slovenia, Sweden, Switzerland); Southern Europe (Italy, Greece, Portugal, Spain, Turkey); the United Kingdom (UK); North America (Canada, United States of America (US)); South America; Africa; Asia; the Middle East; and Oceania.

The UK was not included in the Northern Europe category because the number of UK-affiliated authors and UK-based studies was sufficiently large for it to form its own category. Russia was included in Northern Europe because only one study had been carried out in that country (by US authors). The authors' affiliation countries were based on the location of the university of each researcher: for example, if an article was written by an author affiliated to an Italian university and two authors affiliated to a US university, one location in Italy (in the Southern Europe category) and one in the US (in the North America category) were assigned. With regards to research location, the category 'comparative study' was added to include research comparing different country contexts.

From a methodological point of view, the following typologies were considered: qualitative research; quantitative research; mixed methods (both qualitative and quantitative approaches); literature review; other (contributions where the methodology was not specified or conceptual studies in which no empirical data or literature review were reported).

As recommended for an SLR, a citations measure was included to highlight which articles are most cited and have the highest impact within the literature. Because articles receive few citations in their first few years (Massaro et al., 2016), contributions from 2015 to 2017 were excluded, and only the citation index (provided by Scopus) for contributions published from 2000 to 2014 (60 studies in total) was considered.

In terms of research focus/topic, titles and abstracts were analysed. If necessary (because of limited information included in the abstract), the full paper was examined. Since the implementation of a SLR is considered a 'fluid' and iterative process (Massaro et al., 2016), themes and issues were refined throughout the review.

## DESCRIPTIVE FINDINGS

The literature on women's involvement in FFs has grown exponentially since 2000 (Figure 5.1), the findings demonstrate the dynamism and evolution of this field of research. The greatest attention devoted to women in FFs was in 2014, with a decrease in 2015. However, contributions began to rise again in 2016, and although only the first six months of 2017 were included, a positive trend persists. For instance, dividing the period analysed into 2000–2008 and 2009–2017 demonstrates that publications on women in FFs have more than tripled, from 17 in the first half to 64 in the second half of the study period. This result clearly shows scholars' increasing interest in research on this topic.

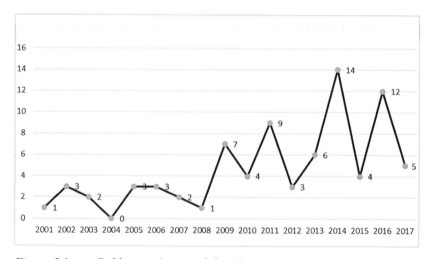

*Figure 5.1      Publication's annual distribution*

Publication of the 68 articles was fragmented, involving a large number of journals (36 in total). The academic journals that published the most papers on women in FFs were the *International Journal of Gender and Entrepreneurship* (11; 17 percent) and the *Family Business Review* (8; 12 percent). Around one in three articles (29 percent) on this topic were published by these two journals. The other 34 journals published the remaining 71 percent of articles, with at most two published in each during the period of observation.

In terms of author affiliation, while scholars from North America dominated early research in the 1990s, since 2000 a relevant and growing contribution has come from European researchers. In fact, 51 percent of the authors' affiliations for the study period were in European countries (including Northern

*Table 5.1     Geographical focus of research*[a]

| Location of research | N.ro | % |
| --- | --- | --- |
| Southern Europe | 13 | 16% |
| Asia | 12 | 15% |
| North America | 11 | 14% |
| Northern Europe | 8 | 10% |
| UK | 8 | 10% |
| Africa | 7 | 9% |
| Oceania | 4 | 5% |
| The Middle East | 3 | 4% |
| South America | 3 | 4% |
| Compared Study | 7 | 9% |
| Not applicable* | 5 | 6% |
| Total | 81 | 100% |

*Note:* [a] The criteria was not applied to the literature reviews and concept papers.

Europe, 17 percent; Southern Europe, 16 percent; and the UK, 18 percent). However, North American has retained its important role, having 31 percent of the authors' affiliations. Scholars affiliated to universities located in Asia (6 percent), Oceania (6 percent), South America (3 percent), the Middle East (2 percent), and Africa (1 percent) have begun to appear on the scene but still represent a minority.

With respect to the location of empirical research, the main geographical focus of contributions was Southern Europe, followed by Asia and North America. Northern Europe, the UK, and Africa were the next most common locations, while Oceania, the Middle East, and South America remained less investigated (Table 5.1). These findings highlight that research interest has progressively moved from regions in which studies on women have a long tradition, such as North America and the UK, toward countries that could be considered 'new lands' for research in this field.

With regards to methodological approach, both qualitative and quantitative approach were employed in research with similar prevalence (32 vs. 31 contributions). Literature reviews were unusual (2) and mixed methodology was seldom used (five contributions). Finally, 11 contributions were classified as 'other'. The prevalence—albeit marginal—of a qualitative approach is consistent with literature on FFs that is characterized by a dominance of descriptive and case studies based on small sample sizes (Benavides-Velasco et al., 2013).

Findings show that the impact of the selected manuscripts was limited. Only 11 contributions (15 percent of the sample) had received more than 10 citations; most (35 contributions; 59 percent) had a number of citations between one and 10. Many contributions (13; 22 percent) had never been cited and five had been heavily cited: Hamilton (2006) (91 citations); Danes and Olson (2003) (73); Vera and Dean (2005) (71); Cruz et al. (2012) (51); and Jimenez (2009) (45).

## RESEARCH FOCUS/TOPIC: THEMES AND ISSUES

Based on the results from the selected contributions, four current themes were identified: (1) women within FFs (30 of 81 studies; 37 percent); (2) succession (24; 30 percent); (3) women-owned FFs and female entrepreneurship (21; 27 percent); (4) copreneurial ventures (5; 6 percent). Figure 5.2 shows the evolution of the four themes during the period analysed. In some cases there is a partial overlap between themes; however a tentative classification was required to provide a global view of the different contributions concerning women in FFs. In the following subsection, themes and associated issues are described, mainly with reference to the most cited contributions in each theme.

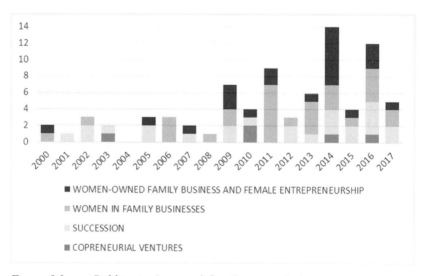

*Figure 5.2     Publication's annual distribution with themes*

**Theme 1:     Women Within Family Firms**

This theme, which represented the main focus of research over the study period, involved studies that analysed women's presence within FFs and how this presence could affect the business. In particular, two groups of contributions were identified within the theme.

The first group included studies that aimed to analyse the presence and role of women within FFs. Lussier and Sonfield (2006) investigated how FFs changed as they grew in size, and compared FFs in the US and France. With regard to women's involvement, they found no differences between small and large FFs in France. Conversely, larger US firms compared to small ones had a smaller percentage of women family members working in the firm and less conflict and disagreement between family members. Curimbaba (2002), examining the dynamics of women's roles as family business managers, maintained that family dimension and composition (order of birth, number of brothers and other men from the same generation) could affect women's involvement and described three daughters' experiences—as professional, invisible, and an anchor. Bjursell and Melin (2011) investigated women's entrepreneurial identity and their 'reactive' and 'proactive' entrance into the FF. The first—employing an 'Alice in Wonderland' narrative—described women who happened to become entrepreneurs or business persons because the FF was there. The second—using a 'Pippi Longstocking' narrative—dealt with conscious choices, drive, and motivation based on an entrepreneurial identification.

Focusing on female representation on Italian corporate boards before the introduction of gender quotas, Bianco et al. (2015) underlined that in the majority of gender-diverse boards, at least one woman had a family tie to the controlling shareholder. Family-affiliated women were more common in companies that were small, had concentrated ownership, were in the consumer sector, and had a larger board: 'Instead, non-family-affiliated women are more common on the boards of companies that are widely held, have younger and more educated boards, have a higher proportion of independent directors, and have a smaller number of interlocked directors' (Bianco et al., 2015, p. 129). With regards to governance-related outcomes, the number of board meetings was negatively correlated with the presence of both family members and female directors. Additionally, women showed lower attendance than men at board meetings.

Hamilton (2006) affirmed that even if women were not directly involved in the business, they may play an important role within the family by influencing male leaders' business decision processes and representing clear resistance and a challenge to patriarchy or paternalism. Investigating the contribution of women to FF from the perspective of the women themselves, Heinonen and Stenholm (2011) showed that women were vital for the functioning of the FF; closeness to the business was crucial and did not depend on formal ownership. Psychological ownership was more important in understanding the development of women's contribution in the FF. Women were themselves aware and did not belittle their contributions, recognizing their own ways of exerting an influence.

Several studies focused on emerging countries and geographical areas with particular economic situations and/or cultural traditions, such as Africa (Binzel and Assaad, 2011), South America (Vergara et al., 2011), India (Jones, 2008), and Southern Europe (Karataş-Özkan et al., 2011). These contributions underlined that in these contexts women were still often invisible and unpaid (Binzel and Assaad, 2011), and their participation was discouraged by factors such as family conflict, work–family imbalances, and the definition of a career (Karataş-Özkan et al., 2011) even if they were gaining prominence in FFs rather than professional corporate setups (Jones, 2008). Lerner and Malach-Pines (2011), focusing on the role played by culture and gender differences in FF, analysed 10 countries: the US, the UK, Australia, New Zealand, Spain, Sweden, Hungary, Brazil, Singapore, and Israel. Results showed consistently large cross-cultural differences among the owners of FFs, but much smaller and less consistent differences between male and female owners of FFs.

Other research adopted a historical perspective and analysed several interesting cases of women's involvement within FFs in the nineteenth and early twentieth centuries (Rutterford and Maltby, 2006; Tweedale, 2013; Nordlund Edvinsson, 2016).

The second group included studies aimed to analyse effects on FFs of women's involvement. In these studies, the focus was mainly on the business, with female involvement included as a variable in analyses (e.g. in a regression model). Scholars investigated if and how women's presence on the board of directors, and/or their participation in managerial roles, and/or in the ownership structure may influence different aspects of the business, such as promotion of corporate social responsibility (CSR) practices (Sundarasen et al., 2016; Rodríguez-Ariza et al., 2017), and business performance (Mínguez-Vera and Martin, 2011). These studies were often based on a comparison between FFs and non-FFs or between women-led and men-led FFs. However, no unequivocal results emerged and further research is needed. For instance, analysing the gender diversity of a sample of Spanish small- and medium-sized enterprises, Mínguez-Vera and Martin (2011) found that women's presence on boards generated a negative impact on firm performance because women directors were less oriented toward risky strategies. In contrast, Cruz et al. (2012) found that women managers knew how to handle conflict between socioemotional and financial goals better than did men, thus improving firm performance. Rodríguez-Ariza et al. (2017) found that the presence of women on the board was less associated with a higher degree of socially responsible commitment in FFs than in non-FFs. In FFs, CSR commitment did not vary significantly with the presence of female directors, as the latter tended to behave in a way that conformed with the family's orientation toward CSR. Conversely, Sundarasen et al. (2016) confirmed that the only variable that positively increased the level of CSR initiatives within FFs was the presence of women directors.

**Theme 2:    Succession**

Studies classified within this theme explicitly and mainly referred to the succession process. Findings confirmed that the succession process from father to daughter remained a crucial theme. Around two out of three contributions on this topic addressed this issue, investigating challenges faced by daughters in family business succession and their path to reach a leadership role (Van den Berghe and Carchon, 2003; Vera and Dean, 2005; Haberman and Danes, 2007; Collins et al., 2016; Gherardi and Perrotta, 2016). In other words, women in family business succession mainly meant daughters in FFs, and the main results confirmed those of Jimenez's (2009) and Wang's (2010) literature reviews. However, some novelty with regards to geographical areas (and consequently cultural contexts) emerged. In fact, growing attention is being devoted to Southern Europe (Howorth and Assaraf Ali, 2001; Cicellin et al., 2015), the Middle East (Ekanem and Alrossais, 2017), and Asia (Janjuha-Jivraj, 2005; Mathew, 2016). With regards to these countries, a 'paradigm shift' (Ekanem and Alrossais, 2017) seems to have arisen, since women are encouraged and given the opportunity to become involved in running their FFs. However, the presence of automatically activated gendered norms (Overbeke et al., 2013), some types of paternalism (Cicellin et al., 2015; Sanchez-Famoso et al., 2017), and the father's predilection for male family members as successors (Glover, 2014), may hinder female succession.

Another important result was the consideration of women as predecessors. Although this remains an overlooked area of research, and succession from mother to offspring still receives little attention by scholars, Cadieux et al. (2002) made an important contribution by analysing how succession unfolds when the incumbent is a woman. However, given the increasing number of female-owned businesses in many economies, succession from mother to son and/or daughter is becoming an extremely relevant topic and should be considered an important direction for future research.

**Theme 3:    Women-Owned Family Firms and Female
        Entrepreneurship**

This theme included studies focused on female entrepreneurs as owners of FFs, investigating their characteristics and the features of their FFs. In general, most attention has been devoted to the early stages of the entrepreneurial cycle of life and factors influencing startup and business growth.

One of the main issues addressed within this theme was barriers and challenges faced by female entrepreneurs in specific geographical contexts; for example, Africa (e.g. Welsh et al., 2013; Welsh, 2016), the Middle East (e.g. Welsh et al., 2014b), and Asia (e.g. Welsh et al., 2014a). Welsh et al. (2014a) focused on Japanese women entrepreneurs and found that their predominately family-owned firms were a growing economic segment in Japan. Investigating the characteristics of Japanese women entrepreneurs and their FFs, they identified barriers and resources that affected success. A customized long-term support system with strong connections between FF supporters and women business owners by both government and private agencies was identified as important for further growth of Japanese women entrepreneurs. Welsh et al. (2013) investigated female entrepreneurs in North Sudan, finding that personal issues, management skills, and obtaining financing were challenges; sources of support for startup and successful running of their FFs included schooling and previous work experience, moral support, and institutional support. Welsh et al. (2014b) explored sources of knowledge and support for Saudi Arabian women entrepreneurs. The findings revealed that women were the principals in the majority (55 percent) of women-owned businesses. Seventy percent of the women owned more than 51 percent of the business and 42 percent started the business by themselves. Saudi Arabian businesswomen were highly educated, received strong support from family and friends, and rated themselves as excellent in terms of people skills and innovation.

The second issue addressed in this theme was the characteristics of women entrepreneurs and their businesses, considering also in this case, particular contexts such as Asia and the Middle East (e.g. Aterido and Hallward-Driemeier, 2011; Rauth Bhardwaj, 2014). Focusing on women entrepreneurs in sub-Saharan Africa, Aterido and Hallward-Driemeier (2011) found that education, management skills, experience and the motivation for being an entrepreneur were most associated with higher productivity. Rauth Bhardwaj (2014) observed that in the emerging market context, entrepreneurial education stimulated women to take up entrepreneurship as a career option and start their FF.

Finally, some contributions focused on how women exercised their leadership role and entrepreneurship in the FF context (Barrett and Moores, 2009a, 2009b). This issue was sometimes strictly related to succession because women may reach an entrepreneurial role taking over leadership of the FF mainly but not exclusively by succeeding their predecessor.

**Theme 4:    Copreneurial Ventures**

Studies included in Theme 4 represented a small percentage of the sample, but this is an emerging field of research. Initial studies on this topic were published in 2003 and then in 2010, and the theme represents an important opportunity for future research. Even if the theme could have been included in Theme 1 (when the man is the leader) or Theme 3 (when the woman is the leader), a specific theme was created because peculiar issues were addressed within this area of research. Studies included in this theme are mainly focused on heterosexual couples and addressed the following issues: (1) how men and women defined their identities, roles, responsibilities, and commitments to both the business and the family (Bensemann and Hall, 2010; Deacon et al., 2014; Kuschel and Lepeley, 2016); and (2) how conflicts between family and work may influence business success and marriage satisfaction (Danes and Olson, 2003; Wu et al., 2010).

Kuschel and Lepeley (2016, p. 181) defined a copreneurial venture as a particular type of FF characterized by 'a male and female couple, integrated as a working team.' They stated that working together allowed each partner to become more aware of mutual skills and strengths and to define their respective roles. Both divided work and family, and had developed a level of mutual trust and commitment so that the business liaison could remain intact even if there was a breakdown in the partners' domestic relationship. According to Deacon et al. (2014), even if there was evidence of duties that could be stereotypically described as either 'men's work or women's work', role tension did not arise between the partners and neither partner's contribution was deemed more valuable than the other's. However, as affirmed by Bensemann and Hall (2010), a gendered ideology persisted even through copreneurial relationships. In fact, copreneurial couples appeared to engage in running their business using traditional gender-based roles mirroring those found in the private home.

Wu et al. (2010, p. 742) found that in copreneurial ventures, 'family boundaries were more permeable than work domains; work–family conflict is negatively related to perceived business success and marriage satisfaction; and work-to-family conflict predicts marriage satisfaction, whereas family-to-work conflict predicts perceived business success.' Finally, Danes and Olson (2003) found that wives were often considered major decision makers, while having more than one decision maker in the business caused different types of tension, and business and family success outcomes varied by level of tensions.

## CONCLUSIONS

This study has reviewed family business studies in the business, management and accounting literature, aiming to explore and outline the state of the art with regards to women's involvement in FFs. Some important findings emerged offering new insights into the topic and integrating more recent literature reviews.

With regards to RQ1—What are the evolutionary trends in the field?—three important tendencies were identified. First, from a quantitative point of view, results confirmed the growing interest of scholars on this topic with a significant increase in number of publications over the period analysed. However, especially with regards to articles, publication was fragmented and distributed over a wide range of journals, and with few exceptions the impact of articles remained limited. Nevertheless, the feeling is that, as a dynamic and emerging field of research, it has 'a niche audience' and is searching for its own identity. Second, this field of research is no longer North American scholar dominated as a relevant and growing contribution is now coming from European researchers (48 percent of the authors' affiliations were located in Europe). At the same time, scholars affiliated to universities located in Asia, Oceania, South America, the Middle East, and Africa have begun to appear on the scene even if they still represent a minority. Finally, the geographical context of research has progressively expanded from North America and the UK toward 'new lands' for empirical investigation, such as Northern and Southern Europe, Asia, and Africa. Locations such as the Middle East and South America remain largely overlooked and require more attention.

With respect to RQ2—What is the focus of literature concerning women's involvement in FFs?—four main themes were identified: women in FFs; succession; women-owned FFs and female entrepreneurship; and copreneurial ventures. The succession process from father to daughter remains a crucial theme in this field of research, as does the analysis of different roles that women may assume within FFs. In contrast, with few exceptions, women as predecessors is an overlooked area of research, and succession from mother to offspring still receives little attention from scholars. With regards to all the themes, there is some novelty in the geographical areas considered and several contributions showed that cultural context has a strong influence on women's experiences within FFs. Increasing attention has also been devoted to female entrepreneurs and their FFs. Finally, a new theme—copreneurial ventures— emerged offering an important novel perspective on research for scholars. To summarize, findings showed that dichotomous descriptions of women in FFs (e.g. excluded–included or visible–invisible) are no longer sufficient because there are several different ways in which women may experience participation and involvement in FFs.

This chapter has several limitations. First, the analysis was limited to a specific area (business, management, and accounting) of a single database (Scopus), and some important keywords were omitted from the literature search (e.g. sister, spouse). Including different areas of research (e.g. sociological and psychological), analysing multiple databases, and using a wider range of keywords would be necessary to ensure that any potentially relevant articles are included in a literature review. Second, if and how different themes and issues were addressed from a gender perspective was not considered. Heinonen and Hytti (2011) focused on this topic and called for research on themes that were more likely to be tackled with a gender perspective. Recent literature reviews presented by Nelson and Constantinidis (2017) and Kubíček and Machek (2018) provided a relevant contribution from this point of view but limited their analyses to the involvement of women in the process of succession. However, as we have seen, the women's involvement in FFs is not limited to succession and there are several angles that could be usefully investigated from a gender perspective.

**Acknowledgments**

This study received financial support from ESU Verona-Italy (Regional Agency for the Right to Study).

## REFERENCES

Aterido, R. and M. Hallward-Driemeier (2011), 'Whose business is it anyway? Closing the gender gap in entrepreneurship in sub-Saharan Africa', *Small Business Economics*, **37** (4), 443–464.

Barrett M. and K. Moores (2009a), 'Spotlights and shadows: Preliminary findings about the experiences of women in family business leadership roles', *Journal of Management and Organization*, **15** (3), 363–377.

Barrett M. and K. Moores (2009b), *Women in Family Business Leadership Roles: Daughters on the Stage*, Cheltenham, UK and Northampton MA, USA: Edward Elgar Publishing.

Benavides-Velasco, C.A., C. Quintana-García and V.F. Guzmán-Parra (2013), 'Trends in family business research', *Small Business Economics*, **40** (1), 41–57.

Bensemann J. and C.M. Hall (2010), 'Copreneurship in rural tourism: Exploring women's experiences', *International Journal of Gender and Entrepreneurship*, **2** (3), 228–244.

Bianco M., A. Ciavarella and R. Signoretti (2015), 'Women on corporate boards in Italy: The role of family connections', *Corporate Governance (Oxford)*, **23** (2), 129–144.

Binzel C. and R. Assaad (2011), 'Egyptian men working abroad: Labour supply responses by the women left behind', *Labour Economics*, **18** (1), S98–S114.

Bjursell, C. and L. Melin (2011), 'Proactive and reactive plots: Narratives in entrepreneurial identity construction', *International Journal of Gender and Entrepreneurship*, **3** (3), 218–235.

Cadieux L., J. Lorrain and P. Hugron (2002), 'Succession in women-owned family businesses: A case study', *Family Business Review*, **15** (1), 17–30.

Campopiano, G., A. De Massis, F.R. Rinaldi and S. Sciascia (2017), 'Women's involvement in family firms: Progress and challenges for future research', *Journal of Family Business Strategy*, **8** (4), 200–212.

Cesaroni F.M. and A. Sentuti (2014), 'Women and family businesses. When women are left only minor roles', *The History of the Family*, **19** (3), 358–379.

Cesaroni F.M. and A. Sentuti (2018), 'The leaders, the outcasts and the others. Which role for daughters in family businesses?', in J. Heinonen and K. Vainio-Korhonen (eds), *Women in Business Families: From Past to Present*, New York: Routledge, 179–198.

Cicellin M., D. Mussolino and R. Viganò (2015), 'Gender diversity and father–daughter relationships: Understanding the role of paternalistic leadership in family firm succession', *International Journal of Business Governance and Ethics*, **10** (1), 97–118.

Cole, P.M. (1997), 'Women in family business', *Family Business Review*, **10** (4), 353–371.

Collins L., J. Tucker and D. Pierce (2016), 'Fathers and daughters', in L. Collins, J. Tucker and D. Pierce (eds), *The Modern Family Business: Relationships, Succession and Transition*, New York: Palgrave Macmillan, 158–178.

Cruz C., R. Justo and J.O. De Castro (2012), 'Does family employment enhance MSEs performance? Integrating socioemotional wealth and family embeddedness perspectives', *Journal of Business Venturing*, **27** (1), 62–76.

Curimbaba F. (2002), 'The dynamics of women's roles as family business managers', *Family Business Review*, **15** (3), 239–252.

Danes S.M. and P.D. Olson (2003), 'Women's role involvement in family businesses, business tensions, and business success', *Family Business Review*, **16** (1), 53–68.

Deacon J.H., J.A. Harris and L. Worth (2014), 'Who leads?: Fresh insights into roles and responsibilities in a heterosexual copreneurial business', *International Journal of Gender and Entrepreneurship*, **6** (3), 317–335.

Denyer, D. and D. Tranfield (2006), 'Using qualitative research synthesis to build an actionable knowledge base', *Management Decision*, **44** (2), 213–227.

Dumas, C. (1989), 'Understanding of father–daughter and father–son dyads in family-owned businesses', *Family Business Review*, **2** (1), 31–46.

Dumas, C. (1992), 'Integrating the daughter into family business management', *Entrepreneurship Theory and Practice*, **16** (4), 41–56.

Dumas, C. (1998), 'Women's pathways to participation and leadership in the family-owned firm', *Family Business Review*, **11** (3), 219–228.

Ekanem I. and L.A. Alrossais (2017), 'Succession challenges facing family businesses in Saudi Arabia', in Philippe W. Zgheib (ed.), *Entrepreneurship and Business Innovation in the Middle East*, Hershey, PA: IGI Global, 122–146.

Ernst & Young Family Business Center of Excellence (2015), 'Women in leadership. The family business advantage. EYGM', accessed September 10, 2017 at https://familybusiness.ey-vx.com/pdfs/ey-women-in-leadership-the-family-business-advantage.pdf.

Gherardi S. and M. Perrotta (2016), 'Daughters taking over the family business: Their justification work within a dual regime of engagement', *International Journal of Gender and Entrepreneurship*, **8** (1), 28–47.

Gillis-Donovan, J. and C. Moynihan-Bradt (1990), 'The power of invisible women in the family business', *Family Business Review*, **3** (2), 153–167.

Glover J.L. (2014), 'Gender, power and succession in family farm business', *International Journal of Gender and Entrepreneurship*, **6** (3), 276–295.

Gnan, L., M. Pellegrini, L. Songini and A. Faraudello (2017), 'The role of women as entrepreneurs in family business: A literature review', in V. Ratten, L.P. Dana and V. Ramadani (eds), *Women Entrepreneurship in Family Business*, London, UK: Routledge, 72–100.

Gupta, V. and N.M. Levenburg (2013), 'Women in family business: Three generations of research', in K.X. Smyrnios, P.Z. Poutziouris and S. Goel (eds), *Handbook of Research on Family Business* (2nd edn), Cheltenham, UK and Northampton, MA, USA: Edward Elgar Publishing, 346–369.

Haberman H. and S.M. Danes (2007), 'Father–daughter and father–son family business management transfer comparison: Family FIRO model application', *Family Business Review*, **20** (2), 163–184.

Hamilton E. (2006), 'Whose story is it anyway?: Narrative accounts of the role of women in founding and establishing family businesses', *International Small Business Journal*, **24** (3), 253–271.

Heinonen, J. and U. Hytti (2011), 'Gender in family firms: A literature review', University of Turku, School of Economics, TSE Entre, Pori Unit.

Heinonen J. and P. Stenholm (2011), 'The contribution of women in family business', *International Journal of Entrepreneurship and Innovation Management*, **13** (1), 62–79.

Hollander, B.S. and W.R. Bukovitz (1990), 'Women, family culture and family business', *Family Business Review*, **3** (2), 139–151.

Howorth C. and Z. Assaraf Ali (2001), 'Family business succession in Portugal: An examination of case studies in the furniture industry', *Family Business Review*, **14** (3), 231–244.

Janjuha-Jivraj S. (2005), *Succession in Asian Family Firms*, New York: Palgrave Macmillan.

Jimenez R.M. (2009), 'Research on women in family firms current status and future directions', *Family Business Review*, **22** (1), 53–64.

Jones N. (2008), 'Governance in the family, the family business and family trusts', in S.L. Spedding (ed.), *Due Diligence Handbook: Corporate Governance, Risk Management and Business Planning*, Amsterdam: Elsevier, 657–681.

Karataş-Özkan M., A. Erdogan and K. Nicolopoulou (2011), 'Women in Turkish family businesses: Drivers, contributions and challenges', *International Journal of Cross Cultural Management*, **11** (2), 203–219.

Kubíček, A. and O. Machek (2018), 'Gender-related factors in family business succession: A systematic literature review', *Review of Managerial Science*, https://doi.org/10.1007/s11846-018-0278-z.

Kuschel K. and M.-T. Lepeley (2016), 'Copreneurial women in start-ups: Growth-oriented or lifestyle? An aid for technology industry investors', *Academia Revista Latinoamericana de Administración*, **29** (2), 181–197.

Lerner M. and A. Malach-Pines (2011), 'Gender and culture in family business: A ten-nation study', *International Journal of Cross Cultural Management*, **11** (2), 113–131.

Lussier R.N. and M.C. Sonfield (2006), 'The effect of family business size as firms grow: A USA–France comparison', *Journal of Small Business and Enterprise Development*, **13** (3), 314–325.

Massaro M, J. Dumay and J. Guthrie (2016), 'On the shoulders of giants: Undertaking a "Structured Literature Review"', *Accounting, Auditing and Accountability Journal*, **29** (5), 767–801.

Mathew V. (2016), 'Women and family business succession in Asia: Characteristics, challenges and chauvinism', *International Journal of Entrepreneurship and Small Business*, **27** (2–3), 410–424.

Mínguez-Vera A. and A. Martin (2011), 'Gender and management on Spanish SMEs: An empirical analysis', *International Journal of Human Resource Management*, **22** (14), 2852–2873.

Nelson, T. and C. Constantinidis (2017). 'Sex and gender in family business succession research: A review and forward agenda from a social construction perspective', *Family Business Review*, **30** (3), 219–241.

Nordlund Edvinsson, T. (2016), 'Standing in the shadow of the corporation: Women's contribution to Swedish family business in the early twentieth century', *Business History*, **58** (4), 532–546.

Overbeke K.K., D. Bilimoria and S. Perelli (2013), 'The dearth of daughter successors in family businesses: Gendered norms, blindness to possibility, and invisibility', *Journal of Family Business Strategy*, **4** (3), 201–212.

Petticrew, M. and H. Roberts (2008), *Systematic Reviews in the Social Sciences: A Practical Guide* (Kindle edn), Oxford, UK: Wiley-Blackwell.

Rauth Bhardwaj B. (2014), 'Impact of education and training on performance of women entrepreneurs: A study in emerging market context', *Journal of Entrepreneurship in Emerging Economies*, **6** (1), 38–52.

Rodríguez-Ariza L., B. Cuadrado-Ballesteros, J. Martínez-Ferrero and I.-M. García-Sánchez (2017), 'The role of female directors in promoting CSR practices: An international comparison between family and non-family businesses', *Business Ethics*, **26** (2), 162–174.

Rowe B.R. and G.-S. Hong (2000), 'The role of wives in family businesses: The paid and unpaid work of women', *Family Business Review*, **13** (1), 1–13.

Rutterford J. and J. Maltby (2006), '"The widow, the clergyman and the reckless": Women investors in England, 1830–1914', *Feminist Economics*, **12** (1–2), 111–138.

Salganicoff, M. (1990), 'Women in family business: Challenges and opportunities.' *Family Business Review*, **3** (2), 125–137.

Sanchez-Famoso V., A. Maseda and I. Erezuma (2017), 'Succession in family businesses: Paternalism and gender', *Espacios*, **38** (11), article n. 24.

Sundarasen D., T. Je-Yen and N. Rajangam (2016), 'Board composition and corporate social responsibility in an emerging market', *Corporate Governance (Bingley)*, **16** (1), 35–53.

Tweedale G. (2013), 'Backstreet capitalism: An analysis of the family firm in the nineteenth-century Sheffield cutlery industry', *Business History*, **55** (6), 875–891.

Van den Berghe L.A.A. and S. Carchon (2003), 'Agency relations within the family business system: An exploratory approach', *Corporate Governance*, **11** (3), 171–179.

Vera C.F. and M.A. Dean (2005), 'An examination of the challenges daughters face in family business succession', *Family Business Review*, **18** (4), 321–345.

Vergara M.P.L., G. Gómez-Betancourt and J.B.B. Ramírez (2011), 'Factors that influence the participation of women in management positions and organs of government in Colombian family businesses', *Cuadernos de Administracion*, **24** (42), 253–274.

Wang C. (2010), 'Daughter exclusion in family business succession: A review of the literature', *Lifestyles*, **31** (4), 475–484.

Welsh D.H.B. (2016), 'Women-owned family businesses in Africa: Entrepreneurs changing the face of progress', in M. Acquaah (ed.), *Family Businesses in Sub-Saharan Africa: Behavioral and Strategic Perspectives*, New York: Palgrave Macmillan, 155–173.

Welsh D.H.B., E. Memili, E. Kaciak and S. Ahmed (2013), 'Sudanese women entrepreneurs', *Journal of Developmental Entrepreneurship*, **18** (2), article n. 1350013.

Welsh D.H.B., E. Memili, E. Kaciak and M. Ochi (2014a), 'Japanese women entrepreneurs: Implications for family firms', *Journal of Small Business Management*, **52** (2), 286–305.

Welsh D.H.B., E. Memili, E. Kaciak and A. Al Sadoon (2014b), 'Saudi women entrepreneurs: A growing economic segment', *Journal of Business Research*, **67** (5), 758–762.

Wu M., C. Chang and W.-L. Zhuang (2010), 'Relationships of work-family conflict with business and marriage outcomes in Taiwanese copreneurial women', *International Journal of Human Resource Management*, **21** (5), 742–753.

PART II

Entrepreneurial mindset and intrapreneurial
orientation

# 6.  Toward a comprehensive measure of entrepreneurial mindset

## Kelly G. Shaver and Immanuel Commarmond

## INTRODUCTION

Any manufacturing process begins with an idea of what the finished product should accomplish. In this case, the finished product should be a comprehensive measure of entrepreneurial mindset that successfully distinguishes people who are entrepreneurs from people who are not. Along the way, "raw materials" must be obtained. Some component parts can be taken "off the shelf," but others must be built for the particular purpose. Individual elements need to be tested for compatibility. Many of these will contribute to the overall product; some will need to be discarded. External constraints will influence the design: The final product must be effective, but it must also be affordable. Ultimately, some users will care only whether the product performs as intended, but others will be comfortable only if they know the details of its construction. This chapter is written for the latter audience. Our goal is to understand the entrepreneurial mindset, but we take pains to describe the "manufacturing" process in enough detail that all of our decisions are open to scrutiny.

Over the last quarter century, investors, educators, researchers, and policy makers have become increasingly interested in trying to understand what factors encourage entrepreneurial activity. National studies of entrepreneurial behavior began in 1995 with the US Panel Studies of Entrepreneurial Dynamics (http://www.psed.isr.umich.edu/psed/home, see Gartner et al., 2004 for the PSED I; Reynolds and Curtin, 2009, for PSED II). International studies of entrepreneurial attitudes and behavior done through the Global Entrepreneurship Monitor (GEM, https://www.gemconsortium.org/) began in 1999 (see Singer et al., 2018 for a recent report). The World Bank Enterprise Surveys provide data on more than 135,000 firms in 139 countries (http://www .enterprisesurveys.org). The Startup Genome project (https://startupgenome .com/) examines the effectiveness of startup ecosystems in more than 30 countries. According to lists maintained by Katz (2018, https://sites.google .com/a/slu.edu/eweb/doctoral-programs-in-entrepreneurship) there are even

83 doctoral programs in entrepreneurship across more than 20 countries. Yet, according to a report from the Kauffman Foundation (https://www.kauffman .org/newsroom/2017/2/entrepreneurship-is-on-the-rise-but-long-term-startup -decline-leaves-millions-of-americans-behind) over the long term there has been a decline in entrepreneurship. Our position on new venture creation—or for that matter its decline—is summarized by Shaver and Scott (1991, p. 39):

> Economic circumstances are important; social networks are important; entrepreneurial teams are important; marketing is important; finance is important; even public agency assistance is important. But none of these will, alone, create a new venture. For that we need a person, in whose mind all of the possibilities come together, who believes that innovation is possible, and who has the motivation to persist until the job is done.

In short, there is tremendous value in a thorough understanding of the individual entrepreneurial mindset. This chapter's contribution is to describe the development of a comprehensive measure of that mindset.

## LITERATURE REVIEW

The first two criticisms applied to any work that describes a new measure of entrepreneurial propensity are "Why bother? Individual differences don't matter!" and "We already have such measures, why are you proposing a new one?" One hopes that the two questions do not originate from within the same critic, because if the first one happened to be correct, there would be no point in asking the second one. It is certainly true that situational influences on entrepreneurial behavior are strong, but only the most hardened behaviorist in the Skinnerian tradition (see for example, Skinner, 1938) would discount personal variables completely. On a more practical level, it is worth noting that investors who consistently "bet on the jockey, not on the horse" are clearly acting as though they believe individual differences matter. Moving to the second question, there are existing measures of entrepreneurial propensity, such as those by Caird (1990), Cassidy and Lynn (1989), Davis et al. (2016), and Robinson et al. (1991). We believe, however, that none of these captures the full breadth of individual differences that can be said to constitute the "entrepreneurial mindset." We hope that when readers finish this chapter, they will agree.

The search for explanations of entrepreneurship is challenging. For every example of a person who intentionally created a company to solve a very large problem, there is an example of a person to whom great success "just happened." Many social psychologists are fond of situational explanations, arguing that the power of circumstances should be paramount, whereas many personality psychologists favor dispositional explanations, arguing that the outcome should be attributed to inherent properties of the person.

In the literature, this debate is well over 40 years old, with a situational position outlined by Mischel (1968) that contrasts with a prior emphasis on individual traits (e.g. Allport, 1937). Unhappy with either pure situationism or pure trait-based approaches, Bowers (1973) argued persuasively that the truth was really somewhere in the *interaction* between person and situation. When situational demands are strong, there will be substantial uniformity of behavior among individuals; when the situational demands are weak, person variables will rise in importance. Not surprisingly, a version of the person–situation debate has appeared in entrepreneurship. Gartner (1988) argued that a pure trait approach should be replaced with a concentration on behavior and activities. Aldrich (1990) focused on environmental conditions, arguing from an ecological perspective that "rates" would be more fruitful than traits. Shaver (1995) argued against a specific set of characteristics that would constitute an "entrepreneurial personality," but Rauch and Frese (2007) countered that it was time to return to the study of traits. Our view of this debate is, obviously, that individual differences do matter, but that it is important to be inclusive in the nature and kind of such variables that are considered.

There is no shortage of individual difference variables (single personality traits, broad personal dispositions, cognitive processes, personal motives, reasons for acting) that have been implicated in entrepreneurial behavior (Carsrud et al., 2017). Some of the single traits include achievement motivation (McClelland, 1961), locus of control (Phares, 1971; Rotter, 1966), risk propensity (Jackson et al., 1972), and desire for autonomy (van Gelderen, 2016). Among the broad personality dimensions are the Big Five (Costa and McCrae, 1992; Ciavarella et al., 2004) or, less frequently, three (Eysenck and Eysenck, 1975), or six (Lee and Ashton, 2004). The Big Five are Openness to experience, Conscientiousness, Extraversion, Agreeableness, and Neuroticism (here arranged in one of the common mnemonic orders, OCEAN). For example, in a meta-analysis of 23 separate studies, Zhao and Seibert (2006) found that compared to managers, entrepreneurs were higher on conscientiousness and openness to experience and lower on neuroticism and agreeableness.

Turning to approaches that are more considered to involve cognitive processes rather than personality dimensions, there are multiple reviews (e.g. Grégoire et al., 2011) and two complete issues of *Entrepreneurship Theory & Practice* on the topic (Mitchell et al., 2004; Mitchell et al., 2007). Some of the approaches based on cognitive processes are the use of entrepreneurial intentions (Krueger, 2009, 2015; Krueger and Carsrud, 1993), expectancies (Gatewood, 2004; Renko et al., 2012), judgment of risk (Palich and Bagby 1995), escalation of commitment (McMullen and Kier, 2016; Staw and Ross, 1987), beliefs in whether an individual's characteristics are fixed or malleable (Dweck et al., 1995), attributions (Diochon et al., 2007; Gartner et al., 2008), overconfidence (Cain et al., 2015; Cooper et al., 1988; Nielsen and Sarasvathy,

2016), and reasons for starting a business in the first place (Carter et al., 2003; Scheinberg and Macmillan, 1988). The list could continue, but this is sufficient to make the point that psychological processes other than personality dimensions might well have something to do with entrepreneurship and entrepreneurial success.

Finally, there are person variables that arguably are influenced by situational factors. Perhaps the best known of these is self-efficacy (Bandura, 1977, 1986, 2012) which, though often considered among the "personality" variables, has features that make it more appropriately described as interactional. First, it is grounded on Bandura's social learning theory—a central tenet of which is learning from the *observation* of others. Second, it is domain-specific. This is the virtual antithesis of a true personality variable expected to operate in roughly the same fashion regardless of the circumstances. Third, although there is a distribution of self-efficacy across individuals, specific training can shift the mean of this distribution. There are other characteristics, which we call "personality variables" for convenience, that technically arise from an interaction between person and situation. One of these is entrepreneurial passion, which, according to Cardon et al. (2009, p. 516) "is not aroused because some entrepreneurs are inherently disposed to such feelings but, rather, that because they are engaged in something that relates to a meaningful and salient self-identity for them." Another is grit (Duckworth and Quinn, 2009, p. 166), defined as "trait-level perseverance and passion for long-term goals." Despite Duckworth's treatment of grit as a lasting individual difference variable, she and Quinn found that grit scores increased with age, which "suggests that grit may increase with life experience" (p, 169). At least in this limited sense, it would seem reasonable to consider grit located in the person–situation interaction.

We take seriously the idea that a comprehensive approach to measuring entrepreneurial mindset must (a) assess cognitive processes and behavioral tendencies as well as traditional personality traits, and (b) do so while paying attention to the varied roles that an entrepreneur might play. Recently, Commarmond (2017) has done just that in a review that is too detailed to be included here. His review begins with the early trait theories of McDougall (1932) and Allport (1937), Cattell (1947), and Fiske (1949) and continues to describe both the Big Five (Costa and McCrae, 1985) and the more recent HEXACO model of six basic factors (Ashton and Lee, 2008). Some of the other approaches that Commarmond considered are Dweck's entity/incremental mindset (Dweck, 2006; Dweck et al., 1995), regulatory focus (Higgins, 1998), and self-monitoring (Snyder, 1974). In his review Commarmond identified 11 key themes that characterize an entrepreneurial mindset. These are lifelong learning and openness to change, engagement in a complex and uncertain world, creativity and innovation, belief in one's own capacity, desire to behave entrepreneurially, the taking of initiative and responsibility for one's actions, pursuit of goal attainment and mastery, recognition of opportunities, grit and perseverance in the face of challenges, taking of acceptable risks, and belief in one's ability to influence others. At the level of single concepts, these themes overlap to a substantial degree with the elements included in other lists of entrepreneurial characteristics. For example, Cromie (2000) suggested seven core attributes—need for achievement, locus of control, calculated risk-taking, tolerance for ambiguity, creativity, need for autonomy, and self-confidence. Baron and Ward's (2004) paper on cognitive processes in entrepreneurship mentioned such things as prospect theory (Kahneman and Tversky, 1979), greater susceptibility to various cognitive biases, regulatory focus (Higgins, 1998), and counterfactual thinking (Epstude and Roese, 2008). Other cognitive processes such as schemata (Bartlett, 1932) congenial to the identification of entrepreneurial opportunities and aspects of metacognition (Gollwitzer and Schaal, 1998) should probably also be considered. Krueger's (2015) "crowd-sourced" list includes action orientation, innovativeness, resilience, persistence, self-efficacy, role identity, entrepreneurial intensity, tolerance for ambiguity, risk acceptance, future orientation, market orientation, value creation, entrepreneurial intentions, and entrepreneurial behavior.

## EXISTING SCALES

Even this abbreviated review illustrates the broad variety of conceptual principles that have been suggested as possible elements of an entrepreneurial mindset. We believe that existing scales, often designed with particular objectives in mind, do not adequately capture the very large and diverse list of constructs that might be offered as explanations for entrepreneurial behavior. First there are the easily-located online tests. These include the Entrepreneurial Personality Test (37 items) offered by *Psychology Today* on the basis of Wagner's book, *The Entrepreneur Next Door* (2006); the *Forbes* Entrepreneurial Instinct Test (31 items) based on Harrison and Frakes' book *Instinct: Tapping Your Entrepreneurial DNA to Achieve Your Business Goals* (2005), which claims to use the Big Five; the Fingerprint for Success based on Duval's interviews with "highly successful entrepreneurs;" the HBR Isenberg Entrepreneur Test (19 yes/no items) authored by the founding director of the Babson Entrepreneurship Ecosystem Project; and the BOSI-DNA based on Abraham's book, *Entrepreneurial DNA: The Breakthrough Discovery That Aligns Your Business to Your Unique Strengths* (2011). No reliability or validity data are available for any of these, so we shall not discuss them further.

Of the scales that appear in the professional literature, one important early entry was an attitude approach to predicting entrepreneurial behavior designed by Robinson et al. (1991). This Entrepreneurial Attitude Orientation (EAO) scale took seriously the view in social psychology that attitudes consisted of three components (cognitive, affective, behavioral). The EAO contained four subscales—achievement in business, innovation in business, perceived personal control over business outcomes, and perceived self-esteem in business. Each subscale contained a cognitive component, an affective component, and a behavioral component. The items in the EAO are themselves very sensible, but the fact that the test as a whole was so closely tied to the concept of a social attitude limits the reach of the scale.

At essentially the same time the EAO appeared, Caird (1990) developed a General Enterprising Tendency (GET) scale at the Open University in the UK. A more recent version (the GET2) is available online (www.get2test .net, accessed September 29, 2017). It uses 54 agree/disagree items to assess achievement, autonomy, creativity, risk-taking, and locus of control. With the GET2, the primary limitation is the restriction to only five of the many constructs that have been suggested as possible contributors to entrepreneurial activity.

Finally, there is the Entrepreneurial Mindset Profile (EMP, Davis et al., 2016). These investigators began with 14 dimensions, some based on prior literature (e.g. four from a model of creativity by Torrance, 1968) and some based on the authors' discussions with entrepreneurs. Seven of the dimensions were regarded as "skills," on the assumption that they could be modified by training or experience, whereas the other seven were regarded as "personality traits" not as susceptible to change. The personality traits include independence, risk acceptance, action orientation, achievement, nonconformity, preference for limited structure, and passion; the skills include future focus, idea generation, execution, self-confidence, optimism, persistence, and interpersonal sensitivity. The authors administered 118 items assessing the 14 dimensions to a convenience sample of 300 people, then used exploratory factor analysis (EFA) to examine the dimensions. Nine dimensions clearly emerged, and then the authors created a second version that clarified some of the prior dimensions and added others. In the second version there were between 7–10 items for each of 14 scales, and these items were administered to another convenience sample of 725 individuals, many of whom had been recruited through connections between their companies and the leadership institute with which two of the authors were affiliated. To create the final version of the 14 scales, the authors chose the five highest-loading items on each scale. This version was published online, and data are reported for 1,872 individuals who completed the final version, some online (for a fee), others as part of either a management training program or a university course. The authors report adequate reliability and validity (Davis et al., 2016) with most scales showing differences between self-identified entrepreneurs and others in the sample. Although the authors report small mean differences between women and men on several of the scales, they did not report factor structures separately by respondent sex.

## SCALE DEVELOPMENT

The limitations inherent in existing instruments suggest that there would be value in creating a conceptually comprehensive test of entrepreneurial mindset. Commarmond's (2017) literature review identified 76 separate descriptors of characteristics that have been considered to be related to entrepreneurial behavior. These 76 characteristics are shown in Table 6.1, with the number of references to the characteristic shown in parentheses in each cell.

Given the diversity of disciplines that have contributed to the entrepreneurship literature, it is not surprising that the descriptions—which Commarmond attempted to keep close to the original—do not all sound like "standard" personal characteristics. Additionally, there are some obvious overlaps. We expect that any author team would reduce this list of 76 separate descriptions to a much shorter list of personal characteristics. Our reduced list is shown in Table 6.2, and contains 37 descriptors, some of which are akin to personality traits, others of which are descriptions of behavior, and still others reflect an entrepreneur's personal preferences.

Even with a dramatically reduced list of terms, there is the danger that distinctions that seem important to experts in any field may not reflect practical differences that are important for others. It is important to have 50 different "words" for snow in the Inuit language, but for someone attempting to clear a drift away from a front door, the only distinction that might matter is whether the snow is wet and heavy or dry and light. It is our expectation that the statistical analyses to be conducted by the completion of this project will likely reduce the effective number of dimensions still further.

Entrepreneurs are almost notoriously short of available time, so an overarching constraint was to keep a final survey short enough that response rates would be high. For a survey in written form, experience suggests that a respondent can answer a single Likert-type item in roughly 7 seconds. At this rate, a total of 75–80 items could be answered in under 10 minutes time, allowing a wide variety of concepts to be assessed. On the other hand, the time limit dictates that essentially no single construct can be measured by a "complete" scale. The Paulhus (1983) Spheres of Control scale, for example, contains 30 items all by itself. As a result of the time limitation, the research strategy involved four steps. For some constructs, we were able to use items from published scales that had been tested on entrepreneurs. In such cases we selected the two (or sometimes three) items that were the best representatives (i.e. those with the highest listed factor loadings). We followed the same procedure when it came to scales measuring concepts related to entrepreneurship, but which concepts

*Table 6.1*    *List of characteristics associated with an entrepreneurial mindset*

| | |
|---|---|
| Ability to exploit contingencies (1) | Independence (2) |
| Achievement orientation (1) | Initiative (2) |
| Action orientation (2) | Innovation (2) |
| Adaptability (2) | Insane hunger to succeed (1) |
| Ambition (2) | Internal locus of control (4) |
| Antagonism (1) | Interpersonal sensitivity (1) |
| Autonomy (1) | Iterative (1) |
| Benefiting others (1) | Learns from criticism (1) |
| Calculated risk-taking (1) | Malleable behaviour (1) |
| Conscientiousness (2) | Mastery-orientated (3) |
| Consistent passion and interest (1) | Mediational judgement (1) |
| Context of relevance: More dynamic, nonlinear, and ecological (1) | Motivation (3) |
| Contextual goal-orientation (1) | Nature of the unknown: Focus on the controllable aspects of an unpredictable future (1) |
| Creativity and imagination (3) | Need for achievement (3) |
| Curiosity (1) | Need for empowerment (1) |
| Dealing with uncertainty (1) | Neuroticism (1) |
| Decision Making: Decisions made by what one is willing to risk (1) | Nonconformity (1) |
| Decision Making: Explores what else could be possible with given means (1) | Open to collaborate and partner (1) |
| Decision Making: Focused on the process and adaptable learning journey (1) | Open to feedback (1) |
| Desire to influence others (3) | Open to experiences (1) |
| Determination (2) | Opportunity recognition (2) |
| Dynamism and complexity (1) | Optimism (1) |
| Effectual (1) | Passionate (2) |
| Effort-oriented (2) | Passion for entrepreneurship (1) |
| Embrace challenges (1) | Persistence (4) |
| Entrepreneurial identity aspiration (1) | Planning ahead (1) |
| Entrepreneurial intention (1) | Preference for a limited structure (1) |
| Entrepreneurial motivation (1) | Probabilistic (1) |
| Entrepreneurial self-efficacy (3) | Recognize Patterns and Linkages (1) |
| Extraversion (1) | Reflective (1) |
| Feeling of empowerment (1) | Resilience (1) |

| | |
|---|---|
| Finds lessons and inspiration in the success of others (1) | Resourcefulness (2) |
| Flexibility (2) | Responds rather than reacts (1) |
| Future focused (1) | Risk-orientation (4) |
| General self-efficacy (3) | Self-belief and self-confidence related (6) |
| Goal-oriented (1) | Tenacious (1) |
| Goals set for learning sake (1) | Tolerance for failure (3) |
| Idea generation (1) | Underlying logic: To the extent we can control the future, we do not need to predict it (1) |

*Table 6.2      A reduced list of personal descriptive terms*

| | |
|---|---|
| action orientation | metacognition |
| adaptability | need for achievement |
| coachability | need for autonomy |
| conscientiousness | neuroticism (stability) |
| creativity | nonconformity |
| curiosity | norms |
| drive | openness to experience |
| effectuation | opportunity recognition |
| effort | optimism |
| emotional intelligence | passion |
| entrepreneurial intentions | perception of failure (resilience?) |
| entrepreneurial self-efficacy | persistence |
| financial goals | personal goals |
| focus | planning |
| general self-efficacy | resourcefulness |
| growth/fixed mindset | risk acceptance |
| innovation | self-confidence |
| leadership | self-reliance |
| locus of control | |

had not yet been tested with entrepreneurial respondents. Next, some of the concepts related to entrepreneurship did not offer publicly available scales, but did provide one or two items that we were able to use as a starting point. Finally, some dimensions that have been suggested as part of the entrepreneurial mindset had neither publicly available scales nor single items that can be used as a place to begin. For these dimensions, we independently wrote items, compared the results, and settled on a wording to be employed. Together these methods produced a total of 116 items.

# PILOT STUDY

With the sponsorship of the Allan Gray Orbis Foundation of South Africa and the GEN Global organization, the pilot study was conducted in South Africa in the late spring of 2017. The field research was accomplished by an exceptionally well-regarded South African market research firm, African Response. In this pilot project the only objective was to create a reliable reduced set of dimensions from the original 116 items. Consequently, there was no attempt to assess the measure's validity by comparing the responses of entrepreneurs to those of people who did not occupy an entrepreneurial role. South Africa is an excellent place to conduct such a pilot study, because the country has 11 official languages and four major racial groups (Black, Colored, Indian, and White). The pilot study was conducted in three metropolitan areas—Cape Town, Durban, and Johannesburg—by field interviewers thoroughly trained by African Response. Although the survey was conducted in English, each field interviewer was fluent in the local language spoken in the particular area to which the interviewer was sent. (Feedback from the interviewers indicated that only rarely was a local translation needed, and then only for occasional words.)

Within the three metropolitan locations, census data were used to identify Enumeration Areas (EAs, basically, local census tracts) selected by stratified random sampling to take the local population probability proportional to size (PPS) into account. Within each EA, households were selected according to a Kish grid. There were three repeat visits before any substitution was permitted, and had substitution been required, the procedures for accomplishing that substitution were specified in advance. Once a household had been selected, the person who answered the door was first asked to enumerate all of the residents of the household, and a Kish grid was used to select the target respondent from among the residents (with the restriction that residents under age 18 were not selected). Interviewers used tablets to collect the data. Every interviewee received the 116 items in a different random order, responses were made in a Likert format (Strongly Disagree to Strongly Agree, scored as a six-point scale), and a concerted effort was made to avoid missing answers. Data were encrypted by the tablets and stored in the cloud.

# RESULTS

On the basis of random selection (no quotas) the pilot study completed interviews with 183 males (46 percent) and 217 females (54 percent). National averages for sex are, respectively, 49 percent and 51 percent. Basic demo-

*Table 6.3    Substitutions required and demographic information*

| Province | Not successful on first visit | Household substituted |
|---|---|---|
| Gauteng (Johannesburg, *n* = 200) | 15.6% | 13.6% |
| KwaZulu-Natal (Durban, *n* = 100) | 28.7% | 22.8% |
| Western Cape (Cape Town, *n* = 100) | 8.0% | 5.0% |
| TOTAL | 17.0% | 13.8% |

| Racial Group | Mean Age | % of Sample |
|---|---|---|
| Black | 38.64  (35.38) | 60.50  (69) |
| Colored | 39.14  (39.68) | 18.00  (18) |
| Indian / Asian | 44.11  (41.22) | 5.80  (1) |
| White | 50.07  (37.84) | 14.80  (13) |

graphic data for this sample of 400 people are shown in Table 6.3 (national averages are shown in parentheses).

Although the mean ages might appear high, they are not that far displaced from the national averages, and across the entire sample, 64 percent of respondents were age 44 or younger.

As a preliminary to the factor analyses, we conducted both the Kaiser–Meyer–Olkin (KMO) test for sampling adequacy and the Bartlett's test of sphericity. The KMO tests for the proportion of variance that might be common (more is better for factor analysis), with higher numbers better. The KMO values were .94 for the 217 females and .90 for the 183 males; values between .90 and 1.0 are considered excellent. The Bartlett's test assesses the null hypothesis that there are no differences in variances of individual items. The result is given as a Chi-square value with $(p*(p-1))/2$ degrees of freedom. The value for females was 22,508.99 and for males was 17,124.38, both highly significant. Because females and males might have produced different factor structures, we analyzed them separately.

SPSS offers six possible methods for factor analysis: principal components analysis (PC), unweighted least squares (ULS), general least squares (GLS), maximum likelihood (ML), principal axis factoring (PAF), alpha factoring (AF), and image factoring (IF). According to Youngblut (1993), PC assumes that all error is random, so the method extracts "real" factors inherent in the data (a geometrically correct result), whether or not that result is related to the original constructs. This is one reason that PC is said to produce "components" rather than "factors" (Nunnally, 1978). Because of differences in the assumptions about error, the conservative course of action is to compare the results of PC to the results of some other extraction technique. Because ULS "does not require any distributional assumptions. It can be used with small samples even when the number of variables is large…" (Jöreskog, 2003, p. 1), it is our choice for an alternative to PC.

## Analysis Strategy

The analysis strategy for the pilot study was to attempt to accomplish three goals. The first goal was to reduce the number of conceptual dimensions from the initial 37 to some much smaller number. The second goal was to account for as much of the variability in the data as possible. The third goal was to rotate the factor structure in $n$-dimensional space to maximize the loadings and enable better identification of the underlying factors. At least two of these goals are in conflict: fewer factors will necessarily explain less of the variance. The amount of variance explained by a factor is its *eigenvalue*, and most statistical programs cause a factor analysis to terminate with a minimum eigenvalue of 1.0, the value equivalent to a single item. We first performed a series of PCA and ULS factor analyses (separately for females and males) with several different eigenvalue criteria: 1.0, 1.2, and 1.3. As it happened, a minimum eigenvalue of 1.2 produced the most easily interpretable outcome. With this eigenvalue, the number of identified factors for males was 20 and the number of identified factors for females was 13, regardless of whether the analysis had been PCA or ULS. Solutions for females were always successfully rotated (both quartimax and varimax) and solutions for males were successfully rotated by quartimax regardless of extraction method. Varimax rotations for males failed regardless of extraction method.

One rule of thumb is that to be retained an item should have a primary loading in excess of ±0.4 and no cross-loading that exceeds ±0.4 (though Costello and Osborne, 2005, suggest that no cross-loading should exceed ±0.32). Thus, in many circumstances, one simply retains items that have high enough primary loadings without being compromised by too-high cross-loadings. Our initial strategy was to do just this, using each of the eight algorithms described above (PC/ULS by Varimax/Quartimax separately for Females and Males). In each of these analyses we counted the number of items with no cross-loadings above an absolute value of 0.32, and identified the specific factor on which each such item loaded. Despite the high number of factors revealed in each analysis, the number of primary items loading on some factor *other than the first* was exceedingly small.

## Exploring Item Standard Deviations

Indeed, the data suggested that instead of the usual case that cross-loaded items are "unclear," it might be that the cross-loaded items were the only ones with sufficient internal variability to appear on some factor other than the first one. To assess this possibility, we looked at the mean and variance for each of the 116 items. Despite the fact that every item had a score range from 1 to 6, the mean scores of nearly all items were around 5.0 (there were only three items with a mean score less than 4.6). The actual values ranged from 4.47 to 5.23 with an overall average of the 116 items = 5.00. Given the mean scores, the standard deviations of items were also restricted, ranging from 0.91 to 1.57, with an overall average $SD = 1.11$. To determine whether the items with higher standard deviations were in fact the ones that had cross-loaded, we counted the number of analyses (out of the eight possible) in which an item had been cross-loaded, and then correlated that number with the standard deviation of the item. The result of this Pearson correlation was highly significant with $r_{(114)} = 0.64$, $p < .0001$. In short, the higher the standard deviation of an item, the more analyses in which it was cross-loaded.

Examination of the content of the cross-loaded items revealed that many of them had originated from publicly available (and previously tested) scales for measuring entrepreneurial potential. Consequently, rather than eliminate these items, we elected to factor analyze them. We included in these analyses the 48 items that had been cross-loaded three or more times (so that the item had to be cross-loaded either for both sexes or in more than one analysis/rotation combination). PCA (varimax rotation) of these 48 items produced five factors for females and seven for males.

Having been able to produce rotated factor structures with the 48 items with the highest item standard deviations, we turned to the items next in descending order of size of standard deviation. Rather than use some form of content criterion for how to create this group of variables to analyze, we simply stopped as soon as the standard deviations dropped below 1.06. PCA (varimax) analysis produced only two dimensions for female respondents and two dimensions for male respondents, with both rotations converging in only three iterations. The next factor analysis performed was on the last 38 items—the ones with the lowest standard deviations.

### Selecting the "Best" Items

Again, the extraction method was PC and the rotation method was varimax. At this point the challenge was to identify the "best" (read, least compromised by cross-loadings) items inherent in all three prior analyses. To accomplish this end, we identified each item in each analysis that had produced only one primary loading (i.e. no cross-loadings) in any dimension for females that had also produced only one primary loading in *some* dimension for males. We counted separately the items that had produced only a primary loading for both sexes on the same numbered factor. The results are as follows. For the 48-item

*Table 6.4     Factor structures for females and males on 62 items*

| 217 female respondents | | | | | | |
|---|---|---|---|---|---|---|
| (KMO = .92; Bartlett = 6937.36)  Factor: | **I** | **II** | **III** | **IV** | **V** | |
| Rotation % of variance accounted for: | 24.65 | 10.57 | 8.92 | 7.99 | 6.47 | |
| Cronbach alpha for scale (CL retained): | .97 | .92 | .88 | .87 | .78 | |

| 183 male respondents | | | | | | | |
|---|---|---|---|---|---|---|---|
| (KMO = .92; Bartlett = 6937.36)  Factor: | **I** | **II** | **III** | **IV** | **V** | **VI** | **VII** |
| Rotation % of variance accounted for: | 15.73 | 9.37 | 7.44 | 5.66 | 5.58 | 5.38 | 3.58 |
| Cronbach alpha for scale (CL retained): | .95 | .88 | .89 | .69 | .76 | .74 | .58 |

analyses, there were 23 items with only a primary loading for both females and males and an additional six items where the primary loadings were on the same numbered factor (total of 29). For the 30-item set, there were three that produced only a primary loading for both sexes, and another seven where the primary loading was on the same numbered factor (total of 10). For the 38-item set, there were 16 with a primary loading for both sexes and another seven where the primary loading was on the same numbered factor (total of 23). Together this created a group of 62 items that had individually produced only primary loadings. This group of 62 was then subjected to PC analysis with varimax rotation. Results of the analysis are shown in Table 6.4.

As in the case of all analyses, this set performed on 62 items showed different factor structures for women and men. Sex differences have previously been obtained in more than a few studies of entrepreneurship, so it is not surprising to find them here as well. Sample items that appeared on Factor I for both males and females included "I am interested in how things work," "I am confident in my skills and abilities," and "when trying an activity for the first time, I am careful and meticulous." Because a large-scale survey was anticipated for South Africa (indeed, it was completed in late December, 2017), the research team elected to add to the 62 items an additional 10—those with the highest factor loadings in any analysis that had not already been incorporated into the 62.

## CONCLUSION

We conclude by noting that this research differs in several important respects from past attempts to assess the entrepreneurial mindset. First and foremost, we did not begin with preconceived ideas about what dimensions we should include. Rather, we began with Commarmond's (2017) review of the literature, abstracted 37 separate constructs from the 76 conceptual statements found, then created 116 items to assess those constructs. The work reported here reduced that number of items to 72 that were subsequently tested in national study of 3,661 individuals (2,404 nationally representative, 791 additional selected from areas with higher concentrations of business, 193 female business owners, and 273 participants in entrepreneurship programs). The results of this large-scale study again showed different factor structures for women and men, while identifying nine core dimensions common to both. These include such things as Confidence, Entrepreneurial Desire, and Resilience. Several of the dimensions successfully distinguish entrepreneurs from non-entrepreneurs. In short, it is possible to begin with a comprehensive review of the existing research and conclude with a reliable and valid measure of entrepreneurial propensity.

### Acknowledgment

Our sincere thanks to Jan Wegelin, the Head of Research for African Response, for his first-rate leadership of the actual pilot project design and data collection effort.

## REFERENCES

Abraham, J. (2011), *Entrepreneurial DNA: The Breakthrough Discovery That Aligns Your Business to Your Unique Strengths*, New York: McGraw-Hill.

Aldrich, H.E. (1990), 'Using an ecological perspective to study organizational founding rates', *Entrepreneurship: Theory & Practice*, *14*(3), 7–24.

Allport, G.W. (1937), *Personality: A Psychological Interpretation*, Oxford: Holt.

Ashton, M.C. and K. Lee (2008), 'The HEXACO model of personality structure', in G.J. Boyle, G. Matthews and D.H. Saklofske (eds), *The SAGE Handbook of Personality Theory and Assessment, Vol 2: Personality Measurement and Testing* (pp. 239–260), Thousand Oaks, CA: Sage Publications.

Bandura, A. (1977), 'Self-efficacy: Toward a unifying theory of behavioral change', *Psychological Review*, *84*, 191–215.

Bandura, A. (1986), *Social Foundations of Thought and Action: A Social Cognitive Theory*, Englewood Cliffs, NJ: Prentice Hall.

Bandura, A. (2012), 'On the functional properties of perceived self-efficacy revisited', *Journal of Management*, *38*(1), 9–44. doi:10.1177/0149206311410606.

Baron, R.A. and T.B. Ward (2004), 'Expanding entrepreneurial cognition's toolbox: Potential contributions from the field of cognitive science',

*Entrepreneurship: Theory & Practice*, *28*(6), 553–573. doi:10.1111/j.1540
-6520.2004.00064.x.

Bartlett, F.C. (1932), *Remembering: A Study in Experimental and Social Psychology*, New York: Cambridge University Press.

Bowers, K.S. (1973), 'Situationism in psychology: An analysis and critique', *Psychological Review*, *80*, 307–336.

Cain, D.M., D.A. Moore and U. Haran (2015), 'Making sense of overconfidence in market entry', *Strategic Management Journal*, *36*(1), 1–18. doi:10.1002/smj.2196.

Caird, S. (1990), 'What does it mean to be enterprising?', *British Journal of Management*, *1*(3), 137–145.

Cardon, M.S., J. Wincent, J. Singh and M. Drnovsek (2009), 'The nature and experience of entrepreneurial passion', *The Academy of Management Review*, *34*(3), 511–532. doi:10.5465/AMR.2009.40633190.

Carsrud, A.L., M. Brännback, J. Elfving and K. Brandt (2017), 'Motivations: The entrepreneurial mind and behavior', in M. Brännback and A.L. Carsrud (eds), *Revisiting the Entrepreneurial Mind* (pp. 185–209), Cham, Switzerland: Springer International Publishing Switzerland.

Carter, N.M., W.B. Gartner, K. Shaver and E.J. Gatewood (2003), 'The career reasons of nascent entrepreneurs', *Journal of Business Venturing*, *18*(1), 13–39.

Cassidy, T. and R. Lynn (1989), 'A multifactorial approach to achievement motivation: The development of a comprehensive measure', *Journal of Occupational Psychology*, *62*(4), 301–312.

Cattell, R.B. (1947), 'Confirmation and clarification of primary personality factors', *Psychometrika*, *12*, 197–220.

Ciavarella, M.A., A.K. Buchholtz, C.M. Riordan, R.D. Gatewood and G.S. Stokes (2004), 'The Big Five and venture survival: Is there a linkage?', *Journal of Business Venturing*, *19*, 465–483.

Commarmond, I. (2017), 'In pursuit of a better understanding of and measure for entrepreneurial mindset', retrieved on October 16, 2017 from http://www.allangrayorbis.org/.

Cooper, A.C., W.C. Dunkelberg and C.Y. Woo (1988), 'Entrepreneurs' perceived chances for success', *Journal of Business Venturing*, *3*(2), 97–108.

Costa, J.P.T. and R.R. McCrae (1985), *The NEO Personality Inventory Manual*, Odessa, FL: Psychological Assessment Resources.

Costa, P.T. and R.R. McCrae (1992), 'Normal personality assessment in clinical practice: The NEO Personality Inventory', *Psychological Assessment*, *4*(1), 5–13. doi:10.1037/1040-3590.4.1.5.

Costello, A.B. and J.W. Osborne (2005), 'Best practices in exploratory factor analysis: Four recommendations for getting the most from your analysis', *Practical Assessment, Research and Evaluation*, *10*(7), 1–9.

Cromie, S. (2000), 'Assessing entrepreneurial inclinations: Some approaches and empirical evidence', *European Journal of Work & Organizational Psychology*, **9**(1), 7–30. doi:10.1080/135943200398030.

Davis, M.H., J.A. Hall and P.S. Mayer (2016), 'Developing a new measure of entrepreneurial mindset: Reliability, validity, and implications for practitioners', *Consulting Psychology Journal: Practice and Research*, **68**(1), 21–48. doi:10.1037/cpb0000045.

Diochon, M., T.V. Menzies and Y. Gasse (2007), 'Attributions and success in new venture creation among Canadian nascent entrepreneurs', *Journal of Small Business & Entrepreneurship*, **20**(4), 335–350.

Duckworth, A.L. and P.D. Quinn (2009), 'Development and validation of the Short Grit Scale (GRIT–S)', *Journal of Personality Assessment*, **91**(2), 166–174. doi:10.1080/00223890802634290.

Dweck, C.S. (2006), *Mindset: The New Psychology of Success*, New York: Random House.

Dweck, C.S., C.Y. Chiu and Y.Y. Hong (1995), 'Implicit theories and their role in judgments and reactions: A world from two perspectives', *Psychological Inquiry*, **6**(4), 267–285. doi:10.1207/s15327965pli0604_1.

Epstude, K. and N.J. Roese (2008), 'The functional theory of counterfactual thinking', *Personality and Social Psychology Review*, **12**(2), 168–192. doi: 10.1177/1088868308316091.

Eysenck, H.J. and S.B.G. Eysenck (1975), *Manual of the Eysenck Personality Questionnaire*, San Diego, CA: Educational and Industrial Testing Service.

Fiske, D.W. (1949), 'Consistency of factorial structures of personality ratings from different sources', *Journal of Abnormal and Social Psychology*, **44**, 329–344.

Gartner, W.B. (1988), 'Who is an entrepreneur? Is the wrong question', *American Journal of Small Business*, **12**(4), 11–32.

Gartner, W.B., K.G. Shaver and J.J. Liao (2008), 'Opportunities as attributions: Categorizing strategic issues from an attributional perspective', *Strategic Entrepreneurship Journal*, **2**(4), 301–315.

Gartner, W.B., K.G. Shaver, N.M. Carter and P.D. Reynolds (2004), *Handbook of Entrepreneurial Dynamics: The Process of Business Creation*, Thousand Oaks, CA: Sage Publications.

Gatewood, E.J. (2004), 'Entrepreneurial expectancies', in W.B. Gartner, K.G. Shaver, N.M. Carter and P.D. Reynolds (eds), *Handbook of Entrepreneurial Dynamics: The Process of Business Creation* (pp. 153–162), Thousand Oaks, CA: Sage Publications.

Gollwitzer, P.M. and B. Schaal (1998), 'Metacognition in action: The importance of implementation intentions', *Personality and Social Psychology Review*, **2**(2), 124–136.

Grégoire, D.A., A.C. Corbett and J.S. McMullen (2011), 'The cognitive perspective in entrepreneurship: An agenda for future research', *Journal of Management Studies*, **48**(6), 1443–1477. doi:10.1111/j.1467-6486.2010 .00922.x

Harrison, T.L. and M.H. Frakes (2005), *Instinct: Tapping Your Entrepreneurial DNA to Achieve Your Business Goals*, New York: Business Plus.

Higgins, E.T. (1998), 'Promotion and prevention: Regulatory focus as a motivational principle', in M.P. Zanna (ed.), *Advances in Experimental Social Psychology* (Vol. 30, pp. 1–46), New York: Academic Press.

Jackson, D.N., L. Hourany and N.J. Vidmar (1972), 'A four-dimensional interpretation of risk taking', *Journal of Personality*, **40**(3), 483–501. doi:10 .1111/j.1467-6494.1972.tb00075.x.

Jöreskog, K.G. (2003), 'Factor analysis by MINRES', retrieved on June 23, 2017 from http://www.ssicentral.com/lisrel/techdocs/minres.pdf.

Kahneman, D. and A. Tversky (1979), 'Prospect theory: An analysis of decision under risk', *Econometrica*, **47**(2), 263–291.

Krueger Jr, N.F. (2009), 'Entrepreneurial intentions are dead: Long live entrepreneurial intentions', in A.L. Carsrud and M. Brännback (eds), *Understanding the Entrepreneurial Mind: Opening the Black Box* (pp. 51–72), Dordrecht, Germany: Springer.

Krueger Jr., N.F. and A.L. Carsrud (1993), 'Entrepreneurial intentions: Applying the theory of planned behaviour', *Entrepreneurship and Regional Development*, **5**, 315–330.

Krueger, N. (2015), 'Entrepreneurial education in practice. Part 1: The entrepreneurial mindset', retrieved on September 29, 2017 from Paris, France: http://www.oecd.org/cfe/leed/skills-for-entrepreneurship.htm.

Lee, K. and M.C. Ashton (2004), 'Psychometric properties of the HEXACO personality inventory', *Multivariate Behavioral Research*, **39**(2), 329–358.

McClelland, D.C. (1961), *The Achieving Society*, New York: D. Van Nostrand Company.

McDougall, W. (1932), 'Of the words character and personality', *Character & Personality; A Quarterly for Psychodiagnostic & Allied Studies*, **1**, 3–16. doi:10.1111/j.1467-6494.1932.tb02209.x.

McMullen, J.S. and A.S. Kier (2016), 'Trapped by the entrepreneurial mindset: Opportunity seeking and escalation of commitment in the Mount Everest disaster', *Journal of Business Venturing*, **31**(6), 663–686. doi:10 .1016/j.jbusvent.2016.09.003.

Mischel, W. (1968), *Personality and Assessment*, New York: Wiley.

Mitchell, R.K., L. Busenitz, T. Lant, P.P. McDougall, E.A. Morse and J.B. Smith (2004), 'The distinctive and inclusive domain of entrepreneurial cognition research', *Entrepreneurship: Theory & Practice*, **28**(6), 505–518. doi:10.1111/j.1540-6520.2004.00061.x.

Mitchell, R.K., L.W. Busenitz, B. Bird, C. Marie Gaglio, J.S. McMullen, E.A. Morse and J.B. Smith (2007), 'The central question in entrepreneurial cognition research 2007', *Entrepreneurship: Theory & Practice*, *31*(1), 1–27. doi:10.1111/j.1540-6520.2007.00161.x.

Nielsen, K. and S.D. Sarasvathy (2016), 'A market for lemons in serial entrepreneurship? Exploring type i and type ii errors in the restart decision', *Academy of Management Discoveries*, *2*(3), 247–271. doi:10.5465/amd .2014.0108.

Nunnally, J.C. (1978), *Psychometric Theory* (2nd edn), New York: McGraw-Hill.

Palich, L.E. and D.R. Bagby (1995), 'Using cognitive theory to explain entrepreneurial risk-taking: Challenging conventional wisdom', *Journal of Business Venturing*, *10*(6), 425–438.

Paulhus, D. (1983), 'Sphere-specific measures of perceived control', *Journal of Personality and Social Psychology*, *44*(6), 1253–1265. doi:10.1037/0022 -3514.44.6.1253.

Phares, E.J. (1971), 'Internal–external control and the reduction of reinforcement value after failure', *Journal of Consulting and Clinical Psychology*, *37*(3), 386–390. doi:10.1037/h0031951.

Rauch, A. and M. Frese (2007), 'Let's put the person back into entrepreneurship research: A meta-analysis on the relationship between business owners' personality traits, business creation, and success', *European Journal of Work & Organizational Psychology*, *16*(4), 353–385. doi:10 .1080/13594320701595438.

Renko, M., K. Kroeck and A. Bullough (2012), 'Expectancy theory and nascent entrepreneurship', *Small Business Economics*, *39*(3), 667–684. doi: 10.1007/s11187-011-9354-3.

Reynolds, P.D. and R.T. Curtin (eds) (2009), *New Firm Creation in the United States: Initial Explorations with the PSED II Data Set*, New York: Springer.

Robinson, P.B., D.V. Stimpson, J.C. Huefner and H.K. Hunt (1991), 'An attitude approach to the prediction of entrepreneurship', *Entrepreneurship: Theory & Practice*, *15*(4), 13–31.

Rotter, J.B. (1966), 'Generalized expectancies for internal versus external control of reinforcement', *Psychological Monographs: General and Applied*, *80*(1), 1–28. doi:10.1037/h0092976.

Scheinberg, S. and I.C. Macmillan (1988), 'An 11 country study of motivations to start a business', in B.A. Kirchhoff, W.A. Long, W.E. McMullan, K.H. Vesper and W.E. Wetzel Jr. (eds), *Frontiers of Entrepreneurship Research* (pp. 669–687), Babson Park, MA: Babson College.

Shaver, K.G. (1995), 'The entrepreneurial personality myth', *Business and Economic Review*, *41*(3), 20–23.

Shaver, K.G. and L.R. Scott (1991), 'Person, process, choice: The psychology of new venture creation', *Entrepreneurship Theory & Practice*, *16*(2), 23–45.

Singer, S., M. Herrington and E. Menipaz (2018), *Global Report 2017–2018*, retrieved on July 31, 2018 from https://gem-2017-2018-global-report -revised-1527266790.pdf/.

Skinner, B.F. (1938), *The Behavior of Organisms*, New York: Appleton-Century-Crofts.

Snyder, M. (1974), 'Self-monitoring of expressive behavior', *Journal of Personality and Social Psychology*, *30*(4), 526–537. doi:10.1037/h0037039.

Staw, B.M. and J. Ross (1987), 'Behavior in escalation situations: Antecedents, prototypes, and solutions', *Research in Organizational Behavior*, *9*, 39–78.

Torrance, E.P. (1968), *Torrance Tests of Creative Thinking*, Wichita, KS: Personnel Press.

van Gelderen, M. (2016), 'Entrepreneurial autonomy and its dynamics', *Applied Psychology: An International Review*, *65*(3), 541–567. doi:10 .1111/apps.12066.

Wagner, B. (2006), *The Entrepreneur Next Door: Discover the Secrets to Financial Independence*, Irvine, CA: Entrepreneur Media.

Youngblut, J.M. (1993), 'Comparison of factor analysis options using the Home/Employment Orientation Scale', *Nursing Research*, *42*(2), 122–124.

Zhao, H. and S.E. Seibert (2006), 'The Big Five personality dimensions and entrepreneurial status: A meta-analytical review', *Journal of Applied Psychology*, *91*, 259–271.

# 7. Technology intrapreneurs – intrapreneurial orientation and potential of IT students

## Christine Blanka, David Rückel, Stefan Koch and Norbert Kailer

## INTRODUCTION

The entrepreneurship field is a well-established discipline exhibiting various theoretical foundations and covering a broad range of research areas (e.g. Landström and Lohrke, 2010). In the last decades, diverse new research agendas emerged at the intersection of entrepreneurship with other disciplines in various contexts (Wiklund et al., 2011). In particular, research combining the fields of entrepreneurship and technology increased, and thus the theory of technopreneurship emerged (Harms and Walsh, 2015). Authors have focused on technology opportunities, spin-offs and the process of technology transfer (Ferreira et al., 2016) and therefore on new venture creation and independent entrepreneurs in a technological context. Nevertheless, technopreneurship research overlooks the possibility of the 'in-the-middle' case (Douglas and Fitzsimmons, 2013) of intrapreneurship. In order to cover the broad definition of entrepreneurship, intrapreneurship should also be taken into account. Intrapreneurs, as entrepreneurial-minded employees, are the key to companies' growth and innovativeness (Veenker et al., 2008) and hence gain in importance in research and practice. In particular, the topic of intrapreneurship in the technological context is emerging, as so-called technology intrapreneurs (Menzel et al., 2007) combine business and technological skills. They are similar to technopreneurs, but instead of being independent entrepreneurs, they use their skills inside an existing organisation and implement innovative ideas. Thus, their intrapreneurial behaviour is essential to foster innovation and competitive advantages in organisations (Williamson et al., 2013; Solymossy and Gross, 2015).

Based on the lack of research on technology intrapreneurs, as well as on the intrapreneurial orientation of individuals in general, this chapter tries to close this gap with regard to future technology intrapreneurs. The terms 'techno-preneurship' and 'technology intrapreneurship' point at the need to bridge the two fields of technology and entrepreneurship/intrapreneurship. The need of a combined skillset and specific knowledge is rooted in adequate education, and hence we draw on students in relevant programs. We estimate that IT students hold the demanded combined skillset and in turn have potential to be future technology intrapreneurs. Therefore, the aim is to provide insights on the intrapreneurial orientation of IT students. Based on a quantitative research approach, we investigate what entrepreneurial, and in particular intrapreneur-ial, potential rests in IT students. We analyse the respective orientations of IT students and assume that non-founders have the chance to function entrepre-neurially as intrapreneurs within an organisation.

By using this broad definition of entrepreneurship, our research offers a holistic view of the potential of IT students. Hence, the contribution of this chapter is twofold: First, by investigating intrapreneurial orientations, we apply a broad perspective on entrepreneurial potential and focus not only on independent entrepreneurial orientation. Intrapreneurial orientation has hardly been examined in previous research, although intrapreneurship is a subfield of entrepreneurship. Therefore, the present research offers a more holistic view and takes into account the idea that non-founding does not automatically mean being non-entrepreneurial. Second, by focusing on the technological context and examining IT students' intrapreneurial orientation, we provide insights at the individual level on possible future technology intrapreneurs.

## THEORETICAL BACKGROUND AND RESEARCH HYPOTHESES

Literature on career intentions looks back on a long history, investigat-ing antecedents and motives for career choices (e.g. Kolvereid, 1996). Entrepreneurship research has focused on entrepreneurial intentions and on the question of possible factors predicting the innovative and entrepreneurial behaviour of individuals (Kautonen et al., 2015; Krueger et al., 2000). Early research on entrepreneurial intentions applied static approaches in order to differentiate intentional founders from intentional employees. By investi-gating the influence of demographic variables and traits, the approaches in use presented mixed results and showed only limited success in comparing founders and employees (e.g. De Pillis and Reardon, 2007). Based on the idea that entrepreneurial skills and an entrepreneurial mindset can be developed, dynamic approaches concentrating on entrepreneurial intentions were applied. Ajzen's Theory of Planned Behaviour (TPB) is one of the most established models (Ajzen and Fishbein, 1975; Ajzen, 1985; Ajzen, 1991) that provide a process-oriented view of individuals' intentions. Rooted in the idea that intentions predict human behaviour, Ajzen explained three factors influencing intentions: (1) attitudes towards a behaviour, (2) subjective norms and (3) perceived behavioural control. Thus, beyond individual-level factors grounded in the individual, Ajzen also integrated the desirability and feasibility of behaviour.

By applying a dynamic perspective on individual behaviour, the TPB model soon became an important theoretical foundation in intention research (e.g. Kautonen et al., 2010). As research on entrepreneurial intentions increased, TPB has become a well-established model to examine entrepreneurial intentions in particular (Moriano et al., 2012). TPB served as trailblazer for a research stream focusing on entrepreneurial behaviour, attitude, factors influencing intentions and the well-known intention-action gap (Ajzen, 2011; Fayolle and Liñán, 2014; Van Gelderen et al., 2008). Based on Ajzen's model, various studies emerged dealing with the validity and refinement of the construct (e.g. Krueger et al., 2000) and longitudinal approaches on entrepreneurial intentions (e.g. Tegtmeier, 2008). In addition, empirical research flourished and huge quantitative online surveys emerged in order to investigate students' intentions. GUESSS (Global University Entrepreneurial Spirit Students' Survey) is one of the largest international entrepreneurship research projects that examine students' entrepreneurial intentions (Global Entrepreneurship Research Association, 2017). Although surveys like GUESSS provide valuable findings concerning founding versus employment intentions (Sieger et al., 2016), the research obscures the alternative case of so-called intrapreneurial behaviour (Douglas and Fitzsimmons, 2013).

The possibility of one's behaving entrepreneurially without founding a company but working as an employee has not been investigated until now. Thus, we identify a clear research gap on students' intrapreneurial intentions. Individual intentions to be a non-founder do not necessarily result in non-entrepreneurial employees. It is rather possible to choose a career path that enables one to behave entrepreneurially but within a corporate context, leading to a career that is also based on innovative thinking and entrepreneurial skills.

**Individuals' Intrapreneurial Potential**

The relevance of entrepreneurial-skilled employees is an up-and-coming topic, rooted in a changed global economy which forces firms to put emphasis on innovation and competitiveness (Antoncic and Hisrich, 2003; Kuratko and Audretsch, 2013). The basic assumption is that innovative and entrepreneurial employees boost the company's performance by facilitating strategic renewal (Dess et al., 2003; Kuratko and Audretsch, 2013; Veenker et al., 2008). The intrapreneurship concept is based upon the work of Pinchot (1985) and underlines the premise that human capital resting in employees leads to self-determined entrepreneurial activity (Åmo and Kolvereid, 2005; Rigtering and Weitzel, 2013; Sinha and Srivastava, 2013). The initiators and main contributors of intrapreneurial activities are employees, and this clearly classifies intrapreneurship as a bottom-up approach (Åmo, 2010). Based on the increased relevance of entrepreneurship activities within established firms (e.g. Parker, 2011), various related concepts besides intrapreneurship deal with this issue. Corporate entrepreneurship, as an organisational-level concept, results either in corporate venturing or strategic entrepreneurship (Kuratko and Audretsch, 2013) and hence is a top-down approach driven by the organisations' management (Kuratko et al., 2005; Rigtering and Weitzel, 2013). Entrepreneurial orientation (EO) is based on the underlying idea that innovation is a result of strategy-making (Wales, 2015) and is observable through the collection of all entrepreneurial behaviours on behalf of the entire organisation (Covin and Wales, 2012). An entrepreneurial-oriented firm is 'one that engages in product-market innovation, undertakes somewhat risky ventures, and is first to come up with 'proactive' innovations' (Miller, 1983, p. 771). We access the research field from the individual-level perspective by applying the intrapreneurship approach and focusing on concepts covering individual proactive behaviour.

Academic research in the field of intrapreneurship focuses not only on organisational antecedents but also on individual attitudes towards intrapreneurship (Åmo and Kolvereid, 2005). Approaches that combine organisational- and individual-level concepts, in particular by linking EO and intrapreneurship (Bouchard and Basso, 2011), have been at the centre. Research has emerged putting emphasis on measurement scales and instruments to access individual orientation or attitude towards entrepreneurship (e.g. Bolton and Lane, 2012; Shetty, 2004). Results show that the same dimensions that characterise the EO of organisations are suitable for investigating individuals' entrepreneurial orientation – innovativeness, risk-taking and proactiveness (Bouchard and Basso, 2011; Covin and Slevin, 1991). A well-established scale to measure individual EO is drawn from the work of Stull and Singh (2005), who also use those three dimensions to gain deeper insights into individual entrepreneurial behaviour. In contrast, research focusing on the term 'individual intrapreneurial orientation' is rare (e.g. Sinha and Srivastava, 2013), but nevertheless, individual EO is said to be an important hint to point at individual intrapreneurial potential (Dess and Lumpkin, 2005). Based on this, we argue that individual EO scales are also suitable to measure the intrapreneurial potential of individuals.

Since Pinchot characterises intrapreneurs as individuals who 'closely resemble entrepreneurs ... who turn ideas into realities inside an organisation' (Pinchot and Pellman, 1999, p.16), intrapreneurs are said to be similar to entrepreneurs with regard to their skills and entrepreneurial mindset (Parker, 2011; Pinchot, 1985). Nevertheless, three differences can be highlighted due to the organisational context: (1) intrapreneurs are able to use existing resources of the established company, (2) they operate within an existing social structure and (3) they are integrated into an organisation that already has established policies and bureaucracy (Baruah and Ward, 2015; Camelo-Ordaz et al., 2012). Research on the individual level also underlines intrapreneurs' and entrepreneurs' similarities but points out differences with regard to their level of risk-taking (e.g. Douglas and Fitzsimmons, 2013).

Despite the similarities, entrepreneurship research has almost entirely neglected examination of intrapreneurial career paths. This is astonishing, as intrapreneurial behaviour is an emerging topic and intrapreneurs can be seen as key in fostering innovation (Veenker et al., 2008). Based on the underlying idea that entrepreneurs and intrapreneurs are quite similar, they should possess the same level of general orientation towards entrepreneurship. We assume that II students show high levels of EO irrespective of their future career choice intention. Based on their career choice, we posit that students intending to found their own business possess *individual entrepreneurial orientation*, and students intending to be employees possess *individual intrapreneurial orientation* (IIO). As research has found no difference concerning the measurement of individual EO and IIO, we imply that future entrepreneurs also possess basic intrapreneurial orientation.

We expect that 'would-be-entrepreneurs' (students intending to found their own business) show the same level of intrapreneurial potential as students intending to be employed. Therefore, a comparison of both with regard to their individual intrapreneurial orientation (IIO) seems interesting:

*Hypothesis 1: Students intending to be founders show the same level of intrapreneurial orientation as students intending to be employees.*

### Proactiveness and Intrapreneurial Orientation

Research in the field of intrapreneurship underlines proactiveness as a specific characteristic that distinguishes intrapreneurs from employees (Bicknell et al., 2010; Edú Valsania et al., 2016; Rigtering and Weitzel, 2013). To emphasise the relevance of this self-determined behaviour of employees, intrapreneurship is defined as a bottom-up approach, and employees are the ones who initiate intrapreneurial projects. There is a consensus that intrapreneurial activities can be defined as initiatives rooted in self-determined employee behaviour and with employees as the main contributors to innovation processes (Åmo, 2010; Rigtering and Weitzel, 2013). In this context, we claim that the individual's proactiveness has a key role in activating intrapreneurial potential, and thus the concept of individual initiative is linked to intrapreneurship. Frese et al. (1997)

investigated the concept of personal initiative and pointed out that this research area will increase further in importance due to employees' influence on organisational effectiveness. When looking at intrapreneurship research, one sees that intrapreneurs are characterised by their willingness to engage beyond their organisational role and show some 'extra-role behaviour' (Moriano et al., 2012; Pinchot, 1985). Based on the idea of individuals' initiative and intrapreneurs' motivation to think and act across the boundaries of organisational units, we argue that personal initiative is an important antecedent of employees showing intrapreneurial behaviour. This also holds for students as potential future intrapreneurs, and therefore the assumption is obvious that self-reported personal initiative and individual intrapreneurial orientation are correlated constructs:

*Hypothesis 2: There is a relationship between students' self-reported personal initiative and their individual intrapreneurial orientation.*

### Student-Specific Factors Influencing Intrapreneurial Orientation

As research on specific factors influencing intrapreneurial intentions of students does not exist, we turn to entrepreneurial intention research. Empirical results on intentions underline various static factors that enhance the entrepreneurial intentions of students. Results of international investigations provide interesting findings as data collection takes place regularly (Global Entrepreneurship Research Association, 2017; Sieger et al., 2016). GUESSS, for instance, identifies two demographic factors that show high relevance. Results indicate that students' entrepreneurial intentions increase over time (e.g. Sieger et al., 2016). This is the result of a logical development: while students prefer working as employees right after studies, they gain relevant work experience. After some years working as employees, their intention to found their own business increases and they tend towards self-employment. In this context, researchers have pointed out that having work experience is an important factor positively influencing entrepreneurial self-efficacy and, in turn, the entrepreneurial intention (Chen et al., 1998; Moriano et al., 2012). In addition, the study period plays a similar role with regard to entrepreneurial intentions. The advanced study phase offers more education and hence access to knowledge and realistic insights on entrepreneurial careers (e.g. Global Entrepreneurship Research Association, 2018). Based on this, students show higher levels of founding intentions at the end of their studies (e.g. Kailer, 2007; Turker and Selcuk, 2009).

We argue that the influence of the mentioned factors is also true for intrapreneurial orientation, and in particular the intrapreneurial orientation of IT students. The importance of intrapreneurship also increases in the techno-logical context, and the changing role of engineers is of particular interest to researchers as well as practitioners (e.g. Menzel et al., 2007; Solymossy and Gross, 2015). Due to changes in the working environment, engineers contrib-ute throughout the whole innovation process and undertake technical as well as managerial tasks (Williamson et al., 2013). This shift from engineering to entrepreneurial tasks emphasises the need to link the technological and busi-ness fields and calls for entrepreneurial but also technical-skilled employees. IT students are actively linking these knowledge areas, and hence are promis-ing future technology intrapreneurs. A specific characteristic of IT students is that they often do internships or freelancing projects during their studies and hence gain their first work experience. Thus, we argue that IT students are, based on their combined skillset, promising future technology intrapreneurs and estimate that possessing work experience influences their intrapreneurial orientation:

*Hypothesis 3a: Students with considerable work experience show higher levels of intrapreneurial orientation than students with no work experience.*

Based on empirical results on entrepreneurial intentions (Sieger et al., 2016) and the idea that entrepreneurs and intrapreneurs are similar concerning the static factor of study period, students at the beginning and at the end of their studies should show different levels of intrapreneurial orientation. Hence we estimate that being close to the final exams also influences the IIO level of IT students:

*Hypothesis 3b: Students close to their final exams show higher levels of intra-preneurial orientation than students at the beginning of their studies.*

## METHODS

### Sample and Procedure

In order to access the research field from the perspective of possible future technology intrapreneurs, we present findings from an online survey among Austrian IT students. The dataset used to test the developed hypotheses concerning intrapreneurship in the technology context derives from an online survey among students in the field of business informatics. We chose this field of study as it is positioned in the intersection of technology and business science and thus is a breeding ground for technopreneurship as well as tech-nology intrapreneurship.

Our quantitative research approach aims at analysing future technology intra-preneurs with regard to the potential of IT students. We call it intrapreneurial 'potential', as we argue that the students already have a general orientation towards intrapreneurship that develops towards real intrapreneurial activities in the future. The questionnaire covers the topics of general career choice intentions, individual orientation towards intrapreneurship as well as personal initiative. The online questionnaire was sent to all students (780) registered in either the bachelor or the master program in business informatics at Johannes Kepler University Linz, Austria. The return rate (after the data clearing process) was 13.59 per cent (106). Thirty-three per cent of the students were female (35) and 67 per cent were male (71). Four per cent (4) were younger than 20, 62 per cent (66) between 21 and 25, 21 per cent (22) between 26 and 30 and 13 per cent (14) older than 30 years. Table 7.1 presents descriptive information on the sample. Seventy per cent of the participants were attending the bachelor programme, 30 per cent the master program. Twenty-seven per cent of the bachelor students were in their first year, 38 per cent in their second year and 35 per cent in their third year. Twenty-two per cent of the students attending the master program were in their first year, 25 per cent in their second year and 53 per cent in their finishing phase, predominantly writing their thesis. The majority of the business informatics students had already gained work experience during their studies, either as employee, founder or even both. Only 34 per cent of the respondents were not working during their studies.

## Measures

The questionnaire that we employed covered various topics related to students' career intentions and intrapreneurial potential. In order to achieve high reliabil-ity, we used objective and established measurement scales whenever available.

## Sociodemographic Variables

The first part of the questionnaire referred to the individual sociodemographic characteristics of the students (gender, age, current phase of studies and per-centage of already successfully completed courses of the studies).

## Career Choices Intention

Students' future career choice intentions were measured by ten items covering a broad range of possible career paths ranging from 'employee in a small busi-ness' to 'other/do not know yet'. We derived these established items from the 2016 international GUESSS report in order to be able to draw a comparison

*Table 7.1*      *Sample of the study*

|  | Gender | Age | Phase of studies | Work experience[a] |
|---|---|---|---|---|
| Male | 71 | | | |
| Female | 35 | | | |
| Up to 20 years | | 3.8% | | |
| 21 to 25 years | | 62.3% | | |
| 26 to 30 years | | 20.8% | | |
| Over 30 years | | 13.2% | | |
| Bachelor program | | | 69.8% | |
| Master program | | | 30.2% | |
| As founder | | | | 8.5% |
| As employee | | | | 54.7% |
| As founder and employee | | | | 2.8% |

*Note*: [a] 66% of the students already gain work experience either as founders (N=9), employee (N=58) or both (N=3); 34% of the students have no work experience.

regarding the general career tendencies of the students. The question concerning career choice was related to the perspectives both directly after studies and five years after graduation. Based on this we constituted the following two categories: *Founders* are students who stated that they intend to (a) found their own business directly after studies, (b) found their own business five years after graduation or (c) found their own business directly and five years after graduation. *Employees* are students who responded with an intent to (a) be employed directly after studies, (b) be employed five years after graduation or (c) be employed directly and five years after graduation, and who in addition at no time stated that they intend to found a business. Based on the idea that family business succession is linked to already-existing firms and structures, we excluded successors from the category of founders.

**Intrapreneurial Orientation**

In order to gain insight into the intrapreneurial potential of IT students, we applied the measurement scale of Stull and Singh (2005). Based on the EO dimensions of innovativeness, proactiveness and risk-taking, those authors developed a scale that captures the individual-level orientation. Five items were developed for each dimension, leading to a scale measuring individual intrapreneurial orientation (IIO). The scale consists of fifteen statements referring to how people approach their work. Students responded to each of the

*Table 7.2      Variables and measurement*

| Variables | Measurement scale |
| --- | --- |
| Career choice intentions | ten items, directly and five years after graduation; four categories built: employee (six items), founders (one item), successors (two items) and others (one item) |
| Individual intrapreneurial orientation (IIO) | Stull and Singh (2005); five-point Likert scale 1=totally disagree to 5=totally agree |
| Individual self-reported initiative | Frese et al. (1997); five-point Likert scale from 1=totally disagree to 5=totally agree, cluster built: weak IIO (coding 1-2) and strong IIO (coding 3-5) |

statements using a five-point Likert scale. To simplify interpretation, clusters for weak IIO (coding 1–2) and strong IIO (coding 3–5) were built.

**Individual Personal Initiative**

Individual initiative has been measured by applying the items of personal initiative identified by Frese et al. (1997), who define personal initiative as behaviour leading to a proactive approach to work and showing more action than is formally required in a job. In particular extra-role behaviour, long-term orientation on goals, self-starting implementation of actions, persistence and proactiveness characterise individual initiative. In particular, the character-istics of proactiveness and extra-role behaviour point at the link of personal initiative with the intrapreneurship concept (Covin and Slevin, 1991; Moriano et al., 2012). Frese et al. (1997) developed various scales to measure different types of initiative. One of the scales is the self-reported initiative referring to people's own concept of their initiative. Based on this, the students responded to seven statements using a five-point Likert scale.

**Reliability and Validity of IIO Scale: Principal Component Factor Analysis**

To assess the reliability and validity of the scale used in reference to the intra-preneurial orientation items (Cronbach's $\alpha = 0.75$), we performed a principal component factor analysis (PCA) with varimax rotation (chi-square = 294.97, $p < 0.05$). Four factors above the eigenvalue of 1.00 emerged, accounting for 66.57 per cent of the variable (Table 7.3), and the rotation required seven iterations to converge.

The results show low cross-loadings among the level of 0.5. Hence, four factors have been generated: *proactiveness* involved five items (Cronbach's $\alpha$ = 0.84), *innovativeness* involved five items (Cronbach's $\alpha$ = 0.84), *risk-taking* was based on three items (Cronbach's α = -0.02) and *change implementing* involved two items (Cronbach's α = -0.25). The Kaiser–Meyer–Olkin (KMO) test returns a value of 0.717 (Barlett significance: p = 0.00), which is a middling result referring to the adequacy of the used items. Only one item shows high factor cross-loadings above 0.5 on two generated factors, namely generating useful new ideas. We argue that these loadings were due to the formulation of the statement using the words *useful* and *new*, which points at both the categories of proactiveness and innovation.

In addition, the results report items showing negative factor loadings. Risk willingness shows a negative alpha value due to the item 'avoid taking calculated risks'. The statement is verbalised in a negative manner (avoiding risks) and therefore presents a negative loading referring to risk willingness. A detailed analysis on Cronbach's α shows that the value of the factor could be increased by dropping the item (Cronbach's α  0.70). Factor four shows negative Cronbach's α as well as negative factor loadings. Based on the statements, we named the factor 'change implementing'. We argue that intrapreneurial-oriented people are at the forefront of innovation and implement change even if uncertainty exists. Therefore, we inverted the item 'approach new projects or activities in a cautious manner' (Cronbach's α = 0.20). As factor four does not exceed the usual reliability criteria of Cronbach's α at or above 0.7, the items loading on this factor were dropped from further analyses. In addition, the item 'avoid taking calculated risks' was excluded from further statistical analyses.

Scale purification and item reduction, based on the findings of the PCA, resulted in a twelve-item scale and therefore three subscales to measure IIO. The proactiveness subscale (IIO Proactiveness) consisted of five items, the innovativeness subscale (IIO Innovativeness) contained five items, and the risk-taking subscale (IIO Risk-taking) consisted of two items. The three built subscales correlate well with the interest in measuring IIO. Proactiveness, innovation and risk-taking are well-established variables to measure individual intrapreneurial behaviour and have been frequently used in prior research (e.g. Bolton and Lane, 2012). The subscales were also significantly correlated (not in the case of risk-taking), further supporting the reliability of the unidimensional construct.

## RESULTS

In order to get detailed insights on possible future career paths of IT students, we first investigated their overall career choice intentions (Figure 7.1). Right after studies, the majority of the respondents intend to be non-founders. Those results show: students planning to be employed in SMEs, 50 per cent; in large companies, 17 per cent; in the public sector, 11 per cent; in academia, 2 per

*Table 7.3      Factor loadings for intrapreneurial orientation items, four factor solution*

| Factor[a] | 1 | 2 | 3 | 4 |
|---|---|---|---|---|
| | Proactiveness | Innovativeness | Risk-taking | Change implementing |
| Eigenvalue | 5.25 | 1.84 | 1.67 | 1.23 |
| Percentage variance accounted for | 25.75 | 20.10 | 12.15 | 8.58 |
| Cronbach's alpha | 0.84 | 0.84 | -0.02 <br> 0.70 <br> (2 item solution) | -0.25 <br> 0.20[b] <br> (inverted solution) |
| *Statements: In the course of my work, I ...* | | | | |
| Actively fix or improve things I don't like. | 0.859 | [a] | | |
| Keep ahead of changes instead of responding to them. | 0.828 | | | |
| Act in anticipation of future problems, needs, or changes. | 0.769 | | | |
| Take the initiative to start projects. | 0.739 | | | |
| Will take calculated risks despite the possibility of failure. | 0.516 | | | |
| Approach business tasks in innovative ways. | | 0.846 | | |
| Often do things in unique ways. | | 0.769 | | |
| Find new ways to do things. | | 0.734 | | |
| Generate useful new ideas. | 0.538 | 0.647 | | |
| Develop new processes, services or products. | | 0.562 | | |
| Do things that have a chance of not working out. | | | 0.836 | |
| Engage in activities that have a chance of not working out. | | | 0.808 | |
| Avoid taking calculated risks. | | | -0.504 | |

| Factor[a] | 1 | 2 | 3 | 4 |
|---|---|---|---|---|
| | Proactiveness | Innovativeness | Risk-taking | Change implementing |
| Tend to implement changes before they are needed. | | | | -0.645 |
| Approach new projects or activeities in a cautious manner. | | | | -0.567 0.567[b] |

*Notes:* [a] Factor loadings smaller than 0.5 have been suppressed; [b] Item has been inverted due to negative value of Cronbach's alpha.

cent. About 10 per cent have other career plans or do not know yet. Concerning intentions towards founding, the results indicate that right after finishing their studies, 8.5 per cent of the respondents intend to start their own business, whereas 23.6 per cent of the students intend to be founders five years after graduation. This overall tendency is in line with the GUESSS survey results, which report an increase in founding intentions over time (Sieger et al., 2016). One frequently stated reason is that after a period of gaining first work experience, students tend towards self-employment, in the form of either founding or succession (e.g. Birley, 2002). The increase of the founding intention is based on a decreased intention over time to be employed.

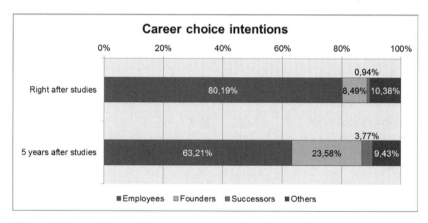

*Figure 7.1        Career choice intentions right after studies and five years after studies*

Further, the students intending to be founders indicate that they have already undertaken steps with regard to their planned business start-up: 34 per cent have already interviewed potential customers, others have designed the first version of the product or service (31 per cent) or analysed the market (24 per cent). Concrete steps like selling items or services, registering the company or developing a business plan have been undertaken by 17 per cent of the students. No student has applied for grants or gathered capital yet, and 45 per cent of the students with founding intentions have not taken any particular steps to plan their future business. Based on their background, the IT students plan their own businesses in the following industry sectors: 66 per cent in information technologies, 14 per cent in managerial consulting, 10 per cent in design and marketing, 7 per cent in trading and 3 per cent in financial services.

Detailed analyses on the intrapreneurial orientation of the IT students provided findings concerning IT students' intrapreneurial potential. The assumption that students also have the chance to behave entrepreneurially within established organisations was examined through the investigation of individuals' intrapreneurial orientation. The descriptive analyses of the mean values point out that the student respondents show high levels, above the average of 3, in almost all items. The results show especially high scores for items referring to innovativeness and proactivity (Table 7.4). Hence, these results underline that besides entrepreneurial intentions, IT students have intrapreneurial potential, and this enables them to take a career path that includes intrapreneurship.

In addition, the analysis on the intrapreneurial orientation in combination with future career choices of the students underlines that future founders and future employees are similar with regard to their intrapreneurial orientation. Results of the non-parametric analysis (Table 7.4) show that founders and employees show the same levels of intrapreneurial orientation among almost all items. Only when it comes to engaging in activities that have a chance of not working out, do founders score significantly higher (3.29) than employees (2.52). This result is explicable, as founders are probably willing to accept more risk and uncertainty when planning activities than employees. Thus, the results show that hypothesis 1 (future founders and future employees show the same level of intrapreneurial orientation) is supported except for the case of engaging in activities that have a chance of not working out. In this case, future founders achieve a significantly higher intrapreneurial orientation.

Correlation analyses on the items of personal initiative (Cronbach's $\alpha = 0.73$) and intrapreneurial orientation reveal interesting findings (see Appendix). Among different items, the results show various significant correlations. The majority of the intrapreneurial orientation items based on the factors of innovation and proactiveness are correlated to personal initiative (significance level 0.05 or 0.01). Only the items referring to risk-taking show no correlations at all. Therefore, hypothesis 2, that individuals' personal initiative and intrapreneurial orientation are correlated, is partly supported.

Finally, individual intrapreneurial orientation has been analysed in detail. Therefore, the assumption that work experience and being close to their final exams influence students' IIO was investigated (Table 7.5). With regard to work experience, we built two groups based on students' working hours per

*Table 7.4     Intrapreneurial orientation (Mann–Whitney test)*

| Statements: intrapreneurial orientation | Overall means | Career Intention | Means |
|---|---|---|---|
| Act in anticipation of future problems, needs, or changes | 4,02 | Founders | 4.38 |
| | | Employees | 3.85 |
| Find new ways to do things | 4,00 | Founders | 4.31 |
| | | Employees | 3.89 |
| Actively fix or improve things I don't like | 3,96 | Founders | 4.33 |
| | | Employees | 3.86 |
| Generate useful new ideas | 3,88 | Founders | 3.92 |
| | | Employees | 3.89 |
| Take the initiative to start projects | 3,72 | Founders | 3.71 |
| | | Employees | 3.72 |
| Take calculated risks despite the possibility of failure | 3,59 | Founders | 3.93 |
| | | Employees | 3.52 |
| Approach business tasks in innovative ways | 3,51 | Founders | 3.77 |
| | | Employees | 3.32 |
| Often do things in unique ways | 3,51 | Founders | 3.79 |
| | | Employees | 3.24 |
| Develop new processes, services or products | 3,47 | Founders | 3.69 |
| | | Employees | 3.46 |
| Keep ahead of changes instead of responding to them | 3,34 | Founders | 3.75 |
| | | Employees | 3.27 |
| Engage in activities that have a chance of not working out | 2,71 | Founders | 3.29* |
| | | Employees | 2.52* |
| Do things that have a chance of not working out | 2,51 | Founders | 2.79 |
| | | Employees | 2.36 |

*Note:* Likert scale: 1=totally disagree; 5=totally agree; * p>0.05.

week during their studies: low work experience (up to 20 hours per week) and high work experience (21 hours and above). A comparison of students with low and high work experience points out that, across the dimensions of proactiveness and innovativeness, the majority of both groups report a strong IIO. With regard to the IIO subscale of risk-taking, the results show a different picture, as the majority of both groups show weak intrapreneurial orientation. This is also in line with prior work that estimates that risk-taking items provide ambiguous results (e.g. Rigtering and Weitzel, 2013). Measure of coherence reports low statistical relationships (Spearman: 0.117; 0.018; -0.134). Whereas proactiveness and innovativeness are weakly correlated with work experi-

*Table 7.5*     *Work experience, final phase of studies and dimensions of IIO*

| | | Work experience | | Bachelor studies | | Master studies | |
|---|---|---|---|---|---|---|---|
| | | Low work experience | High work experience | Beginning/ middle phase | Final phase | Beginning/ middle phase | Final phase |
| IIO | Weak | 26.5% | 15.4% | 30.0% | 14.3% | 25.0% | 22.2% |
| Proactiveness | Strong | **73.5%** | **84.6%** | **70.0%** | **85.7%** | **75.0%** | **77.8%** |
| | | Spearman: 0.117 | | Spearman: 0.0182 | | Spearman: 0.030 | |
| IIO | Weak | 21.6% | 20.0% | 22.7% | 28.6% | 14.3% | 11.1% |
| Innovativeness | Strong | **78.4%** | **80.0%** | **77.3%** | **71.4%** | **85.7%** | **88.9%** |
| | | Spearman: 0.018 | | Spearman: -0.066 | | Spearman: 0.048 | |
| IIO | Weak | **73.0%** | **85.7%** | **72.7%** | **64.3%** | **100.0%** | **88.9%** |
| Risk-taking | Strong | 27.0% | 14.3% | 27.3% | 35.7% | 0.0% | 11.1% |
| | | Spearman: -0.134 | | Spearman: 0.089 | | Spearman: 0.218 | |

*Note:* Coding based on Likert scale: Weak: 1–2; Strong 3–5.

ence, risk-taking shows a weak negative correlation with work experience. Therefore, hypothesis 3a, that students with considerable work experience show higher levels of intrapreneurial orientations than students with no work experience, is partly supported. Both groups, with less and considerable work experience, almost show the same tendencies of IIO.

Further, the phases of studies and IIO were analysed. In order to gain detailed insights, we examined bachelor and master students separately. Table 7.5 shows that the majority of bachelor students at the beginning/middle phase and final phase report a strong IIO on proactiveness and innovativeness. In contrast to this, the majority of both bachelor student groups show a weak orientation on risk-taking. Measure of coherence underlines this and shows weak correlations. Similar results are also presented for master students. The majority of beginners and students at the middle phase as well as students close to their final exams report a strong IIO on proactiveness and innovativeness, but not on risk-taking. Therefore, hypothesis 3b, assuming a correlation between phases of studies and IIO, is partly supported. Nevertheless, the results are somewhat ambivalent, and the variables show low statistical correlations, which points at the need for further research on factors influencing the IIO of IT students. The examination of bachelor and master students also shows that the intrapreneurial orientation (proactiveness and innovativeness) increases over time. The weak orientation with regard to risk-taking intensifies, as all master students and those in the beginning/middle phase report a weak orientation.

To sum up, our tested hypotheses find strong and partial support (Table 7.6). Future founders and future employees show the same level of individual

*Table 7.6     Summary of support of tested hypotheses*

| Hypotheses[a] | | Comparison of means | Correlation analyses | Statistical relationship |
|---|---|---|---|---|
| H 1 | *Founders = employees regarding level of IIO.* | Strong | | |
| H 2 | *Self-reported personal initiative and IIO correlated.* | | Partial[b] | |
| H 3a | *Students with considerable work experience show higher levels of IIO as students with no work experience.* | | | Partial[b] |
| H 3b | *Students close to their final exams show higher levels of IIO as students at the beginning of their studies.* | | | Partial[b] |

*Notes:* [a] blank space indicates not tested; [b] support except risk dimensions of intrapreneurial orientation.

intrapreneurial orientation (H 1). Also, the IIO subscales for innovativeness and proactiveness support the hypotheses that individual intrapreneurial orientation is on the one hand correlated with personal initiative (H 2) and on the other hand related to having work experience (H 3a) and being in a late stage of studies (H 3b). Only the subscale of IIO risk-taking shows weak or even negative correlation with work experience and study stage, leading to ambivalent results and partial support of the tested hypotheses.

## DISCUSSION

The purpose of this research was to examine intrapreneurship in the technology context by focusing on possible future technology intrapreneurs. In doing so, we complemented the view of possible entrepreneurial outcomes like founding and succession by focusing on intrapreneurial potential resting in students. The empirical research undertaken reveals interesting findings concerning IT students' intrapreneurial orientation and underlines their potential as future technology intrapreneurs.

The results of the empirical investigation show that IT students tend towards self-employment in general, and over time this career tendency even increases. But besides this, students report high levels of intrapreneurial orientation. These findings indicate that IT students have intrapreneurial potential, and future careers as technology intrapreneurs are possible. Statistical analyses of intrapreneurial orientation show that future founders and employees report similar levels of IIO, and hence underline that intrapreneurs and entrepreneurs are quite similar, as stated in prior research. A further interesting insight is provided by the detailed analyses of IIO. Based on the PCA, different factors were shaped and resulted in three subscales. The dimensions of innovativeness, proactiveness and risk-taking are in line with the EO literature and with prior research that concentrates on scale development to measure individual intrapreneurial orientation (e.g. Bolton and Lane, 2012). The subscales are based on twelve items measuring IIO, which is different from previous research using fifteen (Stull and Singh, 2005) or ten (Bolton and Lane, 2012) item-solutions. Further analyses of the three subdimensions offer interesting insights on people's IIO. Items of innovativeness and proactiveness showed significant results. Innovativeness and proactiveness are correlated with personal initiative, and thus support the hypothesis that individual initiative is an important key to activating intrapreneurial potential (Åmo, 2010; Rigtering and Weitzel, 2013). In addition, work experience and the stage of studies were also investigated as further antecedents of IIO, and the results show weak correlations with the subscales innovativeness and proactiveness.

In contrast to these results, the dimension of risk-taking offered nonsignificant or negative values: risk-taking items are not correlated with personal initiative and show weak or even negative correlations with having work experience and being at the final stage of studies. Prior empirical research on entrepreneurial orientation also provided mixed results and determined the ambivalent characteristic of risk-taking variables and items (e.g. Douglas and Fitzsimmons, 2013). We argue that specific characteristics of intrapreneurship are possible reasons for nonsignificant and mixed results referring to risk-taking. Intrapreneurship research has shown that especially moderate risk-taking differentiated intrapreneurs from entrepreneurs with higher levels of risk tolerance (Parker, 2011; Pinchot, 1985; Sinha and Srivastava, 2015). Hence, our results probably stress the fairly minor role of risk-taking in intrapreneurship due to the safe setting within an established organisation.

## PRACTICAL IMPLICATIONS

Besides the interesting findings that serve as a foundation for future research, this research also contributes to intrapreneurship in practice. Our research shows that intrapreneurial potential rests in students, but the question is how to foster and activate this potential. Therefore, Entrepreneurship Education (EE) gains in importance. The paradigm of EE has changed in recent years, and one of the main goals of EE has become developing students' skills and behaviour, especially concerning opportunity recognition and creativity (Béchard and Grégoire, 2005; Liñán, 2007; Mwasalwiba, 2010). These enable them to detect opportunities and implement change (e.g. Kirby, 2007), leading to innovation and competitive advantage in various contexts. Hence, the target group of EE is broad, and entrepreneurial outcomes include entrepreneurs but also intrapreneurs, start-up consulters and managers. EE should take into account the goal of fostering entrepreneurial attitudes of students that result in founders, successors or highly skilled employees. As this chapter demonstrates, personal initiative has a key role when it comes to composing intrapreneurial orientation. EE should therefore offer possibilities to engage in proactive behaviour and show initiative. With regard to the increased importance of technology intrapreneurship, we further recommend that entrepreneurship education should be integrated in curricula of technical and natural science. Workshop-based lectures which aim at practising entrepreneurial skills could increase students' attitudes towards intrapreneurship. In addition, students acquire relevant skills, and their perceived ability to be intrapreneurial increases.

Similar to EE at higher education institutions, established organisations should also centre on employees' personal initiative. In order to increase employees' intrapreneurial activities, firms should offer a supportive culture that permits proactiveness and innovativeness within the safe setting of an established organisation. In particular, technology intrapreneurs are of high importance as they are the ones who combine technology and business skills, and this guarantees the growth and competitive advantage of the firms. Hence, companies should create an adequate organisational structure that offers autonomy and possibilities to show intrapreneurial behaviour. In addition, organisations should also offer technically-skilled employees training possibilities of intrapreneurial skills. Practising intrapreneurial behaviour and receiving feedback in turn will lead to an increase in employees' perceived ability. This factor, called entrepreneurial self-efficacy, plays a significant role: engineers in established firms that experience organisational support and the development of intrapreneurial skills are more willing to engage in intrapreneurial behaviour.

## LIMITATION AND THEORETICAL IMPLICATIONS

While the empirical research provides valuable insights on students' IIO, there may be some limitations. The investigation was carried out in one university in Austria, leading to a well-defined sample of IT students. Therefore, attempts should be made in order to test the developed hypotheses on students of other universities at the national and international level. Although the return rate was acceptable, the specific sample (106) and various subgroups of IT students (potential founders, potential employees, etc.) led to statistical results reporting middle or low explanatory power. In order to improve this value, we clearly call for much more empirical research concentrating on intrapreneurial orientation and examining the used variables in different contexts.

Based on the findings and limitations of the research, we highlight various future research agendas. With regard to research fields, we propose that IIO needs more research in order to explain intrapreneurial orientation and to understand factors influencing it. The findings concerning risk-taking items are not clear due to low or negative factor loadings as well as nonsignificant correlations. Therefore, research is needed that examines the role of risk-taking as a subdimension of IIO and also possible mediating or moderating factors. One possibility could be that risk-taking is not a significant dimension, as intrapreneurs in contrast to entrepreneurs operate within a safe setting in an established organisation where access to resources is facilitated and entrepreneurial risk is much lower than operating as an independent entrepreneur. A further research field derives from intrapreneurial intentions and the question of whether intentions are correlated with intrapreneurial orientation. This would offer a detailed view on individual intrapreneurial potential and further antecedents for intrapreneurial intentions. Research on entrepreneurial intentions and EO is available, but the intrapreneurial context has hitherto been nearly disregarded.

Alongside the thematic implications, we also point at research implications in terms of methodology. In order to develop the field of technology intrapreneurs further, more empirical research work on intrapreneurial career paths is needed. International surveys considering intrapreneurship are available but rare and offer no findings on the individual employee level. Thus, quantitative approaches are needed to test measurement scales on IIO. Availability of data is an important condition to work on scale development to measure IIO and to modify available scales if necessary. In addition, the use of longitudinal approaches should be the subject of future research, as they promise detailed insights on IIO over time. Hence, how IIO develops over time and which factors influence the intrapreneurial potential should be future emphases in research. The use of a longitudinal perspective would contribute to the understanding and decoding of intrapreneurial career paths and would further explain how a strong IIO leads to intrapreneurial initiative and, finally, a firm's innovativeness.

## REFERENCES

Ajzen, Icek (1985), 'From intentions to actions: A theory of planned behavior', in Julius Kuhl and Jürgen Beckmann (eds), *Action Control – From Cognition to Behavior*, Heidelberg: Springer, pp. 11–39.

Ajzen, Icek (1991), 'The theory of planned behavior', *Organizational Behavior and Human Decision Processes*, **50**, (2), 179–211.

Ajzen, Icek (2011), 'The theory of planned behaviour: Reactions and reflections', *Psychology & Health*, **26**, (9), 1113–1127.

Ajzen, Icek and Martin Fishbein (1975), *Belief, Attitude, Intention, and Behavior: An Introduction to Theory and Research*, Reading, MA: Addison-Wesley.

Åmo, W. Bjørn (2010), 'Corporate entrepreneurship and intrapreneurship related to innovation behaviour among employees', *International Journal of Entrepreneurial Venturing*, **2**, (2), 144–158.

Åmo, W. Bjørn and Lars Kolvereid (2005), 'Organizational strategy, individual personality and innovation behavior', *Journal of Enterprising Culture*, **13**, (1), 7–19.

Antoncic, Bostjan and Robert D. Hisrich (2003), 'Clarifying the intrapreneurship concept', *Journal of Small Business and Enterprise Development*, **10**, (1), 7–24.

Baruah, Bidyut and Anthony Ward (2015), 'Metamorphosis of intrapreneurship as an effective organizational strategy', *International Entrepreneurship and Management Journal*, **11**, (4), 811–822.

Béchard, Jean-Pierre and Denis Grégoire (2005), 'Entrepreneurship education research revisited: The case of higher education', *Academy of Management Learning & Education*, **4**, (1), 22–43.

Bicknell, Ann, Jan Francis-Smythe and Jane Arthur (2010), 'Knowledge transfer: De-constructing the entrepreneurial academic', *International Journal of Entrepreneurial Behavior & Research*, **16**, (6), 485–501.

Birley, Sue (2002), 'Attitudes of owner-managers' children towards family and business issues', *Entrepreneurship: Theory & Practice*, **26**, (3), 5–19.

Bolton, Dawn Langkamp and Michelle D. Lane (2012), 'Individual entrepreneurial orientation: development of a measurement instrument', *Education & Training*, **54**, (2/3), 219–233.

Bouchard, Véronique and Olivier Basso (2011), 'Exploring the links between entrepreneurial orientation and intrapreneurship in SMEs', *Journal of Small Business and Enterprise Development*, **18**, (2), 219–231.

Camelo-Ordaz, Carmen, Mariluz Fernandez-Alles, José Ruiz-Navarro and Elena Sousa-Ginel (2012), 'The intrapreneur and innovation in creative firms', *International Small Business Journal*, **30**, (5), 513–535.

Chen, C.C., P.G. Greene and A. Crick (1998), 'Does entrepreneurial self-efficacy distinguish entrepreneurs from managers?', *Journal of Business Venturing*, **13**, (4), 295–316.

Covin, Jeffrey G. and Dennis P. Slevin (1991), 'A conceptual model of entrepreneurship as firm behavior', *Entrepreneurship: Theory & Practice*, **16**, (1), 7–25.

Covin, Jeffrey G. and William J. Wales (2012), 'The measurement of entrepreneurial orientation', *Entrepreneurship: Theory & Practice*, **36**, (4), 677–702.

De Pillis, Emmeline and Kathleen K. Reardon (2007), 'The influence of personality traits on persuasive messages on entrepreneurial intention', *Career Development International*, **12**, 382–396.

Dess, Gregory G. and G. Lumpkin (2005), 'The role of entrepreneurial orientation in stimulating effective corporate entrepreneurship', *Academy of Management Executive*, **19**, (1), 147–156.

Dess, Gregory G., R. Duane Ireland, Shaker A. Zahara, Steven W. Floyd, Jay J. Janney and Peter J. Lane (2003), 'Emerging issues in corporate entrepreneurship', *Journal of Management*, **29**, (3), 351–378.

Douglas, Evan J. and Jason R. Fitzsimmons (2013), 'Intrapreneurial intentions versus entrepreneurial intentions: Distinct constructs with different antecedents', *Small Business Economics*, **41**, (1), 115–132.

Edú Valsania, Sergio, Juan A. Moriano and Fernando Molero (2016), 'Authentic leadership and intrapreneurial behavior: Cross-level analysis of the mediator effect of organizational identification and empowerment', *International Entrepreneurship and Management Journal*, **12**, (1), 131–152.

Fayolle, Alain and Francisco Liñán (2014), 'The future of research on entrepreneurial intentions', *Journal of Business Research*, **67**, (5), 663–666.

Ferreira, João J.M., Fernando A.F. Ferreira, Cristina I.M.A.S. Fernandes, Marjan S. Jalali, Mário L. Raposo and Carla S. Marques (2016), 'What do we [not] know about technology entrepreneurship research?', *International Entrepreneurship and Management Journal*, **12**, (3), 713–733.

Frese, Michael, Doris Fay, Tanja Hilburger, Karena Leng and Almut Tag (1997), 'The concept of personal initiative: Operationalization, reliability and validity in two German samples', *Journal of Occupational and Organizational Psychology*, **70**, 139–161.

Global Entrepreneurship Research Association (2017), *Global Entrepreneurship Monitor. Global Report 2016/17*, London: Global Entrepreneurship Research Association.

Global Entrepreneurship Research Association (2018), *Global Entrepreneurship Monitor. Global Report 2017/18*, London: Global Entrepreneurship Research Association.

Harms, Rainer and Steven T. Walsh (2015), 'An introduction to the field of technology entrepreneurship: Editorial to the special issue', *Creativity and Innovation Management*, **24**, (4), 552–557.

Kailer, Norbert (2007), *Gründungspotenzial und -aktivitäten von Studierenden an österreichischen Hochschulen*, Johannes Kepler University Linz, Linz.

Kautonen, Teemu, Ewald Kibler and Erno Tornikoski (2010), 'Unternehmerische Intentionen der Bevölkerung im erwerbsfähigen Alter', *Zeitschrift für KMU und Entrepreneurship: ZfKE*, **58**, 175–196.

Kautonen, Teemu, Marco Van Gelderen and Matthias Fink (2015), 'Robustness of the theory of planned behavior in predicting entrepreneurial intentions and actions', *Entrepreneurship Theory and Practice*, **39**, (3), 655–674.

Kirby, David (2007), 'Changing the entrepreneurship education paradigm', in Alain Fayolle (ed.) *Handbook of Research in Entrepreneurship Education*,

*Volume 1*, Cheltenham, UK and Northampton MA, USA: Edward Elgar Publishing, pp. 21–45.

Kolvereid, Lars (1996), 'Organizational employment versus self-employment: Reasons for career choice intentions', *Entrepreneurship. Theory & Practice*, **20**, (3), 23–31.

Krueger, Norris F., Michael D. Reilly and Alan L. Carsrud (2000), 'Competing models of entrepreneurial intentions', *Journal of Business Venturing*, **15**, (5–6), 411–432.

Kuratko, Donald F. and David B. Audretsch (2013), 'Clarifying the domains of corporate entrepreneurship', *International Entrepreneurship and Management Journal*, **9**, (3), 323–335.

Kuratko, Donald F., R. Duane Ireland, Jeffrey G. Covin and Jeffrey S. Hornsby (2005), 'A model of middle-level managers' entrepreneurial behavior', *Entrepreneurship Theory and Practice*, **29**, (6), 699–716.

Landström, Hans and Franz Lohrke (2010), *Historical Foundations of Entrepreneurship Research*, Cheltenham, UK and Northampton MA, USA: Edward Elgar Publishing.

Liñán, Francisco (2007), 'The role of entrepreneurship education in the entrepreneurial process', in Alain Fayolle (ed.), *Handbook of Research in Entrepreneurship Education, Volume 1*, Cheltenham, UK, Northampton MA, USA: Edward Elgar Publishing, pp. 230–247.

Menzel, Hanns C., Iiris Aaltio and Jan M. Ulijn (2007), 'On the way to creativity: Engineers as intrapreneurs in organizations', *Technovation*, **27**, (12), 732–743.

Miller, Danny (1983), 'The correlates of entrepreneurship in three types of firms', *Management Science*, **29**, (7), 770–791.

Moriano, J.A., M. Gorgievski, M. Laguna, U. Stephan and K. Zarafshani (2012), 'A cross-cultural approach to understanding entrepreneurial intention', *Journal of Career Development*, **39**, (2), 162–185.

Mwasalwiba, Ernest Samwel (2010), 'Entrepreneurship education: A review of its objectives, teaching methods, and impact indicators', *Education & Training*, **52**, (1), 20–47.

Parker, Simon C. (2011), 'Intrapreneurship or entrepreneurship?', *Journal of Business Venturing*, **26**, (1), 19–34.

Pinchot, Gifford (1985), *Intrapreneuring: Why You Don't Have to Leave the Corporation to Become an Entrepreneur*, New York: Harper & Row.

Pinchot, Gifford and Ron Pellman (1999), *Intrapreneuring in Action: A Handbook of Business Innovation*, San Francisco: Berrett-Koehler Publishers.

Rigtering, J.P.C. and U. Weitzel (2013), 'Work context and employee behaviour as antecedents for intrapreneurship', *International Entrepreneurship and Management Journal*, **9**, (3), 337–360.

Shetty, Pramod (2004), 'Attitude towards entrepreneurship in organisations', *The Journal of Entrepreneurship*, **13**, (1), 53–68.

Sieger, Philipp, Urs Fueglistaller and Thomas Zellweger (2016), *Student Entrepreneurship 2016: Insights From 50 Countries. International Report of the GUESSS Project 2016*, St Gallen/Bern: KMU-HSG/IMU.

Sinha, Nupur and Kailash B.L. Srivastava (2013), 'Association of personality, work values and socio-cultural factors with intrapreneurial orientation', *Journal of Entrepreneurship*, **22**, (1), 97–113.

Sinha, Nupur and Kailash B.L. Srivastava (2015), 'Intrapreneurship orientation and innovation championing in Indian organizations', *Global Business Review*, **16**, (5), 760–771.

Solymossy, Emeric and Andrew Gross (2015), 'Taking the engineering path to business leadership and entrepreneurial success in Canada and USA', *International Entrepreneurship and Management Journal*, **11**, (2), 393–408.

Stull, Michael and Jagdip Singh (2005), 'Intrapreneurship in nonprofit organizations examining the factors that facilitate entrepreneurial behaviour among employees', *Case Western Reserve University, May 2005*.

Tegtmeier, Silke (2008), *Die Existenzgründungsabsicht: Eine theoretische und empirische Analyse auf Basis der Theory of Planned Behavior*, Marburg: Tectum.

Turker, Duygu and Senem Sonmez Selcuk (2009), 'Which factors affect entrepreneurial intention of university students?', *Journal of European Industrial Training*, **33**, (2), 142–159.

Van Gelderen, Marco, Maryse Brand, Mirjam Van Praag, Wynand Bodewes, Erik Poutsma and Anita Van Gils (2008), 'Explaining entrepreneurial intentions by means of the theory of planned behaviour', *Career Development International*, **13**, (6), 538–559.

Veenker, Simon, Peter van der Sijde, Wim During and Andre Nijhof (2008), 'Organisational conditions for corporate entrepreneurship in Dutch organisations', *Journal of Entrepreneurship*, **17**, (1), 49–58.

Wales, William John (2015), 'Entrepreneurial orientation: A review and synthesis of promising research directions', *International Small Business Journal*, **34**, (1), 3–15.

Wiklund, Johan, Per Davidsson, David B. Audretsch and Charlie Karlsson (2011), 'The future of entrepreneurship research', *Entrepreneurship Theory and Practice*, **35**, (1), 1–9.

Williamson, Jeanine M., John W. Lounsbury and Lee D. Han (2013), 'Key personality traits of engineers for innovation and technology development', *Journal of Engineering and Technology Management*, **30**, (2), 157–168.

# APPENDIX

*Table 7A.1    Correlation analyses of intrapreneurial orientation and personal initiative*

| | I actively attack problems. | Whenever something goes wrong, I search for a solution immediately. | Whenever there is a chance to get actively involved, I take it. | I take initiative immediately even when others don't. | I use opportunities quickly in order to attain my goals. | Usually I do more than I am asked to do. | I am particularly good at realising ideas. |
|---|---|---|---|---|---|---|---|
| Approach new projects or activities in a cautious manner | -.062 | -.047 | -.290* | -.118 | -.066 | .123 | -.253 |
| Do things that have a chance of not working out | -.070 | .104 | -.098 | -.049 | -.089 | .124 | -.037 |
| Avoid taking calculated risks | -.033 | -.096 | -.016 | -.001 | -.214 | -.052 | -.228 |
| Engage in activities that have a chance of not working out | -.019 | .053 | .069 | .082 | -.246 | -.044 | -.125 |
| Will take calculated risks despite the possibility of failure | .267 | .312* | .293* | .266 | -.001 | -.049 | .206 |
| Keep ahead of changes instead of responding to them | .432** | .399** | .288 | .231 | .197 | .167 | .340* |
| Actively fix or improve things I don't like | .610** | .539** | .525** | .533** | .299 | .238 | .427** |
| Act in anticipation of future problems, needs, or changes | .437** | .342* | .421** | .463** | .110 | -.043 | .337* |
| Take the initiative to start projects | .624** | .420** | .583** | .611** | .293* | .230 | .472** |

| | I actively attack problems. | Whenever something goes wrong, I search for a solution immediately. | Whenever there is a chance to get actively involved, I take it. | I take initiative immediately even when others don't. | I use opportunities quickly in order to attain my goals. | Usually I do more than I am asked to do. | I am particularly good at realising ideas. |
|---|---|---|---|---|---|---|---|
| Tend to implement changes before they are needed | .307* | .131 | .403** | .292* | .236 | .281 | .473** |
| Generate useful new ideas | .533** | .470** | .434** | .613** | .239 | .150 | .603** |
| Develop new processes, services or products | .336* | .232 | .405** | .306* | .183 | .110 | .369* |
| Approach business tasks in innovative ways | .511** | .303* | .417** | .436** | .249 | .247 | .391** |
| Find new ways to do things | .453** | .377* | .322* | .389** | .164 | .113 | .485** |
| Often do things in unique ways | .290* | .008 | .205 | .255 | .216 | .199 | .403** |

*Note:* * p>0.05; ** p>0.01.

# PART III

# Entrepreneurial behaviour, resources and outcomes

# 8. Human capital, external relations, and early firm performance of technology-based start-ups

**Hanna Rydehell, Anders Isaksson and Hans Löfsten**

## INTRODUCTION

Technology-based start-ups (new technology-based firms or NTBFs) in dynamic environments need to utilise existing internal resources and acquire external resources to be able to grow during strategic phases. In such settings, experienced founders are more important than in stable environments (Clarysse et al., 2011) because resources need to be configured into bundles to help firms develop and exploit opportunities. Human capital should be positively related to resource bundling (Sirmon and Hitt, 2003) and provide a base of intangible resources that will most likely lead to competitive advantage (Barney, 1991). Moreover, as most small and young firms, such as NTBFs, rarely have all the resources needed to perform (e.g. Sirmon and Hitt, 2003), they need to rely upon and build relationships with external parties to reduce scarcity. External relationships, including R&D networks, are therefore important for NTBFs' innovative performance (Börjesson and Löfsten, 2012; Löfsten, 2015; Rydehell et al., 2018); by creating alliances, firms can leverage their partners' expertise and technical knowledge, thereby building resource endowments (Lane and Lubatkin, 1998). In terms of NTBFs that base their competitive advantage on technological innovation (Bollinger et al., 1983; Autio and Yli-Renko, 1998; Saemundsson and Candi, 2014), the development of product innovation through internal research and development (R&D) or through collaborations with external partners, such as universities, could enhance young firms' success in launching new products in the market (Ramírez-Alesón and Fernández-Olmos, 2017).

Since the process of resource accumulation is path-dependent and cumulative, and trust and confidence must be developed, new firms need to interact within the business environment to accumulate resources; moreover, these interactions must also begin during the start-up phase (Sirmon and Hitt, 2003). However, we know little about these effects during NTBFs' early phases (the first few years of existence), making it difficult to assess which resources (internal resources related to the founder, or external resources related to external partnerships) or combinations are initially vital for early firm performance. Therefore, this study examines the effects of NTBFs' human capital and external relations on early firm performance (sales and employment).

Studies in the new technology context have attempted to define high technology (Markusen et al., 1986). Monck et al. (1988) state that there are two groups of indicators: (1) measures of resource inputs to high-technology activity, such as R&D effort and expenditure and (2) the employment of qualified personnel and measures of output or performance, such as growth rates, patent records, copyrights and licenses, and technological innovations. In our study, NTBFs (high , medium high, and knowledge intensive high technology firms) were identified using the Eurostat categorisation (Eurostat, 2018) of industries according to technological intensity, an approach pioneered by Butchart (1987) and widely applied thereafter (e.g. Brown and Mason, 2014). Based on the codes of the General Nomenclature of Economic Activities in the European Communities (NACE Rev. 2) we concentrated on firms providing high-, medium-high, and knowledge-intensive high-technology services. Little (1979) identified the following characteristics of a new technology-based firm: (1) It must not have been established for more than 25 years, (2) it must be a business based on potential invention or one having substantial technological risks over and above those of normal business, (3) it must have been established by a group of individuals – not as a subsidiary of an established company, and (4) it must have been established for the purpose of exploiting an invention and/or technological innovation.

New technology-based firms have received significant attention from researchers and policymakers as they have an important impact on an economy's long-term development (Storey and Tether, 1998) and can be seen as drivers of economic growth and innovation (Spencer and Kirchhoff, 2006). In particular, they contribute to the economy through exports, employment, taxes, R&D, and innovation (e.g. Autio and Yli-Renko, 1998; Brinckmann et al., 2011; Colombo and Grilli, 2010). The resources possessed and acquired by NTBFs are therefore important to achieve such contributions (Aspelund et al., 2005). From a resource-based view (RBV), firms' internal human, social, and financial capital are the basis for competitive advantage (Wernerfelt, 1984; Barney, 1991) and therefore important in achieving innovation and economic development. Resources are scarce in the early stages of these new firms. Human capital, such as a founding team's business experience, are important for firm growth and attracting finance (Brinckmann et al., 2011; Clarysse et al., 2011), further facilitating recognition and the exploitation of new opportunities (Davidsson and Honig, 2003). Although initial resources may predict future firm performance, most studies have been conducted in the later phases of NTBFs and we know little about how activities during the early phases set the foundation and constraints of future business growth.

## LITERATURE AND HYPOTHESES

According to RBV, a firm's competitive advantage lies in its unique bundle of internal tangible and intangible resources that are valuable and difficult to imitate (Barney, 1991). It is argued that differences in resources should be utilised, leading to differences in sustainable competitive advantage (Wernerfelt, 1984). Three general categories of firm-specific heterogeneous resources that can provide such competitive advantages are physical, human, and organisational capital (Barney, 1991). Not only do NTBFs lack financial resources and legitimacy (Kollmer and Dowling, 2004; Clarysse et al., 2011; Brinckmann et al., 2011), but organisational assets are also scarce (Bhide, 2000). Consequently, new firms (e.g. NTBFs) will be dependent on their external environment to deal with scarcity and challenges (Pfeffer and Salancik, 2003). Accordingly, in addition to internal resources, research has recognised essential external resources (e.g. Grant, 1991; Das and Teng, 2000, including strategic alliances and collaboration within business networks, as factors explaining firms' competitive advantages and resource acquisition (e.g. Hitt et al., 2000). It is also argued that network resources are difficult to imitate (Gulati, 1999) and it is therefore important for NTBFs to build competitive advantage around their offerings and to influence growth. For example, Davidsson and Honig (2003) showed that being members of a business network had a statistically significant positive effect on first sales and profitability in the earliest stages of entrepreneurial activity. Closeness to universities may further stimulate collaboration and the establishment of R&D networks to provide certain advantages related to, for example, innovative performance (Börjesson and Löfsten, 2012).

Human resources such as skills, education, and previous work experience are especially important for NTBF performance (Colombo and Grilli, 2005, 2010). Bosma et al. (2004) found that previous work experience in the same industry had a positive effect on three entrepreneurial performance measures: survival, profit, and employment, and that managerial experience improved the probability of firm survival. Overall, research on NTBFs shows that while founders (and employees) are highly educated (Löfsten and Lindelöf, 2002; Löfsten and Lindelöf 2005a, 2005b; Brinckmann et al., 2011), the quality of their previous experience distinguishes the firm from competitors and enhances performance. Accordingly, human capital resources are important for firm performance in the start-up phase of NTBFs. Firm behaviour and strategy would depend on the founder(s). Strategic posture can be established along a spectrum, ranging from conservative to entrepreneurial (Miller and Friesen, 1982). Firms with risk-taking behaviour are more likely to allocate resources to opportunities when facing uncertainty, which is important when seeking high growth (Miller, 1983). Therefore, in terms of NTBFs' behaviour and performance, the growth orientation of the founder(s) is a key dimension. Although small firms possess bundles of resources for development, NTBFs need to access resources that often lie outside corporate boundaries (Maine et al., 2010), such as R&D equipment and production facilities. From the perspective of NTBFs in their early start-up phase, human capital (internal resources related to the founder) and external relations (external resources) are important for firm performance. However, existing research is somehow contradictory as to what extent these resources impact on early firm perfor-mance in the first years of start-up, especially concerning human capital. Moreover, there may be a higher level of over-optimism (Lowe and Ziedonis, 2006; Fourati and Attitalah, 2017) or overconfidence (Trevelyan, 2008) among growth-oriented entrepreneurs. Busenitz and Barney (1997) found that entrepreneurs generally express greater overconfidence than managers in more established firms do and one reason could be that nascent entrepreneurs lack relevant business experience that can result in expectations being more biased in high-technology industries (Cassar, 2014). Runyan et al. (2008) studied 267 small entrepreneurs, and found that behavioural tendencies towards innova-tiveness, proactiveness, and risk-taking significantly predict firm performance. The authors specifically focus on owners' perceived performance of their businesses, where founders with higher levels of these behaviours often per-ceive a positive performance, such as sales growth. Performance is obviously a common and important goal for NTBFs (Almus and Nerlinger, 1999).

**Business Experience and Growth Orientation**

Sirmon and Hitt (2003) found that human, social, financial, and survivabil-ity capital, patents, and governance structures are distinct sets of resources available to small firms and that each set of resources can have both positive and negative aspects. From an internal perspective, human capital resources are important to NTBFs' ability to successfully exploit opportunities (e.g. Davidsson and Honig, 2003), and can explain why some NTBFs outperform others (Colombo and Grilli, 2005). Although a positive relationship between human capital and firm performance has been well-established in the literature, the results are conflicting. Gimeno et al. (1997) studied 1,547 entrepreneurs in the US and found that previous managerial and entrepreneurial experience positively affected new firms' economic performance, as did Delmar and Shane (2006) in their study of 223 new ventures in Sweden.

Davidsson and Honig (2003) found that human capital such as years of experience only have small effects on early entrepreneurial activities (e.g. obtaining sales), whereas previous start-up experience and years of education positively predicted such activities. Colombo and Grilli (2005) examined 506 NTBFs in Italy and found that previous entrepreneurial experience influenced growth, meaning that founders' education and previous experience in the same industry are key factors in firm growth. However, West and Noel (2009) analysed 83 new firms in the US and observed that founders' previous start-up experience had no impact on new venture performance. Nevertheless, the experiences of founders have been found to be important for firms' ability to attract initial funding, which influences their performance (Colombo and Grilli, 2005; Brinckmann et al., 2011). In addition, experiences are necessary for developing competencies, as one needs to invest first to experience an outcome. Accordingly, we propose:

*Hypothesis 1: Business experience is positively related to early firm performance*

The strategic behaviour of founders can result in growth (Moreno and Casillas, 2008), especially behaviours such as innovativeness, proactiveness, and risk-taking that allow founders to search for opportunities when facing uncertainty, which is also a behaviour that is important for growth-seeking young firms (Miller, 1983). However, not all firms attempt to or can grow; in fact, few start-ups wish to grow (Storey, 1994). Furthermore, the organisational context is influential in terms of entrepreneurial behaviour (Pittino et al., 2017). Clausen and Korneliussen (2012) studied incubators and NTBFs and found that strategic behaviour has a positive effect on the ability of NTBFs to bring technology to the market quickly, which is important for firms' performance. Runyan et al. (2008) studied 267 small business owners and found that behavioural tendencies towards innovativeness, proactiveness, and risk-taking are significant indicators of performance. The authors specifically focus on owners' perceived performance of their businesses, where founders with higher levels of the aforementioned behaviours often perceive a positive performance such as sales growth to be related to financial performance. Financial performance is a common and important goal for NTBFs (Almus and Nerlinger, 1999). However, research on new and small firms demonstrated differences in growth ambitions (Autere and Autio, 2000) and that not all firms seek to grow (Wiklund et al., 2003; Isaksson et al., 2013). Nevertheless, NTBFs are considered entrepreneurial firms (e.g. Löfsten and Lindelöf, 2005a) and are consequently characterised as risk-taking and growth-oriented (e.g. Miller and Friesen, 1982).

In addition to the experiences and knowledge of NTBF founders, their attitudes and motivations are also essential for firm behaviour and performance (e.g. Löfsten and Lindelöf, 2001). Kirchhoff (1994) underlined that a lack of motivation and resources hinders the development of an innovative small firm. Therefore, the attitudes and motivations of the founders are also key factors for firms to raise funds and achieve growth and profitability. Those firms with dynamic and positive leadership seeking strong growth and financing are therefore more likely to be successful (Löfsten and Lindelöf, 2002). Furthermore, attitudes towards growth have been highlighted by researchers as important determinants of entrepreneurial venture performance (Wiklund and Shepherd, 2003) and there is also evidence to support this relationship. For example, in a study of 1,601 SMEs in Sweden, Isaksson et al. (2013) found that managers' attitudes towards growth have a positive relationship with actual growth outcomes, Yli-Renko et al. (2002) demonstrated that growth orientation is positively related to international sales growth. Thus, it is important to consider the growth orientation of founders when explaining the growth of new firms, especially under great uncertainties (Autio et al., 2000). Accordingly, the attitudes of NTBF founders and firm behaviour, such as growth orientation, can be assumed to have a positive impact on firm performance. Therefore, we propose:

*Hypothesis 2: Growth orientation is positively related to early firm performance*

**R&D Networks**

Other than founding teams' business experience and growth orientation, NTBFs lack financial and organisational assets that are important for their initial growth (Bollinger et al., 1983; Brinckmann et al., 2011). To handle resource scarcity, NTBFs will therefore be dependent on relationships with external parties. As NTBFs have been characterised as entrepreneurial start-ups and spin-offs from technical universities and corporations, numerous studies have focused on their close connection to universities and science parks (Autio and Yli-Renko, 1998; Löfsten and Lindelöf, 2002, 2005b), as universities and other higher education institutions are important sources of new scientific knowledge. Industry can gain access to such knowledge or resources by developing formal and informal links with higher-education institutions (OECD, 1993) to encourage technology innovation and production (Westhead and Storey, 1994). This is consistent with research on NTBFs in their early phases.

R&D networks between universities and other stakeholders, such as customers, is a path-dependent process (Gulati, 1999). Therefore, the network will be idiosyncratic and difficult to imitate (Grant, 1991). However, it also creates barriers in terms of mobility, where resources are firm-specific and property rights are co-specialised (Peteraf, 1993). Formal methods include licensing and cooperative alliances (Lane and Lubatkin, 1998), while informal methods include labour mobility and social meetings and discussions (Pouder and St. John, 1996). For NTBFs, proximity provides opportunities for collaboration that enhance knowledge transfer (Maine et al., 2010; Letaifa and Rabeau, 2013) and access to facilities and R&D equipment (Löfsten and Lindelöf, 2002, 2003) for taking an idea to full commercialisation. Accordingly, the creation of R&D networks provides advantages to NTBFs in the development of their offering (e.g. knowledge and equipment). Therefore, we propose:

*Hypothesis 3: R&D networks are positively related to early firm performance*

## SAMPLE AND METHOD

### Sample

This study focuses on Swedish NTBFs founded between 2013 and 2015. Sweden is known for its advanced company registration system and is therefore a good context from which to collect an NTBF sample. We used the Retriever Business database, which contains information on all Swedish companies (http://business.retriever.se/), to identify our sample and collect secondary business data. To focus on genuine businesses and avoid those related to hobby and lifestyle, we sample only firms registered as limited companies. To control for heterogeneity among new firms (Davidsson, 2007; Wennberg, 2005), we restricted our analysis to independent firms (i.e. not belonging to a business group), thereby avoiding spin-offs from existing businesses and other start-ups that are not true de novo firms. To ensure that the firms in our sample are genuine and have started some kind of operations, we filtered the sample to include only those registered in certain years (2013 to 2015) and active (not deregistered, liquidated, etc.), and thereby liable to pay value-added tax and tax prepayment. We therefore avoid dormant, shelf, and other inactive companies.

Our sampling resulted in a population of 2,329 firms, of which 1,230 (52.8 per cent) were founded in 2013, 812 (34.9 per cent) in 2014, and 287 (12.3 per cent) in 2015. One reason for the skewed distribution in 2013 is that many of the youngest firms were not active and contactable according to our definition. The largest category is knowledge-intensive high-technology services, with 2,096 firms (90.0 per cent), followed by 167 firms (7.2 per cent) in medium-high-technology manufacturing, and 66 (2.8 per cent) in high-technology manufacturing. We received valid responses from 401 firms, a response rate of 17.2 per cent (see Table 8.1), which compares positively with mail surveys of small- and medium-sized firms (e.g. see Chandler and Hanks, 1994, 19 per cent; Yli-Renko et al., 2001, 24 per cent). The main reasons for non-response were that some firms could not be located (e.g. wrong numbers, answering machines, managers being abroad), while others stated that they did not have any activity, did not have the time, or simply refused to participate.

Table 8.1 summarises the characteristics of the respondents and compares these with non-respondents. Non-respondents have somewhat lower sales, profits, and profitability, but also higher total assets. The only significant difference between respondents and non-respondents is the founding year (significant at the 0.05 level). The table reveals no large difference between them apart from this. Respondents are small in terms of employment (mean: 1.80) and have high returns on total capital (mean: 16.47 per cent). Respondents' average firm age is 28.3 months. The oldest firms started in January 2013 (39 months; the survey was conducted during March–April 2016) and the youngest firms are six months old (see Table 8.1).

## Data Collection

We developed the survey in two stages before finalising it. First, we conducted a pilot study as part of study operationalisation and development. We interviewed 26 NTBFs to further develop the measures (the method is described in detail in Rydehell and Isaksson, 2016). Second, the survey was tested and modified through a pre-test with six NTBFs (not previously interviewed) via telephone to identify uncertainties and avoid misunderstandings. The final survey was conducted during March–April 2016. To further ensure sample validity, we collected all data for the questionnaire by phone using one of Sweden's largest and most respected marketing research companies (TNS-Sifo: National Institute for Consumer Research). TNS-Sifo also double-checked the questionnaire regarding language and ease of understanding.

Inter-rater reliability was further increased by using randomly selected experienced professional callers. To ensure response consistency and quality, the interview process was monitored and recorded. If there were any problems with the manuscript, this would have been captured during monitoring. To ensure that the sample did not show any significant differences between firms founded in different years, independent sample T-tests were conducted, which compared the means of the same variable in two unrelated groups. We separated the groups (start year 2013 and 2014, 2013 and 2014, 2014 and 2015) by creating a grouping variable called 'start year'. The tests (Levene's test for equality of variances and T-test for equality of means, sig. two-tailed) showed no significant differences between the nine variables regarding business experience, growth orientation, and R&D networks – university over 2013–2015.

*Table 8.1     Descriptive statistics for the surveyed new technology-based firms, 2016*

1. *Sample and response rate:*

Firms

| N (population): 2459 | No valid firms: 130 |
| n (response): 401 | Response rate (%): 17.2 |
| No responses: 1,928 | |

2. *Business data – Means and standard deviations*

| | Sample | | | No response | | | |
| | 401 firms | | | 1928 firms | | | |
| | N | Mean | SD | N | Mean | SD | Sig (2-tailed) |
|---|---|---|---|---|---|---|---|
| Start year[a] | 401 | 2,013.52 | 0.70 | 1,928 | 2,013.61 | 0.70 | 0.013* |
| Employment[b] | 377 | 1.80 | 6.62 | 1,812 | 1.72 | 10.53 | 0.858 |
| Sales[c] | 377 | 2,177.26 | 10,724.77 | 1,812 | 2,071.82 | 10,346.82 | 0.636 |
| Total capital[c] | 377 | 1,388.20 | 5,324.68 | 1,812 | 1,896.56 | 20,688.24 | 0.636 |
| EBIT[c] | 377 | 234.72 | 779.00 | 1,812 | 208.99 | 1,356.28 | 0.722 |
| Retrun on assets[d] | 377 | 16.47 | 47.32 | 1,812 | 12.25 | 95.75 | 0.403 |

3. *Technology level, founding year, and firm age (responding firms)*

| Technology level | Founding year and number of firms | | | | |
| | Year 2013 | Year 2014 | Year 2015 | Sum | Percent |
|---|---|---|---|---|---|
| High-tech | 15 | 3 | 0 | 18 | 4.49 |
| Mid-tech | 21 | 11 | 2 | 34 | 8.48 |
| Knowledge intensive | 205 | 99 | 45 | 349 | 87.03 |
| Sum | 241 | 113 | 47 | 401 | 100.00 |

Firm age (months)

| N | Minimum | Maximum | Mean | SD |
|---|---|---|---|---|
| 401 | 6 | 39 | 28.32 | 8.59 |

4. *Sectors – frequencies (%)*

| | | Sample | |
| | | Response | No Response |
|---|---|---|---|
| Manufacturing | | 8.50 | 7.28 |
| Construction | | 0.25 | 0.57 |

| | | |
|---|---|---|
| Wholesale and retail trade | 1.50 | 2.27 |
| Transportation and storage | 0.25 | 0.15 |
| Accommodation and food service activities | 0.00 | 0.21 |
| Information and communication | 75.00 | 79.55 |
| Financial and insurance activities | 0.50 | 0.05 |
| Real estate activities | 0.00 | 0.05 |
| Professional, scientific, and technical activities | 13.25 | 7.75 |
| Administrative and service support activities | 0.25 | 0.41 |
| Education | 0.00 | 0.31 |
| Human, health and social work activities | 0.25 | 0.78 |
| Arts, entertainment, and recreation | 0.25 | 0.46 |
| Other service activities | 0.00 | 0.16 |
| Sum | 100.00 | 100.00 |

*Notes:* [a] Year; [b] Number of employees; [c] 1,000 SEK; [d] Per cent; * $p<0.05$.

However, there were significant differences regarding sales between 2013 and 2015, 2014 and 2015, and with employment in the same periods. A total of 241 NTBFs in the sample were founded in 2013, 113 in 2014, and only 47 in 2015.

**Measures and Statistical Analysis**

Nearly all measures in the questionnaire were measured on a five-point Likert-type or a binary scale (Yes = 1, No = 0). The empirical base consists of nine variables and three control variables (see Table 8A.1 in Appendix). We used early firm performance (sales and employment) as the dependent variable in our regression model. We gathered the sales and employment measures for the 2015 accounting year during spring 2016. We used the Retriever Business database from the Chalmers University Library to collect secondary business data on firm performance. However, a clear understanding of performance as the major dependent construct of this chapter is problematic. Measuring firm performance is at the heart of strategic management (Venkatraman and Ramanujam, 1986) and there is no generally accepted definition of firm performance as it is both complex and multi-dimensional. Scholars have defined and used a large variety of indicators to assess firm performance. Overall, these indicators can be classified into objective and subjective indicators. Accounting measures are examples of objective firm performance indicators and are the most commonly used indicators of firm performance among business academics; they are also used by academics due to a variety of advantages. These measures are based on performance data generated in line with the corresponding accounting principles of a firm, that is, their financial statements. Additionally, firm growth itself is often also regarded as a performance indicator (Davidsson et al., 2009).

We used business experience (two items, measured in number of years), growth orientation (three items), and R&D–university networks (four items) as independent variables. Nearly all independent variables were measured on a five-point Likert scale. The analysis also includes five control variables for firm age and size based on secondary data sources (annual reports) – measured in months and employment and sales, respectively – and firm age (years), number of patents and incubator localisation (Yes/No). The statistical analysis has three steps. First, we apply principal component analysis (PCA) to convert potentially correlated variables into linearly uncorrelated variables (principal components). Exploratory procedures are more accurate and multiple variables represent each factor in the analysis with, ideally, between three and five measured variables per factor (MacCallum, 1990; Safón, 2009). The Kaiser–Meyer–Olkin measure is calculated to determine sampling adequacy. Second, a correlation analysis identified the statistically significant measures (latent and control variables). Third, regression analysis is used to test the link between dependent and independent latent variables.

## RESULTS

The PCA reveals three significant latent variables related to business experience, growth orientation, and R&D networks. Principal components are developed for business experience ($\alpha = 0.596$), growth orientation ($\alpha = 0.604$), and R&D networks–university ($\alpha = 0.699$). According to Hair et al. (1995), the generally accepted lower limit for Cronbach's alpha is 0.700, although this may decrease to 0.600 in exploratory research. According to George and Mallery (2003), $\alpha > 0.500$ can be perceived as poor, and $\alpha < 0.500$ is unacceptable. Therefore, we used three latent variables in the analysis and then performed a Pearson correlation analysis to predict statistically significant latent variables and variables (significant at least at the 0.05 level, see Table 8.2). The correlation matrices present simple relationships between latent variables and variables (Pearson correlation, -1–1). The results show correlations between early firm performance and business experience, and between sales and R&D networks. Correlations were also found between growth orientation and the control variable 'incubator localisation', and between the control variables 'patent' and 'incubator localisation'.

*Table 8.2        Correlation matrix*

|  | 1. | 2. | 3. | 4. | 5. | 6. | 7. |
|---|---|---|---|---|---|---|---|
| *Principal components* | | | | | | | |
| 1. Business experience | | | | | | | |
| 2. Growth orientation | 0.168** | | | | | | |
| 3. R&D networks – university | 0.185 | 0.205 | | | | | |
| *Control variables* | | | | | | | |
| 4. Firm age | 0.054 | -0.070 | 0.035 | | | | |
| 5. Patent | 0.033 | 0.077 | 0.035 | 0.008 | | | |
| 6. Incubator localisation | -0.073 | 0.265** | 0.060 | 0.028 | 0.197** | | |
| *Early film performance* | | | | | | | |
| 7. Sales | 0.164* | 0.092 | 0.254* | 0.029 | 0.002 | -0.024 | |
| 8. Employment | 0.131* | 0.098 | -0.088 | 0.028 | 0.009 | -0.001 | 0.972** |

*Note:* * $p<0.05$; ** $p<0.01$.

## Regression Analysis

Regression analysis, based on the latent variables constructed from the aggregated statistical means of underlying measures, is the third step in the statistical analysis. Since nearly all measures were expressed on Likert-type scales, extreme values could not have affected the aggregated means. The regression model below tests the relationship between the dependent variable 'early performance' (sales and employment in 2015) and the three independent latent variables:

$$EP = \beta_0 + \beta_1 BE + \beta_2 GO + \beta_3 RN \qquad (8.1)$$

where EP = Early performance;
    BE = Business experience;
    GO = Growth orientation;
    RN = R&D networks – university.

Table 8.3 reports the results of the regression analysis. One of the regression models is significant at the 0.005-level (dependent variable: Early firm

*Table 8.3*     *Regression analysis (Hypotheses 1–3 including collinearity statistics – dependent variable: Early firm performance - sales[abc])*

| Model[abc] | Standardised coefficients, beta | t | Sig. | Collinearity tolerance | Statistics VIF |
|---|---|---|---|---|---|
| (Constant) | | -1.657 | 0.0102 | | |
| Business experience | 0.409 | 3.813 | 0.000*** | 0.968 | 1.033 |
| Growth orientation | 0.173 | 1.610 | 0.112 | 0.960 | 1.042 |
| R&D networks – university | 0.146 | 1.332 | 0.187 | 0.930 | 1.075 |

*Notes:* [a] Dependent variable: Early firm performance – sales; [b] Model summary: R square = 0.255, adjusted R square = 0.222 and standard error of estimate=2921.544; [c] The model: Sig.= 0.000*** (ANOVA); * p<0.05; ** p<0.01; *** p<0.005.

performance–sales), while the other is not (sig. = 0.279, dependent variable: Early firm performance–employment). Predictors that are highly collinear or linearly related can affect regression coefficient estimates. Multicollinearity occurs in regression analysis when there is a high correlation between at least one independent variable and a combination of the other independent variables. Table 3 shows the collinearity statistics (tolerance and variance inflation factor, VIF). Although a VIF above 5 signals multicollinearity, and a tolerance below 0.20 is a cause for concern, this is not the case. The regression model in Table 8.3 is significant (p < 0.000). However, only one principal component is significant, business experience, which has a positive impact on sales. The R-squared is 25.5 per cent and the adjusted R-squared is 22.2 per cent. The next section discusses the implications of these results for theory and practice.

## DISCUSSION

In the early stages of a start-up, NTBFs' business performance depends on both internal and external resource dimensions that build a basis for competitive advantage. From a resource-based perspective, bundles of resources facilitate firm development, but in the early start-up phase, only a few resources are available for development and initial firm performance. Founders' human capital and their strategic orientation towards growth are two internal resource dimensions NTBFs possess and can utilise, but networks with external actors are also important for firm performance and future prospects. Regarding internal founder resources (e.g. human capital), our results show a positive relationship between founders' business experience and sales. This supports Hypothesis 1 and is in line with the argument that the previous work and managerial experience of founders have a positive effect on firm performance (e.g. Gimeno et al., 1997; Colombo and Grilli, 2005). For early-phase NTBFs, founders' business experience may enhance firms' prospects of attracting employees and initiating first sales, also demonstrated by the correlation between business experience and sales and employment. Hence, business experience in the early stage facilitates early growth and can therefore explain founders' perceived satisfaction with their early firm performance. Although business experience (i.e. previous experience) has been found to have limited effect on initial sales (Davidsson and Honig, 2003), our results indicate that for the perception and satisfaction regarding early firm performance, business experience is still influential.

Contrary to expectations, growth orientation has no significant effect on early firm performance, and the same is true for their correlation. Moreover, in the early phase, NTBFs seem to be less growth-oriented, demonstrating the lower growth ambitions of high-tech ventures (e.g. Autere and Autio, 2000). However, growth is important for NTBFs, and founders with higher ambitions may easily feel dissatisfaction with early firm performance. Our results also demonstrate correlations between growth orientation and business experience; hence, founders with previous experience are more knowledgeable about the industry and about how to orient their firms towards growth. From an RBV, growth orientation as an internal resource dimension related to NTBF founders seems less important in the early stages. However, this may have consequences regarding firms' attitudes towards seeking and exploiting opportunities, thus hindering firm development (e.g. Kirchhoff, 1994).

In terms of firm behaviour, NTBF founders seek support from science parks and incubators for advice and growth acceleration through network resources (e.g. Löfsten and Lindelöf, 2003; Löfsten, 2015). Incubators are set up to accelerate NTBF development (Aaboen, 2009) and, according to Löfsten and Lindelöf (2002), science parks, including incubators, probably attract a more motivated group of founders than off-park locations, especially during early stages. This is because they create conditions for development, including close contact with universities, which facilitate the early development of patents. In a more recent study of six European incubators, van Weele et al. (2017) found that entrepreneurs were not aware of their resource shortages and therefore had difficulties using the incubator to develop resources that were lacking. Such problems may also result in a negative relationship to performance, due to founders having difficulties developing resources needed for the firm's progress. Nevertheless, our findings reveal a positive correlation between growth orientation and incubator localisation, where science parks may attract more motivated founders.

Following a resource-based perspective, we study the effects of founders' experiences and attitudes (internal resources) and external R&D networks on the early firm performance of NTBFs. Our study adds to the literature on

NTBFs by demonstrating the effects of both internal and external resource dimensions (e.g. human capital and external relations) on performance in the very early phase of start-ups, rather than in later phases, which can reduce the risk of memory bias. In terms of resources at founding, founders' business experiences enhance early firm performance. This strengthens the resource-based literature on high-tech ventures, arguing that human capital as well as social capital play important roles in firm development and performance (e.g. Gimeno et al., 1997; Davidsson and Honig, 2003; Bosma et al., 2004). Conversely, firm behaviour and founders' attitudes regarding growth orientation may be an initial obstacle, rather than a competitive advantage. There is a tendency in research on high-tech ventures such as NTBFs to assume growth orientation as a given. Previous research has demonstrated that initial choices have long-lasting effects on firms' future prospects (Boeker, 1989), and accordingly has proposed that less growth-oriented behaviour in the early stages may create difficulties for later growth (Autere and Autio, 2000).

Because the choices made at the point of inception of a new start-up have a significant impact on its development well beyond the start-up phase (Bamford et al., 2013), scholars should investigate whether the initial configuration of a new start-up has significant consequences on its subsequent development (e.g. Beckman and Burton, 2008; Colombo and Piva, 2012; Tornikoski and Renko, 2014). Stinchcombe (1965) introduced organisational research to the concept of imprinting, which describes how organisations take on elements of their founding environment and how these elements persist well beyond the founding phase. This concept has attracted interest in a wide array of fields, from organisational and institutional ecology to network analysis and career research (Marquis and Tilcsik, 2013).

For practitioners, this study has managerial implications concerning the utilisation and acquisition of resources for new firms in their early start-up phase. In the early phase after founding, it is also essential to consider what resources the founder or founding team has to be able to handle changes in the (unstable) environment of high-tech ventures. Moreover, founders should consider not only the time and additional resources needed for initial growth, but also their growth orientation for future development. Growth ambitions and initial resources may also be important factors to be considered by advisors at science parks and incubators when giving advice on how early growth orientation may influence firms. Finally, the study raises some interesting questions for future research regarding how to develop incubators that offer better support to high-tech NTBFs during the early stages.

## CONCLUSION

This study examines the effects of NTBFs' human capital and external relations on early firm performance, demonstrating that both internal and external resource dimensions are important for NTBFs in their early start-up phase. The previous business experience of founders is an important internal resource for achieving higher sales and employment. This dimension enhances initial (early) firm performance. However, growth orientation and the attitudes of founders, as another internal resource dimension, do not seem to have a significant impact in the early stages. Accordingly, NTBFs may benefit from utilising their human capital (significant in this study) but should also consider their growth orientation and external R&D relations in terms of their future prospects.

## REFERENCES

Aaboen, L. (2009), 'Explaining incubators using firm analogy', *Technovation*, **29** (10), 657–670.

Almus, N. and E.A. Nerlinger (1999), 'Growth of new technology-based firms: Which factors matter?', *Small Business Economics*, **13** (2), 141–154.

Aspelund, A., T. Berg-Utby and R. Skjevdal (2005), 'Initial resources' influence on new venture survival: A longitudinal study of new technology-based firms', *Technovation*, **25** (11), 1337–1347.

Autere, J. and A. Autio (2000), 'Is entrepreneurship learned? Influence of mental models on growth motivation, strategy, and growth', Working Paper series, 7/2000. Institute of Strategy and International Business. Helsinki University of Technology, Espoo.

Autio, E. and H. Yli-Renko (1998), 'New, technology-based firms in small open economies – an analysis based on the Finnish experience', *Research Policy*, **26** (9), 973–987.

Autio, E., H. Sapienza and J. Almeida (2000), 'Effects of time to internationalization, knowledge-intensity, and imitability on growth', *Academy of Management Journal*, **43** (5), 909–924.

Bamford, C.E., T. Dean and P. McDougall-Covin (2013), 'An examination of the impact of initial founding conditions and decisions upon the performance of new bank start-ups', *Journal of Business Venturing*, **15** (3), 253–277.

Barney, J. (1991), 'Firm resources and sustained competitive advantage', *Journal of Management*, **17** (1), 99–120.

Beckman, C.M. and M.D. Burton (2008), 'Founding the future: Path dependence in the evolution of top management teams from founding to IPO', *Organization Science*, **19** (1), 3–24.

Bhide, A. (2000), *The Origin and Evolution of New Businesses*, New York: Oxford University Press.

Boeker, W. (1989), 'Strategic change: The effects of founding and history', *Academy of Management Journal*, **32** (3), 489–515.

Bollinger, L., K. Hope and J.M. Utterback (1983), 'A review of literature and hypotheses on new technology-based firms', *Research Policy*, **12** (1), 1–14.

Börjesson, S., and H. Löfsten (2012), 'Capabilities for innovation in small firms: A study of 131 high-tech firms and their relation to performance', *International Journal of Business Innovation and Research*, **6** (2), 149–176.

Bosma, N., M. van Praag, R. Thurik and G. De Wit (2004), 'The value of human and social capital investments for the business performance of start-ups', *Small Business Economics*, **23** (3), 227–236.

Brinckmann, J., S. Salomo and H.G. Gemuenden (2011), 'Financial management competence of founding teams and growth of new technology-based firms', *Entrepreneurship Theory and Practice*, **35** (2), 217–243.

Brown, R. and C. Mason (2014), 'Inside the high-tech black box: A critique of technology entrepreneurship policy', *Technovation*, **34** (12), 773–784.

Busenitz, L.W. and J.B. Barney, (1997), 'Differences between entrepreneurs and managers in large organizations: Biases and heuristics in strategic decision-making', *Journal of Business Venturing*, **12** (1), 9–30.

Butchart, R.L. (1987), 'A new UK definition of the high technology industries', *Economic Trends*, **400**, 82–88.

Cassar, G. (2014), 'Industry and startup experience on entrepreneur forecast performance in new firms', *Journal of Business Venturing*, **29** (1), 137–151.

Chandler, G.N. and S.H. Hanks (1994), 'Market attractiveness, resource-based capabilities, venture strategies and venture performance', *Journal of Business Venturing*, **9** (4), 331–349.

Clarysse, B., J. Bruneel and M. Wright (2011), 'Explaining growth paths of young technology-based firms: Structuring resource portfolios in different competitive environments', *Strategic Entrepreneurship Journal*, **5** (2), 137–157.

Clausen, T. and T. Korneliussen (2012), 'The relationship between entrepreneurial orientation and speed to the market: The case of incubator firms in Norway', *Technovation*, **32** (9), 560–567.

Colombo, M.G. and L. Grilli (2005), 'Founders' human capital and the growth of new technology-based firms: A competence-based view', *Research Policy*, **34** (6), 795–816.

Colombo, M.G. and L. Grilli (2010), 'On growth drivers of high-tech start-ups: Exploring the role of founders' human capital and venture capital', *Journal of Business Venturing*, **25** (6), 610–626.

Colombo, M.G. and E. Piva (2012), 'Firms' genetic characteristics and competence-enlarging strategies: A comparison between academic and non-academic high-tech start-ups', *Research Policy*, **41** (1), 79–92.

Das, T.K. and B.S. Teng (2000), 'A Resource-based Theory of Strategic Alliances', *Journal of Management*, **26** (1), 31–61.

Davidsson, P. (2007), 'Strategies for dealing with heterogeneity in entrepreneurship research', Paper presented August 7th at the Academy of Management Conference, Philadelphia.

Davidsson, P. and B. Honig (2003), 'The role of social and human capital among nascent entrepreneurs', *Journal of Business Venturing*, **18** (3), 301–331.

Davidsson, P., P.R. Steffens and J.R. Fitzsimmons (2009), 'Growing profitable or growing from profits: putting the horse in front of the cart?', *Journal of Business Venturing*, **24** (4), 388–406.

Delmar, F. and S. Shane (2006), 'Does experience matter? The effect of founding team experience on the survival and sales of newly founded ventures', *Strategic Organization*, **4** (3), 215–247.

Eurostat (2018), 'Glossary: High-tech classification of manufacturing industries', Retrieved 12 December 2018 from https://ec.europa.eu/eurostat/statistics-explained/index.php/Glossary:High-tech_classification_of_manufacturing_industries.

Fourati, H. and R.B. Attitalah (2017), 'Entrepreneurial optimism, the nature of entrepreneurial experience and debt decision for business start-up', *International Journal of Innovation Management*, **22** (3), 1–26, doi.org/10.1142/S136391961850024X.

George, D. and P. Mallery (2003), *SPSS for Windows Step By Step: A Simple Guide and Reference*, 11.0 update, 4th edn, Boston, MA: Allyn & Bacon.

Gimeno, J., T. Folta, A. Cooper and C. Woo (1997), 'Survival of the fittest? Entrepreneurial human capital and the persistence of underperforming firms', *Administrative Science Quarterly*, **42** (6), 750–783.

Grant, R.M. (1991), 'The resource-based theory of competitive advantage', *California Management Review*, **33** (3), 114–135.

Gulati, R. (1999), 'Network location and learning: The influence of network and firm capabilities on alliance formation', *Strategic Management Journal*, **20** (5), 397–420.

Hair, J.F., R.E. Anderson, R.L. Tatham and W.C. Black (1995), *Multivariate Data Analysis*, 3rd edn, New York: Macmillan Publishing Company.

Hitt, M.A., M.T. Dacin, E. Levitas, J.L. Arregle and A. Borza (2000), 'Partner selection in emerging and developed market contexts: Resource-based and organizational learning perspectives', *Academy of Management Journal*, **43** (3), 449–467.

Isaksson, A., V. Vanyushyn. and P. Hultén (2013), 'The impact of managers' attitudes on SMEs' growth in northern Sweden', *International Journal of Entrepreneurship and Small Business*, **18** (3), 298–312.

Kirchhoff, B. (1994), *Entrepreneurship and Dynamic Capitalism*, Westport, CT: Praeger.

Kollmer, H. and M. Dowling (2004), 'Licensing as a commercialisation strategy for new technology-based firms', *Research Policy*, **33** (8), 1141–1151.

Lane, P. and M. Lubatkin (1998), 'Relative absorptive capacity and inter-organizational learning', *Strategic Management Journal*, **9** (5), 461–477.

Letaifa, S.B. and Y. Rabeau (2013), 'Too close to collaborate? How geographic proximity could impede entrepreneurship and innovation', *Journal of Business Research*, **66** (10), 2071–2078.

Little, A.D. (1979), *New Technology-based Firms in UK and Federal Republic of Germany*, London: Wilton House Publications.

Löfsten, H. (2015), 'Critical resource dimensions for development of patents: An analysis of 131 new technology-based firms in incubators', *International Journal of Innovation Management*, **19** (1), 1550006.

Löfsten, H. and P. Lindelöf (2001), 'Science parks in Sweden: Industrial renewal and development?', *R&D Management*, **31** (3), 309–322.

Löfsten, H. and P. Lindelöf (2002), 'Science parks and the growth of new technology based firms: Academic-industry links, innovation and markets', *Research Policy*, **31** (6): 859–876.

Löfsten, H. and P. Lindelöf (2003), 'Determinants for an entrepreneurial milieu: Science Parks and business policy in growing firms', *Technovation*, **23** (1), 51–64.

Löfsten, H. and P. Lindelöf (2005a), 'Environmental hostility, strategic orientation and the importance of management accounting: An empirical analysis of new technology-based firms', *Technovation*, **25** (7), 725–738.

Löfsten, H. and P. Lindelöf (2005b), 'R&D networks and product innovation patterns – academic and non-academic new technology-based firms on Science Parks', *Technovation*, **25** (9), 1025–1037.

Lowe, R.A., and A.A. Ziedonis (2006), 'Overoptimism and the performance of entrepreneurial firms', *Management Science*, **52** (2), 173–186.

MacCallum, R.C. (1990), 'The need for alternative measures of fit in covariance structure modeling', *Multivariate Behavioral Research*, **25** (2), 157–162.

Maine, E.M., D.M. Shapiro and A.R. Vining (2010), 'The role of clustering in the growth of new technology-based firms', *Small Business Economics*, **34** (2), 127–146.

Markusen, A., P. Hall and A. Glasmeier (1986), *High Tech America: The What, How, Where and Why of the Sunrise Industries*, Boston, MA: George Allen and Unwin.

Marquis, C. and A. Tilcsik (2013), 'Imprinting: Toward a multilevel theory', *The Academy of Management Annals*, **7** (1), 195–245.

Miller, D. (1983), 'The correlates of entrepreneurship in three types of firms', *Management Science*, **29** (7), 770–791.

Miller, D. and P.H. Friesen (1982), 'Innovation in conservative and entrepreneurial firms: Two models of strategic momentum', *Strategic Management Journal*, **3** (1), 1–25.

Monck, C.S.P., R.B. Porter, P. Quintas, D.J. Storey and P. Wynarczyk (1988), *Science Parks and the Growth of High Technology Firms*, London: Croom Helm.

Moreno, A.M. and J.C. Casillas (2008), 'Entrepreneurial orientation and growth of SMEs: A causal model', *Entrepreneurship Theory and Practice*, **32** (3), 507–528.

OECD (1993), *Small and Medium-Sized Enterprises: Technology and Competitiveness*, Paris: Organisation of Economic Co-operation and Development.

Peteraf, M.A. (1993), 'The cornerstones of competitive advantage: A resource-based view', *Strategic Management Journal*, **14** (3), 171–191.

Pfeffer, J. and G.R. Salancik (2003), *The External Control of Organizations: A Resource Dependence Perspective*, Stanford, CA: Stanford University Press.

Pittino, D., F. Visintin and G. Lauto (2017), 'A configurational analysis of the antecedents of entrepreneurial orientation', *European Management Journal*, **35** (2), 224–237.

Pouder, R. and C.H. St. John (1996), 'Hot spots and blind spots: Geographical clusters of firms and innovation', *Academy of Management Review*, **21** (4), 1192–1225.

Ramírez-Alesón, M. and M. Fernández-Olmos (2017), 'Unravelling the effects of science parks on the innovation performance of NTBFs', *The Journal of Technology Transfer*, **43** (2), 482–505. doi.org/10.1007/s10961-017-9559-y.

Runyan, R., C. Droge and J. Swinney (2008), 'Entrepreneurial orientation versus small business orientation: What are their relationships to firm performance?', *Journal of Small Business Management*, **46** (4), 567–588.

Rydehell, H. and A. Isaksson (2016), 'Initial configurations and business models in new technology-based firms', *Journal of Business Models*, **4** (1), 63–83.

Rydehell, H., A. Isaksson and H. Löfsten (2018), 'Effects of internal and external resource dimensions on the business performance of new technology-based firms', *International Journal of Innovation Management*, **23** (1), 195001-1–195001-29, doi: 10.1142/S1363919619500014.

Saemundsson, R.J. and M. Candi (2014), 'Antecedents of innovation strategies in new technology-based firms: interactions between the environment and founder team composition', *Journal of Product Innovation Management*, **31** (5), 939–955.

Safón, V. (2009), 'Measuring the reputation of top US business schools: A mimic modeling approach', *Corporate Reputation Review*, **12** (3), 204–228.

Sirmon, D. and M. Hitt (2003), 'Managing resources: linking unique resources, management, and wealth creation in family firms', *Entrepreneurship Theory and Practice*, **27** (4), 339–351.

Spencer, A.S. and B.A. Kirchhoff (2006), 'Schumpeter and new technology based firms: Towards a framework for how NTBFs cause creative destruction', *International Entrepreneurship and Management Journal*, **2** (2), 145–156.

Stinchcombe, A. (1965), 'Social structure and organizations', in March, J.G. (ed.), *Handbook of Organizations*, New York: Rand McNally & Company, pp. 142–193.

Storey, D. (1994), *Understanding the Small Business Sector*, London: Routledge.

Storey, D.J. and B.S. Tether (1998), 'New technology-based firms in the European Union: An introduction', *Research Policy*, **26** (9), 933–946.

Tornikoski, E. and M. Renko (2014), 'Timely creation of new organizations: The imprinting effects of entrepreneurs' initial founding decisions', *Management*, **17** (3), 193–213.

Trevelyan, R. (2008), 'Optimism, overconfidence and entrepreneurial activity', *Management Decision*, **46** (7), 986–1001.

van Weele, M., F.J. van Rijnsoever and F. Nauta (2017), 'You can't always get what you want: How entrepreneur's perceived resource needs affect the incubator's assertiveness', *Technovation*, **59** (1), 18–33.

Venkatraman, N. and V. Ramanujam (1986), 'Measurement of business performance in strategy research: A comparison of approaches', *The Academy of Management Review*, **11** (4), 801–814.

Wennberg, K. (2005), 'Entrepreneurship research through longitudinal databases: measurement and design issues', *New England Journal of Entrepreneurship*, **8** (2), 9–19.

Wernerfelt, B. (1984), 'A resource-based view of the firm', *Strategic Management Journal*, **5** (2), 171–180.

West, G. and T. Noel (2009), 'The impact of knowledge resources on new venture performance', *Journal of Small Business Management*, **47** (1), 1–22.

Westhead, P. and D.J. Storey (1994), *An Assessment of Firms Located On and Off Science Parks in the United Kingdom*, London: HMSO.

Wiklund, J. and D. Shepherd (2003), 'Aspiring for, and achieving growth: The moderating role of resources and opportunities', *Journal of Management Studies*, **40** (8), 1921–1941.

Wiklund, J., P. Davidsson and F. Delmar (2003), 'What do they think and feel about growth? An expectancy-value approach to small business managers' attitudes toward growth', *Entrepreneurship Theory and Practice*, **27** (3), 247–270.

Yli-Renko, H., E. Autio and H.J. Sapienza (2001), 'Social capital, knowledge acquisition, and knowledge exploitation in young technology-based firms', *Strategic Management Journal*, **22** (6–7), 587–613.

Yli-Renko, H., E. Autio and V. Tontti (2002), 'Social capital, knowledge, and the international growth of technology-based new firms', *International Business Review*, **11** (3), 279–304.

# APPENDIX

*Table 8A.1     Variables used in the study*

| Measures | Mean | SD | Scale |
|---|---|---|---|
| *Business experience* | | | |
| Founders' work experience (total) in the same industry at the start-up year | 19.83 | 15.35 | Years |
| Founders' managerial experience (total) at the start-up year | 8.05 | 12.33 | Years |
| *Growth orientation* | | | |
| High growth–employees–important firm objective | 1.56 | 1.03 | 1–5 |
| High growth–sales–important firm objective | 2.99 | 1.55 | 1–5 |
| Rapid geographic expansion on new markets–important firm objective | 2.05 | 1.43 | 1–5 |
| *R&D networks – university* | | | |
| Firms' R&D-projects–university staff | 2.19 | 1.54 | 1–5 |
| Common R&D-projects–university | 2.43 | 1.61 | 1–5 |
| Use of R&D equipment–university | 2.03 | 1.49 | 1–5 |
| Recruitments–university | 1.96 | 1.42 | 1–5 |
| *Control variables* | | | |
| Firm age | 28.32 | 8.58 | Months |
| Percent | 0.10 | 0.78 | Number |
| Incubator localisation | 0.10 | 0.294 | Yes/No (1/0) |

# 9. Disembeddedness, prior industry knowledge and opportunity creation processes

**Karin Hellerstedt, Caroline Wigren-Kristoferson, Maria Aggestam, Anna Stevenson and Ethel Brundin**

## INTRODUCTION

The role of prior industry experience has attracted attention from entrepreneurship scholars for decades. In particular, industry experience can be beneficial because it provides access to customer and supplier networks as well as important rules and norms (Gimeno et al., 1997; Delmar and Shane, 2006). The knowledge corridor principle has gained strong acceptance since its introduction by Ronstadt (1988). In short, this principle predicts that entrepreneurs are more likely to see and pursue opportunities in areas where they have been professionally active. However, many breakthrough innovations are made by entrepreneurs who enter new markets and question taken-for-granted ways of doing things.

The opportunity creation process is complex and contingent on factors ranging from individual personality traits, prior knowledge and social networks to favorable circumstances in the environment (Ardichvili et al., 2003). Additionally, personal interest in the topic can influence the process (Tobias, 1995). Therefore, the role of prior industry experience is difficult to isolate. Instead, it may be fruitful to gain insight into how the process unfolds when a specific experience is lacking. Thus, the purpose of this study is to investigate *how entrepreneurs handle a lack of industry embeddedness in their venturing process*. We address this purpose by building on the literature on prior knowledge and embeddedness phenomena to further our understanding of the entrepreneurial process.

Prior industry knowledge is often emphasized as beneficial for opportunity creation processes (Shane, 2000). However, the potential benefits of prior industry experiences may also represent limitations and cause lock-in effects that impose limits on the innovative height of new products and services. Although there is an extensive body of literature investigating the role of prior industry experience for the survival and success of new firms, prior industry experiences can place cognitive limits on the types of opportunities a person may see and develop, such that "increased prior knowledge could make thinking 'outside the box' more difficult and the identification of more innovative opportunities unlikely" (Shepherd and DeTienne, 2005, p. 104). Put differently, embeddedness in certain contexts, such as industries, has been viewed as important for entrepreneurial processes but a lack of specific industry knowledge also means that the individual is disembedded from that context and might be better equipped to come up with novel and more radical innovations.

Radical change and innovations are often depicted as crucial for economic development and growth (e.g. Baumol and Strom, 2007). Policy makers and researchers assert that these factors are important for a country's prosperity and development. As such, they are highly prioritized by policy makers. This is clearly articulated in the European Union's 2020 Growth Strategy document, which notes that smart growth, which builds on innovations and knowledge, is a high priority. Researchers have been intrigued by the role of radical innovations since Schumpeter's (1934) theory of economic development and the process of creative destruction. A large body of existing literature has aimed to clarify whether new or incumbent firms are key sources of radical innovations (Hill and Rothaermel, 2003). As Schumpeter put it:

> In general it is not the owner of stagecoaches that builds railways. (Schumpeter, 1934, p 66)

According to this quote (Schumpeter, 1934), radical innovations are often initiated by entrepreneurs venturing into new contexts, such as a new industry. AirBnB is an example of the founders drastically changing the conditions for firms within the hospitality industry and the hotel and lodging industry in particular. The founders of AirBnB came from a different industry background. In Sweden, there are companies such as Spotify and the well-known grocery bag concept firms Middagsfrid and Linas Matkasse in which the founders lacked prior industry-specific experiences.

Previous research shows that entrepreneurs frequently start businesses in industries in which they have experience (Shane, 2000). In addition, much of the entrepreneurship literature emphasizes the importance of prior industry experience for firm survival and growth (cf. Delmar and Shane, 2006). However, although prior industry experience can be an important resource and can increase success rates for firms in general, it does not necessarily spark radical innovations. In a recent article, Dencker and Gruber (2015) find that industry experience is more important when pursuing low-risk opportunities, whereas managerial experience is more important for exploiting high-risk opportunities. In a similar vein, Gabrielsson and Politis (2011) find that diverse functional experience is more likely to lead to new business ideas, while deep industry experience has a negative effect. At the same time, Venture Capitalists and investors tend to invest in and favor entrepreneurs with extensive industry-related competencies (cf. Hoenig and Henkel, 2015) and prior start-up experience (Hsu, 2007).

Building on the work of Dencker and Gruber (2015), we believe it is important to adopt a more nuanced view of the role of prior industry experience. In other words, there might be more variance in the performance of firms that are started by individuals who lack prior industry experience. Thus, these firms may be more likely to fail in general, but there may also be interesting outliers that are highly innovative and successful. Interestingly, there is a lack of knowledge concerning the process by which radical innovations come about and the role of context in this process (Autio et al., 2014). Welter (2011) notes that "context is important for understanding when, how, and why entrepreneurship happens and who becomes involved" (p. 166).

In this chapter, we explore how disembeddedness and the process of becoming embedded can contribute to our understanding of the impact of opportunity creation processes on the entrepreneurial process. More specifically, we intend to explore how entrepreneurs handle being disembedded in an industry into which they venture. To do this, we conduct three exploratory case studies with entrepreneurs to illustrate how they manage to change their position from disembedded to embedded in their venturing process.

This study extends previous literature that has assumed that previous industry experience is decisive for the success of entrepreneurs. Our research challenges this assumption by showing how disembeddedness in an industry can contribute to radical innovations. Theoretically, this study contributes by considering the role of disembeddedness in the entrepreneurial process and arguing that it is not fruitful to classify the opportunity creation process into dichotomies of embeddedness and disembeddness. Rather, depending on the context and the unfolding of the process, the entrepreneur may move between being embedded and disembedded. Our study discusses entrepreneurs who have brought novel ideas to markets where they lack prior knowledge and where they began as disembedded.

Further, our findings show that entrepreneurs who lack particular experiences perceive challenges but are also able to adopt an open view in the opportunity creation process. A lack of knowledge causes these entrepreneurs to make mistakes or to be unable to foresee things they otherwise would have addressed. At the same time, they seem to have low attachment to certain industries and do not seem to be restricted by industry boundaries. Instead, they have an open approach to markets and applications.

Even so, these entrepreneurs make strong use of existing networks and prior knowledge in other spheres (such as connections to certain suppliers). Therefore, it is clear that embeddedness and disembeddedness are a matter of degree on a scale and on different levels, ranging from micro- to macro-levels. This ability to compensate for the lack of knowledge at a certain level by drawing on resources that are embedded at another level appears to be important for the opportunity creation process.

We also find that depending on their previous experiences, entrepreneurs adopt different approaches when entering a new industry. They rely on story-telling to build a strong brand and acceptance in the market or use prior knowledge and experiences from other industries to build a convincing offering. It is also possible to use a combination of both approaches.

The chapter is structured as follows. In the next section, we cover literature on prior knowledge and embeddedness. Subsequently, we explain the chosen method. Following that, we present the empirical material and the analyses and discussion. Finally, we offer implications and new research questions and discuss limitations in our research.

## FRAME OF REFERENCE

### The Role of Prior Knowledge

The role of prior industry experience has attracted attention from entrepreneurship scholars for several decades. Industry experience can be beneficial because it provides access to customer and supplier networks as well as important rules and norms (Gimeno et al., 1997; Delmar and Shane, 2006). Nevertheless, these potential benefits may also represent limitations and cause lock-in effects that impose limits on the innovative height of new products and services. The knowledge corridor principle has gained strong acceptance since its introduction by Ronstadt (1988). In short, this principle predicts that entrepreneurs are more likely to see and pursue opportunities in areas where they have been professionally active. In an influential study on the role of prior knowledge in the opportunity discovery process, Shane (2000) refined the principle into *prior market knowledge, prior knowledge about how to serve certain markets* and *prior knowledge of customer problems*. A qualitative case study (Shane, 2000) showed how an individual's idiosyncratic knowledge influences the opportunity development process. His findings show that prior knowledge has a strong influence on what opportunities individuals see and how they develop them. Although the author acknowledges that prior knowledge can be gained in many different ways, he places a strong emphasis on market and industry knowledge. Interpreted differently, this means that prior industry experiences can also place cognitive limits on the types of opportunities a person may see and develop. This argument is in line with Ko and Butler (2006), who study the role of cognitive approaches in the opportunity creation process. They find that bisociative thinking causes more novelty than associative thinking. The former would be more likely when venturing into new domains than when staying in a familiar context. Additionally, Baron (2006) argues that cognitive perspectives, such as the pattern recognition perspective, can enable a holistic view of the opportunity creation process and the way prior knowledge, such as industry experience (or lack thereof), is interrelated with the other dimensions. Corbett (2005) also shows how learning can be important for understanding the role of prior knowledge in the opportunity creation process. In sum, much research assumes that prior industry experience is good for radical innovations. Nevertheless, research based on cognitive perspectives also claims that ideas based on such knowledge might be less novel. Therefore, given that there are many empirical examples of individuals venturing into new areas with radical innovations, it is interesting to learn how the opportunity creation process unfolds when market and industry knowledge is limited.

Although there is an extensive body of literature investigating the role of prior industry experience in the survival and success of new firms, the results are mixed and inconclusive (Delmar and Shane, 2006). Cassar (2014) found that industry experience had a positive influence on entrepreneurs' forecast performance. Delmar and Shane (2006), while correcting for venture failure, found that prior start-up and industry experience enhanced survival and sales. However, these effects were non-linear and varied depending on the age of the firm (Delmar and Shane, 2006), and the authors did not assess the relationship to innovativeness. Other studies have shown that managerial (Dencker and Gruber, 2015) and entrepreneurial experience (Ucbasaran et al., 2009) could be more important for the type and number of opportunities an individual might envision. In a study on new firm performance, Dencker and Gruber (2015) studied the role of managerial and industry experience. They found that managerial experience had a stronger influence on firm performance when the firm was based on a high-risk opportunity. For low-risk opportunities, industry experience was more important. In sum, prior knowledge is important for the new venture development process, but we know relatively little about how entrepreneurs deal with the lack of certain knowledge as they venture into new domains.

The opportunity creation process is complex and contingent on factors ranging from individual personality traits, prior knowledge and social networks to favorable circumstances in the environment (Ardichvili et al., 2003). In addition, personal interest in the topic or the situation can influence the process (Tobias, 1995). Therefore, the role of prior industry experience is difficult to isolate. It would be fruitful to gain more insight into how the process of developing embeddedness unfolds when an individual lacks a particular experience.

## Embeddedness, Disembeddedness and the Opportunity Creation Process

At the core of this research lies what we call the disembedded entrepreneur, who is disembedded in the sense that he or she is entering into a new industry context when starting a firm. From previous research, we know that entrepreneurs are embedded in networks (cf. Granovetter, 1973, 1985; Uzzi, 1996), and networking activities are embedded in social contexts. One social context is the industry. The entrepreneurs we focus on are not embedded in the industry context in which they start the firm but in other contexts. That is, we do not argue that they lack embeddedness in general. Starting the firm is also a process of becoming embedded in the industry context of the firm.

Aldrich and Zimmer (1986) focus on entrepreneurship as "embedded in a social context, channeled and facilitated or constrained and inhibited by people's positions in social networks" (Aldrich and Zimmer, 1986, p. 4). Their perspective views "entrepreneurship as embedded in networks of continuing social relations" (p. 8). Burt (1992) underlines that for entrepreneurs, what you know is less important than who you know. Knowledge and resources are embedded in the network of the entrepreneur. Burt (1992) states that people tend to develop relationships with those who are like them; he adds that people who are similar, independent of their interests, meet in the same places where relationships are created and maintained.

The way opportunities are formed varies systematically (Venkataraman, 2003), and the way an opportunity is formed might influence how it is exploited (Alvarez and Barney, 2010). Generally speaking, two perspectives dominate in the literature. According to the first and most established perspective, opportunities are formed by exogenous shocks to preexisting markets or industries, which entrepreneurs discover (Shane, 2003). The second perspective, which has recently been developed further, suggests that entrepreneurs form opportunities endogenously by creating them (Alvarez and Barney, 2007, 2010). In this research, opportunities are understood as created by entrepreneurs.

Fletcher (2006, p. 425) addresses the issue "why people enact opportunities in the way (and at the time) that they do in relation to broader societal, economic and political processes" and she argues that the discovery approach to opportunities has attributed agency to specific individuals who, because of their market skills, see opportunities and that less attention has been paid to the societal, economic and cultural structures or patterns that shape entrepreneurial practice.

In entrepreneurship research, there has been a strong focus on the importance of being in control of resources (Sarasvathy, 2001; Baker and Nelson, 2005) and being embedded in networks and industries. For Kotha and George (2012), entrepreneurs are embedded in a web of social relations that help to create new companies, while the ability to draw beneficial resources from the network depends on the combination of ties (family/professional) and industry and start-up experience. Santarelli and Tran (2013) stressed the importance of the entrepreneur's individual and social capital deriving from personal networks for firm performance. Selden and Fletcher (2015) remarked that important factors for new ventures that internationalize early and lack prior knowledge of international markets and prior international work experience are improvisation, effectuation and network constituencies. The authors concluded that networks and *idiosyncratic* prior knowledge are critical resources that entrepreneurs hold and that are useful in the internationalization process

Some research, however, hints that newcomers or outsiders might have an advantage. Desa (2011) argued that less-embedded actors can still survive; when entrepreneurs are not locked in preexisting institutional structures, they can use various activities that challenge the rules and norms of existing institutional arrangements. Bechky and Okhuysen (2011) found that individuals then restructure their activities by role shifting, reorganizing routines, and reassembling the work. Gras and Nason (2015) examined the family as the context for acquiring resources and found that increasing family household diversity is likely to bring creativity-related performance benefits because it generates innovative resource combinations.

Although social capital can initially facilitate knowledge transfer and creation, Weber and Weber (2011) found that social network structures that once were enriching can eventually become a social liability, which is referred to as the "dark side" of social capital.

Despite extensive studies on embeddedness, research on disembeddedness is scarce in the field of entrepreneurship, and researchers have conceptualized it differently. Gonin (2015) discussed the need for businesses to interact with their social context from a social responsibility perspective and identified four disembeddedness factors that challenge the embeddedness of individuals, businesses and society. Arguing that the enterprise is no longer subject to the values of the entrepreneur because it has gained the status of a disconnected, legal person, changes in the ownership structure and the transformation of the entrepreneurial role toward an agency role, and changes in the relation to the local community contribute to the disembeddedness of businesses (Gonin, 2015).

Muellerleile (2013) integrated Karl Polanyi's conception of disembedded markets and Michel Callon's performativity thesis and suggested that these two concepts are necessary for an analysis of contemporary financial markets and their relationship to the socio-economy. In contrast to Muellerleile (2013), we focus on individual entrepreneurs and their firms in their local contexts rather than on the industry level. Our research has some similarities with the research conducted by Amezcua et al. (2013), who study agro-food systems and how different strategies can lead to contributions to rural regional development. These authors found that local actors may not always benefit from territorial embeddedness; in some cases, rural development depends on the extent to which local actors manage to disembed themselves from the territorial context. While these authors focused on embedded entrepreneurs who disembed themselves, we focus on in-migrating entrepreneurs who engage in a process of becoming embedded in a local context. Our focus is on entrepreneurs who engage in entrepreneurial creation processes in an industry that is new to them.

## METHOD

To fulfil the purpose of investigating how entrepreneurs handle being disembedded in terms of lack of previous industry experiences in the opportunity creation process, three empirical case studies were used to illustrate the phenomena studied. This enabled a rich and contextualized understanding of the research question at hand (Stake, 1995). We used purposeful sampling in which the chosen cases had the following in common: (1) they were started by entrepreneurs who did not have previous industry experiences in the industry in which they started the firm; (2) they contributed to the industry by doing something that was considered novel in the industry context; and (3) they had succeeded in establishing themselves in the market, that is, they were firms that were up and running. We used ethnographic interviewing techniques (Spradley, 1979) with descriptive, structural and contrast questions. Because we had a main interest in the early stage of the opportunity creation process, we relied on narratives and retrospective data collection. All interviews were recorded, transcribed, coded and analyzed. When coding, we grouped the material into themes. As a first step, we wrote case descriptions that are presented in the findings section. Based on the cases and our coding, we grouped the material into themes showing how the entrepreneurs developed their ideas and how they handled being disembedded in their industry context.

Using a qualitative approach, we aim to extend previous literature that has assumed that resources at hand and knowledge, such as prior industry experience, are of decisive importance for the entrepreneur. To fulfil the purpose of investigating how disembeddedness, in terms of a lack of previous industry experiences influences the opportunity creation process, we conduct three narrative studies with founders/owners of young entrepreneurial ventures who have recently entered a market that was new to the founders and that brought about novel offerings and solutions. The empirical material consists of three two-hour face-to-face interviews and is complemented with extensive media follow-up and company presentations as secondary information.

Qualitative data offer possibilities to incorporate a critical and reflective perspective (Alvesson and Sköldberg, 2009). Because we have a main interest in the early opportunity creation process, we primarily rely on retrospective data collection to understand the embedding process in the industry.

The main sampling criteria were that the entrepreneur had started a firm in an industry with no previous industry experience in that particular industry. When sampling, we also searched for differences between the cases. We selected (1) firms from different industries and (2) entrepreneurs with different backgrounds and levels of business experience.

We focused on the entrepreneurial process and retrospectively developed an understanding of why and how entrepreneurs enacted opportunities in the way they did and at the time they did so (cf. Fletcher, 2006). However, to avoid an overly long time frame from the start-up, the entrepreneurial venture could not be farther back in time than three to five years. As stressed above, we consider opportunities as created and embedded in societal, economic and political contexts. This implies that the context of the entrepreneurial process is important and acknowledged in our research. We also focus on the process of becoming embedded in the new industry context over time.

The empirical material is the basis for an exploratory study. From the empirical work, we are able to study the embedding process when an entrepreneur is new to an industry and initially does not have access to industry networks, knowledge and skills related to this specific industry.

The two theoretical frames we used when planning and conducting the empirical study were embeddedness and opportunity creation. We focus on entrepreneurs who are new to the industry where they establish their firms and label this disembeddedness. Disembeddedness can be linked to relational and structural embeddedness, mixed embeddedness, family embeddedness, political embeddedness, cultural embeddedness and network embeddedness. As a process, the mixed embeddedness approach involves several contexts and levels of embeddedness, such as political embeddedness, cultural and cognitive embeddedness. Political embeddedness focuses on the sources and means of economic action (Zukin and DiMaggio, 1990) and denotes institutional limits on economic power and incentives; cultural embeddedness is associated to the cognitive dimension of society and emphasizes the shared collective memories, historical reciprocity which privileges aspects of societal belongings (Denzau and North, 1994) that also represents shared beliefs and values that shape economic aims. Cognitive embeddedness represents symbols, frameworks and structured mental processes of an entrepreneur which they could only facilitate through contextually aware embeddedness (Jack and Anderson, 2002).

We also used secondary material, such as news articles, media information, and public company presentations. The data were examined in detail, focusing on embeddedness building in the early stage of venturing. Independently, we iteratively discussed and reviewed our data in relation to their current context. These data were coded and incorporated into the analyses. Our group collaboration and discussion was helpful in building confidence for our understanding and our interpretations. Our study was restricted to a small number of cases that inhibits generalizability (Chandler and Hanks, 1994). However, methodological techniques were useful to explore and illustrate the ways in which resource capabilities were developed and identified (Chandler and Hanks, 1994).

## ILLUSTRATIVE CASES

### Case 1: Gaia Biomaterials

The founder of Gaia Biomaterials is the serial entrepreneur Åke. He founded several companies before starting Gaia Biomaterials. In the past, he has been involved in starting twelve companies. In 1976, he started a company called Masterplast; in the 1980s, he founded the company Filltech, a company that later was sold to a German company, and in the late 1990s, he founded a third company, Ecolean, all in the packaging industry. Additionally, he has participated in several spin-off processes started by former employees. Both Filltech and Ecolean are currently global companies with plants all over the world. After Åke graduated in engineering, he obtained a mentor, Hans Rausing, who was the son of the founder of the company Tetra Pak. Hans Rausing agreed to act as a mentor for Åke, and they became good friends. They agreed at an early stage that Åke should not start working in the large company Tetra Pak but rather should start a firm so that they could develop new things. Åke stated that he has never been interested in developing me-too products; the driving force has always been to develop radically new products. His parents were teachers, and he stressed that the world of academia is very different from working in industry.

In Greek mythology, Gaia was Mother Earth, so the name Gaia Biomaterials is related to Mother Earth and biomaterials. The company has developed a renewable, degradable and compostable material called Biodolomer. A driving force for the company is to contribute to a more sustainable society by replacing fossil-based and energy-intensive plastic and packaging materials. In the interview with Åke, he stated that Margot

Wallström was an environmental commissioner in the European Union, and in a meeting, she stressed the need to find a material that could replace plastics. Today, Åke envisions a future where the company produces and delivers different types of products, such as knives, forks, mugs, trays, soup bags, and laundry bags. This implies that Gaia Biomaterials' core product is the new material that can be applied in several different industry contexts. Thus, it is possible to position the company in the materials sector, where it produces a new competitive biomaterial. The company was thus started in a new industry context compared to the packaging industry, which was the location of the previous companies founded by Åke.

Åke started to work with biomaterial in 1974; he produced golf tees and could follow how they were degradable. However, from his perspective, this was far too early to introduce biomaterial to the market. In earlier processes, he used plastic as the binding material.

### Case 2: Orbital Systems

The founder of Orbital Systems is Mehrdad. In 2012, Mehrdad, at the end of his education in industrial design at the Faculty of Engineering LTH at Lund University, was given the task, in cooperation with NASA, to find a solution that would enable minimal water usage during a round trip to Mars. The project was successful in finding a solution, and Mehrdad realized that this type of technology could also be used on earth. In an article by Almi,[1] Mehrdad explains that he realized that he had a business idea:

> [W]hen I looked at the market and saw that the ones who build showers do not care about water consumption and the ones who purify water are often municipal companies without knowledge in construction technology and with no financial incentives. A classic mismatch where neither one has the know-how about the other thing. I decided to create a business that can do both parts.

This was the start of what was to become Orbital Systems. Mehrdad built the first prototype of a shower using water-recycling technology together with his cousins in the basement of a relative's house. The technology was patented, and Mehrdad began seeking financing. At the end of 2012, the company won the Green Mentorship Award, which meant that Mehrdad would be the mentee of Niklas Zennström, the founder of Skype, for one year. Six months later, Niklas became a part owner and has since financed Orbital Systems together with a few other investors. Orbital Systems currently employs almost 100 people, located either at the headquarters in Malmö, Sweden, or at their sales offices in Sausalito, California; Berlin, Germany; and Copenhagen, Denmark. In the same Almi article, Mehrdad ascribes the success to "an idea of questioning how things have been done before. That permeates all our work; we call it internal avant-garde. If we had wanted to do what everyone else does, we wouldn't have been here."

The first product, V1, was expensive and only produced on a small scale. A hospital in Kristianstad, Sweden, and Ribersborgs Kallbadhus, a public sauna and bathing house in Malmö, were among the first to purchase this product, which enabled the company to use this as a reference for further sales. At this point, V1 had a number of growing pains that needed attention, which provided important knowledge for the new product. This is also believed to be one of the success factors: testing the prototype against the market and obtaining input from customers at an early stage instead of continuing the technological development in an isolated lab environment.

In June 2017, the company was able to launch its first commercially scalable application, called Oas. This product is a shower that saves up to 90 percent of water usage (80 percent of energy usage is normally wasted when showering). The water is recycled as it runs through a built-in Micron filter that removes 99.9 percent of undesirable particles and chemicals and a UV light that neutralizes bacteria. The cleaned water is then pushed up through the showerhead again. Through this technology, it is possible to limit water usage to approximately ten liters regardless of the time spent showering.

Stephan, Quality Director at Orbital Systems, explains that it takes a certain amount of time before the market can accept a new type of product like this. People are worried that the water might not actually be clean or that it is not safe to use the shower. Internally, Orbital Systems is not seen as having revolutionized an industry but rather as having created a new industry. The company is also the first actor to have a commercially viable product because competitors with comparable products are still in the small-scale development phase. The product is sold directly to the end customer, mainly business clients such as hotels or gyms that need multiple showers in their facilities. This strategy enables the technology to reach a broad market (that is, a broad range of customers) more quickly. The water-saving technology was first applied in the shower, which represents the greatest water usage within a household, but the company has a clear vision of changing the way people view water usage through a complete integration of their technology in all household applications.

Stephan further explains that with a new product such as this, there are no standardizations and certifications to which to refer. There is, for example, no standardized distinction between drinking water, grey water and black water on an EU level. Local interpretations of such matters create challenges for the company, and Orbital Systems must act as a lobbyist to set the standard on matters relating to water quality.

**Case 3: Global Warning System**

The founder of the Global Warning System is the serial entrepreneur Lars. Before starting the Global Warning System, he started the company Scandimed and the company Bone Support. Lars is a medical doctor in orthopedics; he became a doctor in 1970. In 1973, he received his PhD, and soon after he became an associate professor. In 1986, he became a full professor. According to Lars, orthopedics is a technical specialty. He began to develop different details to make it possible to conduct better surgery. The reason for starting the Global Warning System is related to three incidents that Lars experienced. The first incident was when he was invited by the Swedish Research Council to participate in a trip to Thailand, China and Hong Kong. During the trip, they visited hospitals. When Lars returned to Sweden, he realized that he had been in the epicenter of SARS. The second incident was the tsunami in Thailand, when he flew to Thailand to help. When he experienced the catastrophe, he began to think that it is not possible that people cannot be tracked through their mobile phones, a Swedish innovation from the company Ericsson. Furthermore, it should have been possible to warn the people through their mobile phones that there was a tsunami coming. Finally, he participated in a conference in India when there was a terror attack at the hotel in Bombay, and he realized how difficult it was to get in contact with all participants in the conference. When he returned from India, he wrote a patent for a solution that aimed to track people to warn them and to ensure that they are safe.

Today, this patent is the core of the Global Warning System. The Global Warning System has a group of analysts who constantly follow social media with the purpose of identifying different catastrophes in the world. When analysts realize that something is happening, they communicate with those who buy their service. The customers of Global Warning System are primarily large companies that have employees all over the world and insurance companies. Companies with employees abroad shoulder the responsibility for their employees, and they want to know that their employees are safe. The system communicates with the person who is close to the geographical area of the catastrophe; he or she receives a message and should confirm that he or she is safe and that this information is communicated to the company/employer.

When Lars was in the process of starting the company, he decided to bring Andreas Rodman on board. Andreas had a background in computer science and had been part of a couple of previous start-ups. When starting the company, it was decided that Lars would own the majority of the company but also cover the costs.

## ANALYSIS

Our analysis relates to how the entrepreneurs have handled being disembedded in the industry and how they have approached the market. A theme we chose to call *storytelling* emerged strongly from our coding. In particular, all three cases show strong tendencies to build a story around their company and their offerings. This story is then refined and communicated in several channels, such as in media and marketing campaigns. Their stories have become part of their company descriptions and are stated on their web pages. In the early interviews with Orbital, we see that they highlighted certain aspects at early stages. For the founder of Orbital, the link to NASA has existed since the beginning, before there was a prototype (or even a legal entity), as a way to build a story around the opportunity development. Being able to use the name of NASA is clearly a door opener and a way to obtain positive attention. In the storytelling examples, we can also see that they emphasize aspects that can give them higher status. For the founder of Orbital, this involved drawing on the reputation of NASA, Lund, and the names of other collaborators. For the founder of Global Warning System, the technical qualities of the company were highlighted. Therefore, we can see that both social and spatial contexts are used in storytelling and as ways to establish a hierarchy or certain status.

What was particularly interesting in our case samples of respondents was that they seemed to draw extensively on frictions within the company. Åke mentioned tensions at the working table with potential customers. He refers to his past experiences: "I was technical and have been an adviser to one of the biggest moguls, from whom I have learned a lot. I was very careful to highlight those who did it before me. I was extremely attentive to the stories the other people have to tell. That gave me experience to act now in my new business situations."

### Embedded Niches

In general, the literature provides evidence that embeddedness is the non-economic logic of how entrepreneurs, firms and industry combine many reciprocal relationships as configuring elements of business processes. Embeddedness thus emphasizes the importance of the specifics in shaping the entrepreneurial process. These specifics form personal knowledge, develop entrepreneurial experience and build particular niches of competence and capabilities. Beyond being inspired by the stories of others, we found that our respondents were actively involved in various arrangements focused on building embeddedness in the new industries. This was directed by the entrepreneurs' new industry situation through their enactive action to advance the creation of embedding. The environmental process was directed by the person–environment (context) relationship (Weick, 2001), which indicates that context is constituted by action and stored within the entrepreneurial experience base. Within this process, enactive practices from the past serve as a new situated embedding and belong to the embedded niche of capabilities. These specifics turn them toward unique embeddedness niches that are affiliated socially, industrially and locally. Being embedded within the industrial context in the past provides entrepreneurs with resources, networks, connections and, importantly, practical knowledge. By building new embeddedness, it was much easier, one of the respondents said, to turn to their own "library of experiences" to recognize what was required and accessible. The element that we associate with the enactment of experience is what Piaget (1962, pp. 191–193) called "surging in extension of his own activities." In our study, entrepreneurs continuously perform cognitive work by collecting various events until these events become useful in their particular industry niche in the new embedding building process. An entrepreneur, in our study, is not applying events from outside of the context but, as Weick (2001, p. 186) posits, "is punctually enacting the flow of experiences, the results of these activities being retained in a network of causal sequences or a causal map."

The other response has been to talk about the importance of the context and particular knowledge about the rules of the game in that context. For example, one of the respondents said, "It is crucial to understand the context and rules of the game of the partners you intend to trade with. Contexts that differ are bound to national rules of the game and have to be applied accordingly for rich success." When the entrepreneurs had extensive experience from other industries and prior start-up experience, they did not only rely on storytelling. The founder of BioGaia often talked about how he challenged existing practices and brought new materials to the market. In addition, he tried to convince potential customers that he would deliver what he promised. One example of that is when he explained how he had rented a helicopter to show the facilities of his business to interested customers. However, the customers were unaware that he showed them a different location. By doing so, he was accepted by the clients, and they placed an important order. At the same time, he has drawn on his extensive experiences from other industries, which leads us to the theme of the role of other industry experience. By drawing on previous successes and business experiences, Åke of BioGaia has gained acceptance, which has served as a vehicle to approach the market. Global Warning System's founder does not show clear signs of storytelling. Instead, he has drawn on his previous successful experiences and professional niches and brought them into new contexts when approaching the market.

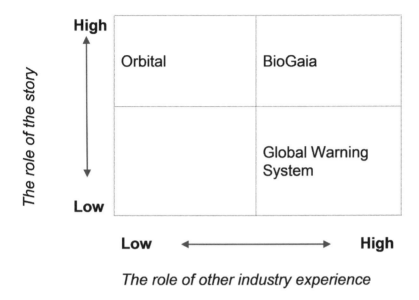

*Figure 9.1     The role of storytelling and other industry experience when handling being disembedded*

Figure 9.1 portrays how the different cases fall into a categorization of how they have approached the market and handled being disembedded. When they have extensive previous experiences from other contexts, they build on this to become accepted by the market. In this sense, they make use of the halo effect, which enables them to draw on the cognitive bias in which success in one domain is also expected in another domain. In other words, they draw on their success in previous ventures and industries in order to gain legitimacy in the new industry context.

BioGaia and Global Warning System have been able to break out from their existing knowledge corridors and have entered a new corridor, seeing novel solutions that others have not seen. This ability to transfer between contexts has enabled them to introduce and create novel solutions to the market. By default, transferring between contexts is something that a serial entrepreneur does frequently. However, the size of this shift varies. Nonetheless, it appears that they are entering a knowledge elevator rather than being stuck in their existing context. At the least, it makes their corridors more nuanced and broad.

Those who enter into new contexts develop or display certain characteristics that are important for entrepreneurial processes. The topics we observed among our empirical cases could be classified as courage, general market knowledge, creating one's own capability niche, ability to handle uncertainty and ability to build stories and new networks.

In this process of approaching the market, building a story and drawing on knowledge from other contexts, we see clear links to the concept of enactive action, which describes the process by which experience arises when situated embeddedness is needed. According to Fletcher (2011), entrepreneurial change can only occur when experiences and knowledge are enacted into actions. Enactment in this regard seems to be a mechanism by which disembedded entrepreneurs build stories and draw on prior industry experiences from other contexts to approach the market. Our research challenges this assumption by showing how disembeddedness can positively contribute to the opportunity creation process. We also argue that we contribute to theories on embeddedness.

## DISCUSSION, CONCLUSIONS AND FUTURE RESEARCH

Entrepreneurship research rests on the underlying assumptions that social networks and prior experience (such as industry experience) are pivotal for the creation of new firms and their success. Practitioners, investors and policy makers are often influenced by these beliefs. Our project, inspired by empirical radical innovations, aims to question some of these widely held beliefs. We do not question the important insights obtained in extant research. However, we believe that there is room to gain important insights and further extend the accumulated knowledge by adopting a novel perspective and focusing on some of the outliers rather than the mainstream cases. This argumentation is very much in line with the work on innovation on the periphery which claims that radical innovations are likely to come from outside the industry boundaries (Anthony, 2012). For example, Kudic et al. (2015) study how innovation can take place in the periphery rather than the core of an industry network. They argue that firms in the periphery of an industry network might need to adopt unorthodox methods and be more risk-taking and creative when addressing technical problems (Kudic et al., 2015). Kudic et al. (2015) also claim that firms tend to move from the periphery to the core over time, which is similar to what we see in the process of the disembedded entrepreneur becoming embedded in the new industry context.

Focusing on outliers enables us to develop conceptual insights into the creation of radical innovations, which corresponds to the call made in the EU's 2020 Growth Strategy. We also observe that there are tools that entrepreneurs use to handle being disembedded and lacking particular experience or prior knowledge. Future research could further disentangle how these tools have been applied and their interplay with opportunity creation. This could ideally be done by following a few cases in depth over a longer time period, for example, in an ethnographic study.

One of our cases targets end consumers, while two cases are business-to-business firms. It is plausible that the role of storytelling and prior experiences also varies based on the characteristics of the market. Therefore, we believe that future research would benefit from considering the characteristics of the new context, such as who the customer is. Furthermore, it would be valuable to explore what role the characteristics of the market play in the embedding process.

## NOTE

1. Almi is an organization offering advisory and financing services to Swedish start-ups. http://almistories.se/orbital-systems-mehrdad-mahdjoubi/.

## REFERENCES

Aldrich, H. and C. Zimmer (1986), 'Entrepreneurship through social networks', in Sexton, D.L. and Smilor, R.W. (eds), *The Art and Science of Entrepreneurship*, Cambridge, MA: Ballinger, 2–23.

Alvarez, S.A. and J.B. Barney (2007), 'Discovery and creation: Alternative theories of entrepreneurial action'. *Strategic Entrepreneurship Journal*, **1**(1–2), 11–26.

Alvarez, S.A. and J.B. Barney (2010), 'Entrepreneurship and epistemology: The philosophical underpinnings of the study of entrepreneurial opportunities', *Academy of Management Annals*, **4**, 557–583.

Alvesson, M. and K. Sköldberg (2009), *Reflexive Methodology: New Vistas For Qualitative Research* (2nd edn), London: Sage Publications.

Amezcua, A.S., M.G. Grimes, S.W. Bradley and J. Wiklund (2013), 'Organizational sponsorship and founding environments: A contingency view on the survival of business-incubated firms, 1994–2007', *Academy of Management Journal*, **56**(6), 1628–1654.

Anthony, S.D. (2012), 'Go innovate on the periphery'. *Harvard Business Review*, April 26.

Ardichvili, A., R. Cardozo and S. Ray (2003), 'A theory of entrepreneurial opportunity identification and development', *Journal of Business Venturing*, **18**, 105–123.

Autio, E., M. Kenney, P. Mustar, D. Siegel and M. Wright (2014), 'Entrepreneurial innovation: The importance of context', *Research Policy*, **43**, 1097–1108.

Baker, T. and R.E. Nelson (2005), 'Creating something from nothing: Resource construction through entrepreneurial bricolage', *Administrative Science Quarterly*, **50**, 329–366.

Baron, R.A. (2006), 'Opportunity recognition as the detection of meaningful patterns: Evidence from comparisons of novice and experienced entrepreneurs', *Management Science*, **52**, 1331–1344.

Baumol, W.J. and R.J. Strom (2007), 'Entrepreneurship and economic growth', *Strategic Entrepreneurship Journal*, **1**, 233–237.

Bechky, B.A. and G.A. Okhuysen (2011), 'Expecting the unexpected? How SWAT officers and film crews handle surprises', *Academy of Management Journal*, **54**, 239–261.

Burt, R.S. (1992), 'The social structure of competition', in N. Nohria and R. Eccles (eds), *Networks and Organizations: Structure, Form and Action*, Boston, MA: Harvard Business School Press, 57–91.

Cassar, G. (2014), 'Industry and start-up experience on entrepreneur forecast performance in new firms', *Journal of Business Venturing*, **29**, 137–151.

Chandler, G. and S. Hanks (1994), 'Market attractiveness, resource-based capabilities, venture strategies, and venture performance', *Journal of Business Venturing*, **9**, 331–347.

Corbett, A.C. (2005), 'Experiential learning within the process of opportunity identification and exploitation', *Entrepreneurship Theory and Practice*, **29**, 473–491.

Denzau, A. and D. North (1994), 'Shared mental models: Ideologies and institutions', *Kyklos*, **47**, 3–31.

Desa, G. (2011), 'Resource mobilization in international social entrepreneurship: Bricolage as a mechanism of institutional transformation', *Entrepreneurship Theory and Practice*, **36**, 727–751.

Delmar, F. and S. Shane (2006), 'Does experience matter? The effect of founding team experience on the survival and sales of newly founded ventures', *Strategic Organization*, **4**, 215–247.

Dencker, J.C. and M. Gruber (2015), 'The effects of opportunities and founder experience on new firm performance', *Strategic Management Journal*, **36**, 1035–1052.

Fletcher, D.E. (2006), 'Entrepreneurial processes and the social construction of opportunity', *Entrepreneurship & Regional Development*, **18**, 421–440.

Fletcher, D.E. (2011), 'A curiosity for contexts: Entrepreneurship, enactive research and autoethnography', *Entrepreneurship & Regional Development*, **23** (1–2), 65–76.

Gabrielsson, J. and D. Politis (2011), 'Career motives and entrepreneurial decision-making: Examining preferences for causal and effectual logics in the early stage of new ventures', *Small Business Economics*, **36**, 281–298.

Gimeno, F.J., T.B. Folta, A.C. Cooper and C.Y. Woo (1997), 'Survival of the fittest? Entrepreneurial human capital and the persistence of underperforming firms', *Administrative Science Quarterly*, **42**, 750–783.

Gonin, M. (2015), 'Adam Smith's contribution to business ethics, then and now', *Journal of Business Ethics*, **129**, 221–236.

Granovetter, M. (1973), 'The strength of weak ties', *American Journal of Sociology*, **78**, 1360–1380.

Granovetter, M. (1985), 'Economic action and social structure: The problem of embeddedness', *American Journal of Sociology*, **91**, 481–510.

Gras, D. and R. Nason (2015), 'Bric by bric: The role of the family household in sustaining a venture in impoverished Indian slums', *Journal of Business Venturing*, **30**, 546–563.

Hill, C. and F. Rothaermel (2003), 'The performance of incumbent firms in the face of radical technological innovation', *The Academy of Management Review*, **28**, 257–274.

Hoenig, D. and J. Henkel (2015), 'Quality signals? The role of patents, alliances, and team experience in venture capital financing', *Research Policy*, **44**, 1049–1064.

Hsu, D.H. (2007), 'Experienced entrepreneurial founders, organizational capital, and venture capital funding', *Research Policy*, **36**, 722–741.

Jack, S. and A. Anderson (2002), 'The effects of embeddedness on the entrepreneurial process', *Journal of Business Venturing*, **17**, 467–487.

Ko, S. and J.E. Butler (2006), 'Prior knowledge, bisociative mode of thinking and entrepreneurial opportunity identification', *International Journal of Entrepreneurship and Small Business*, **3**, 3–16.

Kotha, R. and G. George (2012), 'Friends, family, or fools: Entrepreneur experience and its implications for equity distribution and resource mobilization', *Journal of Business Venturing*, **27**, 525–543.

Kudic, M., W. Ehrenfeld and T. Pusch (2015), 'On the trail of core-periphery patterns in innovation networks: measurements and new empirical findings from the German laser industry', *The Annals of Regional Science*, **55**, 187–220.

Muellerleile, C. (2013), 'Turning financial markets inside out: Polanyi, performativity and disembeddedness', *Environment and Planning A*, **45**, 1625–1642.

Piaget, J. (1962), *La construction du reel chez l'enfant*, Neuchatatel: Delachaux and Niestle.

Ronstadt, R. (1988), 'The corridor principle', *Journal of Business Venturing*, **3**, 31–40.

Santarelli, E. and H. Tran (2013), 'The interplay of human and social capital in shaping entrepreneurial performance: The case of Vietnam', *Small Business Economics*, **40**, 435–458.

Sarasvathy, S. (2001), 'Causation and effectuation: Toward a theoretical shift from economic inevitability to entrepreneurial contingency', *The Academy of Management Review*, **26**, 243–263.

Schumpeter, J.A. (1934), *The Theory of Economic Development* (8th edn), Cambridge: Harvard University Press.

Selden, P. and D. Fletcher (2015), 'The entrepreneurial journey as an emergent hierarchical system of artifact-creating processes', *Journal of Business Venturing*, **30**, 603–615.

Shane, S. (2000), 'Prior knowledge and the discovery of entrepreneurial opportunities', *Organization Science*, **11**, 448–469.

Shane S. (2003), *A General Theory of Entrepreneurship. The Individual–Opportunity Nexus*, Cheltenham, UK and Northampton, MA, USA: Edward Elgar Publishing.

Shepherd, D.A. and D.R. DeTienne (2005), 'Prior knowledge, potential financial reward, and opportunity identification'. *Entrepreneurship Theory and Practice*, **29**, 91–112.

Spradley, J.P. (1979), *The Ethnographic Interview*, New York: Holt, Reinhart & Winston.

Stake, R.E. (1995), *The Art of Case Study Research*, London: Sage Publications.

Tobias, S. (1995), 'Interest and metacognitive word knowledge', *Journal of Educational Psychology*, **87**, 399–405.

Ucbasaran, D., P. Westhead and M. Wright (2009), 'The extent and nature of opportunity identification by experienced entrepreneurs', *Journal of Business Venturing*, **24**, 99–115.

Uzzi, B. (1996), 'The sources and consequences of embeddedness for the economic performance of organizations: The network effect', *American Sociological Review*, **61**, 674–698.

Venkataraman S. (2003), 'Foreword', in S. Shane (ed.), *A General Theory of Entrepreneurship. The Individual–Opportunity Nexus*, Cheltenham, UK and Northampton, MA, USA: Edward Elgar Publishing, xi–xii.

Weber, C. and B. Weber (2011), 'Exploring the antecedents of social liabilities in CVC Triads: A dynamic social network perspective', *Journal of Business Venturing*, **26**, 255–272.

Welter, F. (2011), 'Contextualizing entrepreneurship: Conceptual challenges and ways forward', *Entrepreneurship Theory and Practice*, **35**, 165–184.

Weick, K. (2001), *Making Sense of the Organization*, London: Blackwell Publishing.

Zukin, S. and P. DiMaggio (1990), *Structure of Capital: The Social Organization of the Economy*, Cambridge, MA: Cambridge University Press.

# 10. "Dear crowd, let me tell you a story." The influence of emotions, authenticity and sense of community on entrepreneur's ability to acquire funds via crowdfunding

Amélie Wuillaume, Amélie Jacquemin and Frank Janssen

## INTRODUCTION

Acquiring funds constitutes a crucial and challenging activity for an entrepreneur (Mollick, 2014). Demonstrating the potential of their new venture to potential resource providers is not an easy task (Lounsbury and Glynn, 2001). In this challenging activity, scholars consider narrative as an effective mechanism (Lounsbury and Glynn, 2001; Martens et al., 2007; Allison et al., 2013; Lurtz and Kreutzer, 2014; Jennings et al., 2015) because of its capability to shape investors' decision making (Martens et al., 2007; Herzenstein et al., 2011; Pollack et al., 2012; Allison et al., 2013; Fischer and Reuber, 2014).

The influence of narratives on traditional money providers as business angels (Pollack et al., 2012), institutional investors (Martens et al., 2007) or peer-to-peer lenders (Herzenstein et al., 2011; Allison et al., 2013) has been demonstrated. Yet alternative forms of financing are now emerging (Belleflame et al., 2014; Mollick, 2014; Agrawal et al., 2015; Kuppuswamy and Bayus, 2017). Amongst these mechanisms, crowdfunding provides entrepreneurs with a novel means of acquiring funds. If this alternative is not new, it has recently gained visibility and become increasingly popular (Mollick, 2014). This financing option directly appeals to the public ("the crowd") through an online platform (Belleflamme et al., 2014). Despite the enthusiasm crowdfunding generates, our comprehension of its mechanisms is still limited and the need to deepen research has been highlighted (Bruton et al., 2015).

Narratives constitute an avenue to enhance our understanding of crowdfunding, since their role is even more central in this context (Allison et al., 2015) gathering projects that are nascent and thus, lack records. The early research carried out about narratives in crowdfunding rather fuels a traditional and "economic" school of thought—narratives are considered to be effective for their capability to shape resource providers' perceptions of economic dimensions (Martens et al., 2007). These dimensions do not seem to be the primary ones in crowdfunding. Indeed, it has to be distinguished from traditional sources of entrepreneurial financing (McKenny et al., 2017) in the sense that funders are driven by emotions to some extent (Fisher et al., 2017).

While both narratives (Allison et al., 2015) and emotions (Jennings et al., 2015) play a key role in crowdfunding, there has been limited attempt to investigate whether the emotional aspect of narrative influences funders' decision making in crowdfunding, Therefore, focusing on the emotional appeal of narratives, we seek to analyze *how entrepreneurial narratives may influence funders in crowdfunding platforms*.

Following McKenny et al.'s (2017) advice to appeal to theory from other literatures to nourish entrepreneurial crowdfunding understanding, we study the social effects of emotions in light of psychology literature (van Kleef et al., 2009; Côté et al., 2013). Based on the EASI theory (van Kleef et al., 2009), we hypothesize that the emotional dimension of narratives positively influences the decision of crowdfunders (McKenny et al., 2017). We further suggest that the feeling of being part of a community is another key driver for funders (Jung et al., 2015). Then, we further predict that the relation between the emotional content of narratives and backers' support for a crowdfunding project is moderated by the narratives' authenticity (Roberts, 2005).

In addition to that, we further make a distinction between crowdfunders' profiles since Skirnevskij et al. (2017) advise scholars to compare the platforms and to take into account backers' views and drivers. Crowdfunders visit different crowdfunding platforms according to their main interests (pure donation, reward-based donation, lending or equity-based platform) (Schwienbacher and Larralde, 2010; Mollick, 2014). We argue that individuals visiting donation platforms (with or without reward) attach less importance to economic considerations (Ahlers et al., 2015; Davis et al., 2017), while the ones on lending-based and equity-based platforms are motivated more by economic dimensions (Kuppuswamy and Bayus, 2017). Since people searching for emotion-inducing situations are more influenced by emotions in their decision making while people looking for cognitive activities tend to be more affected by cognitive information (van Kleef et al., 2015), we suggest the hypothesized relation between the emotional tone of narratives and funders' support for a crowdfunding project to be stronger on platforms that meet "emotional" motivations (donation and reward) than on the ones that primarily meet economic motivations (equity and lending).

The setting for our empirical analysis is a unique dataset combining data from two crowdfunding platforms: (1) Ulule,[1] one of the most important platforms operating with pure donation and reward-based donation systems, from which we created and examined a dataset of narratives and publicly available information on 492 projects posted between 2010 and 2016 and (2) MyMicroInvest,[2] an equity and lending platform gathering crowdfunders and professional investors, from which we created and examined a dataset of narratives and publicly available information on 56 projects posted between 2013 and 2016.

We test our claims in two steps. In the first step, we examine the relationship between multiple narratives' dimensions and funders' support based on Ulule database. In the second step, employing data from MyMicroInvest, we assess the extent to which our first results vary according to the type of platform mechanisms. Our findings indicate that the emotional content of narratives positively influences funders' participation in a crowdfunding project using donation and reward-based models, but only in the presence of a social dimension in the narratives. Results also show that the emotional dimension is less salient in narratives presented on the platform using lending and equity mechanisms, compared to the ones appearing on donation and reward-based platforms. Furthermore, because MyMicroInvest gathers two types of funders, nonprofessional and professional ones, we are able to observe that nonprofessionals appear to prefer emotionally charged narratives, while professionals favor cognitive messages. The social dimension is as influential in donation and reward-based models as in lending and equity-based.

Our study contributes to the literature in entrepreneurship in multiple ways. First, this chapter provides further evidence of the "hot" role of emotions in entrepreneurship (Cardon et al., 2012; Shepherd, 2015). Then, it highlights the "emotional" way to influence resource acquisition, while previous studies focused almost exclusively on their ability to shape resource providers' perceptions of economic dimension (Martens et al., 2007). Finally, taking into account the multiple drivers in crowdfunding and comparing platforms, we answer the call of Skirnevskij et al. (2017) to compare funders' views and motivations for a better understanding of crowdfunding.

The chapter unfolds as follows. We begin by reviewing the relevant literature on narratives and crowdfunding. Then, we develop a research model and the corresponding research hypotheses. Next, we present the empirical study. Finally, we conclude by discussing the findings and drawing some implications for theory and practice.

## THEORETICAL BACKGROUND

In this section, we discuss the theoretical background for the hypotheses guiding our research. First of all, we look at the literature on narratives. Then, we address crowdfunding. Finally, we examine the various motivations of funders.

Narratives are recognized to be a strategic and effective tool used by entrepreneurs to influence financial resource providers. However, while different authors agree that narratives constitute a critical dimension of entrepreneurial success in resource acquisition, it has not been considered for its emotional dimension nor in the crowdfunding context. Allison et al. (2015) point out the central role of the entrepreneurial narrative, being one of the few available pieces of information for crowdfunding solicitation in particular (Moss et al., 2015).

**Narratives**

Narratives represent "accounts of events" and constitute a set of stories (Dalpiaz et al., 2014). There are "constitutive of human understanding and [as] integral to meaning-making, identity building and purposeful acting" (O'Connor, 2002) and allow to link "individual human actions and events with interrelated aspects to gain an understanding of outcomes" (Smith and Anderson, 2004). Three basic elements compose narratives; a subject, an object (goal) and an addressee organized through a temporal sequence, creating a sense of plot (Lounsbury and Glynn, 2001; Martens et al., 2007). Entrepreneurial narratives specifically depict the entrepreneur, his/her venture or both (Martens et al., 2007) and are employed to create and convey meaning (Smith and Anderson, 2004).

As the "fundamental, preferred and ... effective means" for authors (Martens et al., 2007, p. 1110) to communicate, make and give sense (Boje, 1991), narratives allow entrepreneurs to accomplish some crucial activities (Wolfe and Shepherd, 2015), as shaping funders' interpretations of the new venture (Lounsbury and Glynn, 2001). In this sense, narratives are "an essential component of an entrepreneur's toolkit" (Martens et al., 2007, p. 1107).

Empirical research provides strong evidence of the role of narratives as an effective mechanism for seeking resources (Lounsbury and Glynn, 2001; Dalpiaz et al., 2014; Martens et al., 2007; Allison et al., 2013; Lurtz and Kreutzer, 2014; Jennings et al., 2015) because it shapes investors' perceptions (Rawhouser et al., 2016) and decision making (Martens et al., 2007; Herzenstein et al., 2011; Pollack et al., 2012; Allison et al., 2013; Fischer and Reuber, 2014). These efforts have largely highlighted the ability of narratives to shape traditional money providers' perceptions regarding important economic dimensions specifically: uncertainty, return (Martens et al., 2007; Herzenstein et al., 2011; Allison et al., 2013), information asymmetry and risk (Pollack et al., 2012) in the context of IPO or venture capital lending (Martens et al., 2007; Allison et al., 2013).

## Crowdfunding

Crowdfunding constitutes one of the emerging financing alternatives that has gained prominence and visibility over these last few years (Bruton et al., 2015) because of the development of the Internet and online transactions (Mollick, 2014). This alternative is a way for entrepreneurs of for-profit, artistic, cultural and social ventures to raise funds from a large audience (crowdfunders) through an online platform, without standard financial intermediaries (Belleflamme et al., 2014; Mollick, 2014). This platform constitutes a virtual meeting place for entrepreneurs seeking resources and resource providers (Belleflamme et al., 2014). Crowdfunding enables entrepreneurs to gather small contributions from a large number of individuals instead of soliciting a smaller group of sophisticated investors offering larger amounts (Belleflamme et al., 2014; Mollick, 2014). These individuals from the "crowd" are said to be small and "unsophisticated" (Ahlers et al., 2015): they invest relatively small amounts of money and lack financial sophistication (knowledge and experience) to assess investment alternatives (Ahlers et al., 2015; Davis et al., 2017) as professional investors, who make informed decisions based on a mindset and valuated tools from years of professional experience (Victoravich, 2010).

Crowdfunding platforms may take four main forms: donation-, reward-, lending- and equity-based platforms (Cholakova and Clarysse, 2015). Donation-based platforms allow philanthropist donation without rewards. The reward-based model provides non-financial (tangible or intangible) rewards in return. Lending-based platforms offer a lending contract and, the equity-based model gives a shareholding contract (Cholakova and Clarysse, 2015). In addition to encompassing diverse goals for entrepreneurs (acquiring money, testing the project...) (Mollick, 2014), crowdfunding platforms also allow money providers themselves to achieve different objectives. On donation- and reward-based platforms, funders can support a cause (Mollick, 2014), help someone or take part in a project (Allison et al., 2013; Cholakova and Clarysse, 2015; Mollick, 2014). On lending- or equity-based platforms, crowdfunders rather look for potential returns (Galak et al., 2011; Cholakova and Clarysse, 2015) or equity shares primarily (Ahlers et al., 2015).

Early studies on the funders' activating motivations to participate in crowd-funding activities (Schwienbacher and Larralde, 2010; Galak et al., 2011; Mollick, 2014; Cholakova and Clarysse, 2015; Ahlers et al., 2015) tend to consider the crowdfunders' community as a homogenous group and have so far produced conflicting findings. Some show that crowdfunding projects are particularly successful in raising resources from individuals not primarily motivated by financial rewards (Collins and Pierrakis, 2012). Others rather demonstrate that financial/utility considerations drive crowdfunders' support in a project (Cholakova and Clarysse, 2015).

We call on narrative as a strategic device to address previous inconsistent results. We know that narratives are an effective tool, able to shape the way people understand things (Smith and Anderson, 2004), particularity used by entrepreneurs (Martens et al., 2007). It should especially be true in crowdfunding. Because market information on a microenterprise is very limited, microlenders significantly rely on entrepreneurial narratives as a key piece of information (Moss et al., 2015). Moreover, the interests by which people are animated affect their perception of the message (Huskinson and Haddock, 2004). Diverse interests are observed within the crowdfunders' community which may influence the way people perceive, comprehend and react to narratives.

## HYPOTHESES DEVELOPMENT

### Emotional Tone

Prior research on funding decision has focused on how a message shapes individuals' perceptions of economic indicators and therefore influences resource allocation decisions (Chen et al., 2009). However, the emotional appeal of narratives has started to be pointed out as an alternative route (Davis et al., 2017).

Psychology literature informs us about the social influence of emotions (van Kleef et al., 2009; Côté et al., 2013). Emotions are not only internal states, they are also expressed and thus, observed by others. They subsequently influence others' emotions, cognition and behaviors (van Kleef et al., 2009; Côté et al., 2013, Mikolajczak et al., 2014). Specifically, the *emotions as social information theory* (EASI) indicates that the emotional framing of narratives[3] may influence observers' attitude and subsequent behavior because observers use others' emotional expressions as pieces of information, depending on their willingness to process this emotional information (van Kleef et al., 2009, 2011, 2015).

Specifically, the attitude of someone toward an object is built on a combination of both affective and cognitive elements. The weight given to each of these considerations varies from person to person (van Kleef et al., 2015). While people are more motivated to approach/avoid emotion-inducing situations, they are likely to form their attitude based on affect to a great extent. When individuals rather want to engage in effortful cognitive activities, they look for information primarily. Whether someone's attitude is primarily based on affect or cognition determines which type of message is the most influential on him/her (See et al., 2008). Affective messages are more influential among individuals who engage in emotion-inducing situation (Huskinson and Haddock, 2004). Conversely, cognitive information is more influential among individuals who are engaged in rather cognition-based activities (Huskinson and Haddock, 2004).

Because they rather search an emotional connection with the entrepreneur or the project and do not receive financial reward (Fisher et al., 2017; McKenny et al., 2017), funders on reward-based and donation platforms can be characterized by the pursuit of an emotional dimension. Because individuals who engage in an emotion-inducing situation are more influenced by affective messages (Huskinson and Haddock, 2004), we expect the emotional appeal to be particularly influential among them. Thus, we formulate the following hypothesis:

*H1: Funders will support more a project on a pure donation or reward-based platform if its narrative is strongly emotionally toned (compared to more neutral narrative).*

Because they are rather motivated by potential returns (Galak et al., 2011; Cholakova and Clarysse, 2015) or equity shares (Ahlers et al., 2015) primarily, we expect funders on lending- and equity-based platforms to act under an economic logic and to make their decision in a more cognitive manner (Huskinson and Haddock, 2004; van Kleef et al., 2015; Davis et al., 2017). We thus expect them to be less influenced by an emotional message but more by an informational and neutral message. Thus, we propose the following hypotheses:

*H2.a: Funders will support a project on a lending or equity platform less if its narrative is strongly emotionally toned (compared to a more neutral narrative).*

*H2.b: Funders will support more a project on a lending or equity platform if its narrative is strongly cognitively toned (compared to a more emotional narrative).*

## Community and Authenticity

### Community
Emotions expressed act as social information (van Kleef et al., 2009, 2011, 2015), but also play a key role in social cohesion: expressing emotions strengthens social links between people (Mikolajczak et al., 2014; Rimé, 2009). The feeling of belonging to a community and interacting with similar others (Cholakova and Clarysse, 2015) seems to be determinant for a campaign success (Gerber and Hui, 2013). It even supersedes the economic dimensions (Jung et al., 2015). This is under such a "community logic" that financial resources are provided to entrepreneurs (Fisher et al., 2017).

Hence, we hypothesize that social dimension mediates the relationship between emotions expressed through narratives and crowdfunders' support. In other words, the expression of emotions strengthens social relationship that, in turn, influences money providers' support. Thus, we propose the following hypothesis:

*H3: The sense of community membership mediates the positive relationship between emotional content narratives and funders' support for a crowdfunding project: the emotional tone of narratives strengthens the sense of community that, in turn, positively influences the number of funders on a pure donation or reward-based platform.*

### Authenticity
We have argued that the expression of emotions through narratives may strategically be used by entrepreneurs to gain support from the crowd. Based upon the work of Roberts (2005) and van Kleef et al. (2015) showing the potentially detrimental effects of feigned emotional expressions, this strategic use of emotions should be handled with care.

The manipulative acting of emotions may lead observers to doubt their authenticity and subsequently, create mistrust (Côté et al., 2013). In the professional sphere, if someone is perceived as inauthentic, he/she is likely "to experience negative consequences on well-being, relationships, and performance" (Roberts, 2005, p. 700).

If it is true in the professional sphere, we may anticipate that the use of some exaggeratedly feigned emotions may also be counterproductive in crowdfunding—interpersonal relationships also being of particular importance in this context. Moreover, because the authenticity of displayed emotions moderates the impact of traditional impression management (Roberts, 2005; Côté et al., 2013), we expect the emotions' authenticity to moderate the relation between emotional content and backers' support in crowdfunding. Thus we state the following hypothesis:

*H4: The authenticity of the narrative mediates the positive relationship between emotional content narratives and funders' support for a crowdfunding project: the authenticity strengthens the influence of the emotional tone of narratives on the number of funders on a pure donation or reward-based platform.*

## DATA AND METHOD

### Sample and Data Sources

The setting for our empirical analysis is composed of two crowdfunding platforms; a donation- and reward-based platform, Ulule, and a lending- and equity-based platform, MyMicroInvest[4].

### Ulule

Ulule is one of the three largest crowdfunding platforms in the world with Kickstarter and Indiegogo. Since its launch in October 2010, 28,155 projects have been financed by users from 194 countries. This platform has a "success" rate of 73 percent and is available in seven languages. According to the website, Ulule values diversity with projects from 15 broad categories: Film & Video, Music, Charities & Citizen, Publishing & Journal, Stage, Games, Art & Photo, Sports, Crafts & Food, Technology, Fashion & Design, Comics, Childhood & Education, Heritage and Other projects.

To participate, the entrepreneur must create a profile and join the community. Before being authorized to start the campaign, the campaign is discussed (and adapted) with a platform staff member. The campaign is then made accessible to the community of money providers.[5] The web page developed by the creator explains (1) who he/she is, (2) what the project is and (3) the reason(s) for the fundraising. In addition to this narrative, the funding goal (amount or number of presales), the duration of the campaign (days) and the proposed rewards appear on the right side of the page.

Ulule follows an "all-or-nothing" model (which is opposed to the "keep-it-all" model); the project must be fully funded before the deadline; otherwise no money is transferred. If the project has reached its anticipated goal, it can still continue to receive contributions until the end date.

Backers on Ulule receive no financial returns, but tangible (i.e. a postcard) or intangible (i.e. an autograph) rewards for their support or pre-buy products/

services. Pure donations are also allowed: crowdfunders (i.e. family members of the entrepreneur) give money, but decide not to receive the proposed reward.

To constitute our database, we have extracted the narratives describing the entrepreneur, the project and the reason for the funding for all closed projects written in English from April 2011 to November 2016. In addition, we also collected all the relevant information publicly shown on the platform, that is, the category of the project, the goal in terms of amount or presale, the amount or presale acquired, the number of news posted during the campaign, the number of contributors and the fact that the creator has already launched a fundraising on the platform before or not. After cleaning all the narratives for inaccuracies, misspelling or typing errors and inserted pictures, we obtained information on 492 projects.

Out of these 492 projects, 446 were successfully funded (percentage of success equal or above 100 percent) and 46 did reach their targeted goal (percentage of success below 100 percent). This is higher than the percentage of success announced on Ulule (68 percent). However, some unsuccessful projects chose to be deleted from the platform right after the campaign ended (hence, they are not present in our dataset).

**MyMicroInvest**
MyMicroInvest, launched in 2012, targets "promising European startups and growing businesses". The money providers' community is composed of non-professional crowdfunders and professional investors (angel investors, venture capitalists, and industry professionals).

Entrepreneurs apply to feature on the platform and a professional team of financial analysts vets their financial details to select the companies with enough potential. Selected businesses are then presented to a community of more than 35,000 crowd investors and professional investors. In addition to the information provided by the entrepreneur, the platform also provides company data, risk analysis, and legal information.

As Ulule, MyMicroInvest follows an "all-or-nothing" model. Funders[6] are offered a lending contract or a shareholding contract (the project owner chooses the mechanism).

To constitute our database, we extracted the narratives describing the project, the team, the market, the financials and the reason of the funding for all closed projects written in English from 2013 to 2016. In addition, we also collected all the relevant information publicly shown on the platform, that is, the category of the project, the goal for the crowd, the amount acquired by the crowd, the number of crowdfunders and the amount committed by professional contributors. After cleaning all the narratives for inaccuracies, misspelling or typing error and inserted pictures, we obtain information on 57 projects. Out of these 57 projects, 44 were successfully funded and 13 did reach their targeted goal.

## EMPIRICAL STUDY

In this section, exploiting the above-mentioned databases, we empirically test our hypotheses. We first test our hypotheses on the Ulule database and then complement our results with the MyMicroInvest database.

## VARIABLES DEFINITION

### Dependent Variable

*The number of funders.* Following Ahlers et al. (2015), Bi et al. (2017) and Josefy et al. (2017), this variable counts the number of individuals participating in the project. This variable is indicative of the appeal of the venture (Drover et al., 2017). A high volume of funders should indicate an appreciation of the project which can be translated into market demand (Drover et al., 2017).

### Independent Variables

To test our hypotheses, we use a measure for the emotional tone (both positive and negative), the cognitive tone, the community dimension and for the authenticity.

Consistent with previous studies (Wolfe and Shepherd, 2015), we use the Linguistic Inquiry and Word Count (LIWC) dictionary to determine the *emotional content* of narratives (Tausczik and Pennebaker, 2010). This dictionary (of almost 6,400 words, word stems and select emoticons) was developed based on the fact that the words people use provide rich insights concerning their beliefs, fears, thinking patterns, social relationship and personality.

*Emotional tone.* We use the emotional tone variable to capture the emotional dimension of narratives (Pennebaker et al., 2015). This is a summary variable recently integrated in the LIWC 2015 version and constructed from LIWC basic variables. Emotional tone puts the negative and positive emotions dimension into a single variable (Cohn et al., 2009), by subtracting negative emotions from positive emotions. The obtained number is then rescaled along a scale going from 0 to 100. The algorithm is built so that the higher the number, the more positive the tone. Numbers below 50 account for a more negative emotional tone.[7]

*Positive* and *negative emotions* are also part of the dictionary. The LIWC list for positive emotions contains 620 words (such as *sweet*, or *love*). The list of negative emotion words contains 744 words (such as *ugly* or *hurt*). The number obtained are percentages of total words within a text.

*Cognitive tone.* To capture the cognitive tone of a narrative, we call on the *cognitive processes* variable from LIWC dictionary (Pennebaker et al., 2015). The list of cognitive words contains 797 words (such as *cause, know* or *ought*). This dimension captures the degree to which people use words suggesting formal, logical, and hierarchical thinking patterns. People low on analytical thinking tend to use language focusing on the here-and-now, and personal experiences.

*Community dimension.* To capture the social dimension of a narrative, we call on the *affiliation* variable from LIWC dictionary, which denotes language used by people looking for relationships with others (Pennebaker et al., 2015). Affiliation includes 248 words as *help, friend, family* or *we*. The calculated numbers for affiliation are percentages of total words within a text.

*Authenticity dimension.* To capture the authenticity dimension, we call on the summary variable *authenticity*. As for the other summary variables, it has been constructed on an algorithm made from various LIWC variables. The numbers are standardized scores converted to percentiles ranging from 0 to 100. The higher the score, the higher the degree of authenticity. When people reveal themselves in an authentic or honest way, they are more personal, humble, and vulnerable.

**Control Variables**

We also include other variables in the analysis in order to control for possible alternative explanations for the relationships. We incorporate the number of words, the experience in crowdfunding campaign and the support provided by a well-known organization.

*Narratives length* (word count). Consistent with previous research on pitches in crowdfunding (Davis et al., 2017), we include narrative length in our estimation models to account for differences across funding narratives. Writing longer narratives allows for further details and information.

*Crowdfunding experience.* If entrepreneurs have already developed a campaign on the platform, they can benefit from this past experience, as a source of identity (Fisher et al., 2017). Experienced entrepreneurs are already known by the backers and might know what kind of narrative content is the most influential. We control for entrepreneur's experience in crowdfunding campaign by including a binary variable (0: no campaign previously launched on the same platform; 1: at least one campaign previously launched on the same platform).

*Support from a well-known organization.* Some of the projects are visibly supported by a famous organization (well-known TV channel or bank group). Since ties with associations serve to establish legitimacy (Fisher et al., 2017), it can positively influence funding success. We control for the support provided by a well-known organization by including a binary variable (0: not supported by a well-known organization, 1: supported by a well-known organization).

*Category.* Consistent with previous research (Allison et al., 2015), we control for the project's category, since it can affect funders' intention to fund. We operationalized category by developing a dummy variables corresponding to the sectors in which our sample projects were classified.

*Goal.* Following previous research (Davis et al., 2017) and to account for the potential influence of the amount to raise, we control for the funding goal (dollars).

## MAIN RESULTS

To test our hypotheses, we use Hayes' (2013) mediation and moderation regression models for the development of our models through computational modeling tools on SPSS (Hayes, 2013; Spiller, 2013). Hayes' (2013) models allow for indirect effect and interaction between variables. These methods are particularly popular in psychology and examples of research on emotions using these are numerous (Preacher et al., 2007).

We ran a regression of the number of funders on three independent variables: (i) emotional tone; (ii) the social dimension; and (iii) the authenticity (interaction term) of the narrative. We ran a mediation model with a moderation (model 1) and three simple mediations (model 2, 3 and 4). Tables 10.1a and 10.1b present the coefficients and significance for variables included in our models. Since cognitive tone did not significantly explain funding success in any of the models, we excluded it.

### Direct Effects

Hypothesis 1 (model 1 and 2) predicted that backers' support for a project on a pure donation or reward-based platform would be higher if the narrative was strongly emotionally toned (compared to more neutral narrative). Run on the macro PROCESS of Preacher and Hayes (2008) with 5,000 bootstraps, the analysis indicates, quite surprisingly, that the coefficient for emotional tone is statistically significant but negative in the mediation with moderation model (1a) and in the simple mediation model (1b). The direct effect of the emotional tone on the number of funders is thus negative.

Thus, in order to test if the influence of the emotional tone was driven by positive emotions, negative ones or both, we conducted further analyses. We used the macro PROCESS of Preacher and Hayes (2008) with 5,000 bootstraps again. We ran two additional simple mediations (model 3 and 4) replacing "emotional tone" by "positive emotional tone" (model 3) and by "negative

*Table 10.1a     Hayes regression model for funders' number*

| | Coefficient (β) | Sig. (p) |
|---|---|---|
| Model 1 | | $R^2 = 0.0784$ |
| Outcome: *affiliation* | | |
| Constant | 2.5809 | 0.0000*** |
| Emotional tone | 0.9425 | 0.0000*** |
| Organization support | | |
| Narrative length | | 0.2768 |
| | | 0.0652 |
| Goal | | 0.2572 |
| Category | | 0.5539 |
| | | |
| Outcome: nb of funders | | $R^2 = 0.5652$ |
| Constant | | 0.3132 |
| Affiliation (M) | 11.2311 | 0.0105* |
| Emotional tone (X) | -66.4420 | 0.0035** |
| Authenticity (W) | | 0.0761 |
| Int. 1 (X*W) | | 0.5041 |
| Ind. Eff. (X*M) | 10.5853 | 0.0000*** |
| Organization support | 522.1033 | 0.0000*** |
| Narrative length | 0.1061 | 0.0000*** |
| Goal | 0.0165 | 0.0000*** |
| Category | | 0.8252 |

*Notes:* *** significant at the 0.001 level; ** significant at the 0.01 level; * significant at the 0.05 level; Model 1: *Mediation with moderation, X=emotional tone.*

emotional tone" (model 4) successively. The direct influence of emotions on the number of funders is significant for positive emotions, but not for negative emotions.

Figure 10.1 illustrates the three types of emotional dimension we have identified and provides example for each of them.

As presented in Tables 10.1a and 10.1b, a second direct effect is the one of the emotional tone on the social dimension. Hypothesis 3 suggested that the emotional tone affected the sense of affiliation to the community. This hypothesis is supported (model 2). This direct effect of emotions on the social dimension is significant and positive for positive emotions (model 3) and also significant but negative for negative emotions (model 4).

*Table 10.1b    Hayes regression models for funders' number*

| | Coefficient (β) | Sig. (p) | Coefficient (β) | Sig. (p) | Coefficient (β) | Sig. (p) |
|---|---|---|---|---|---|---|
| Model | 2 | $R^2 = 0.0784$ | 3 | $R^2 = 0.1067$ | 4 | $R^2 = 0.0328$ |
| Outcome: *affiliation* | | | | | | |
| Constant | | 0.0000*** | 2.5435 | 0.0000*** | 3.2180 | 0.0000*** |
| Emotional tone | | 0.0000*** | 1.1563 | 0.0000*** | -0.4023 | 0.0340[4] |
| Organization support | 2.5809 | 0.2768 | | 0.1895 | | |
| Narrative length | | 0.0652 | 0.0003 | 0.0396* | 0.0003 | 0.2427 |
| Goal | 0.9425 | 0.2572 | | 0.3928 | | 0.0372* |
| Category | | 0.5539 | | 0.2882 | | 0.2516 |
| | | | | | | 0.6537 |
| | | | | | | |
| Outcome: nb of funders | | $R^2 = 0.5615$ | | $R^2 = 0.5568$ | | $R^2 = 0.5526$ |
| Constant | | 0.9563 | | 0.7372 | | 0.4232 |
| Affiliation (M) | 12.3732 | 0.0044** | 11.9337 | 0.0072** | 9.2977 | 0.0299* |
| Emotional tone (X) | -53.9887 | 0.0015** | -38.7992 | 0.0291* | | 0.6562 |
| Indirect effect (X*M) | 11.6618 | 0.0000*** | 13.7992 | 0.0000*** | -3.7409 | 0.0000*** |
| Organization sup. | 522.7610 | 0.0000*** | 517.0097 | 0.0000*** | 521.4496 | 0.0000*** |
| Narrative length | | 01908 | | 0.2278 | | 0.2178 |
| Goal | 0.0166 | 0.0000*** | 0.0167 | 0.0000*** | 0.0166 | 0.0000*** |
| Category | | 0.7301 | | 0.6328 | | 0.7174 |

*Notes:* *** significant at the 0.001 level; ** significant at the 0.01 level; * significant at the 0.05 level; Model 2: *Simple mediation, X=emotional tone*; Model 3: *Simple mediation, X=positive emotional tone*; Model 4: *Simple mediation, X=negative emotional tone.*

| Content dimension | Examples |
|---|---|
| Positive emotional tone | *"After the award-winning two short films Alia and Deema YASMINE is the concluding and breathtaking finale in this Trilogy that merges expressionistic art with narrative film."* |
| | - Yasmine Narrative |
| Negative emotional tone | *"Natan, a solitary young man, lives as a recluse in the big family home with his overbearing mother and his authoritarian father who both spy on him."* |
| | - Captif Narrative |
| Neutral tone | *"It will have taken at least 18 months of in-depth studies and of collecting scientific and analytical data, along with other assessments, to determine the suitability and necessity, or otherwise, of an eventual intervention, and its feasibility."* |
| | - Restoring "L'atelier du Peintre" Narrative |

*Figure 10.1    Content dimension and examples for positive, negative emotional tone and neutral tone*

## Indirect Effects

Hypothesis 3 also predicted a mediation relationship between the emotional tone and the number of funders through the sense of affiliation communicated in the narrative. We tested this hypothesis via the macro PROCESS from Preacher and Hayes (2008) with 5,000 bootstraps. It is supported in the sense of Zhao et al. (2010) since the indirect effect of the emotional tone on money providers through the social dimension is positive and significant for model 1, model 2, model 3 and significant but negative for model 4. Schematic

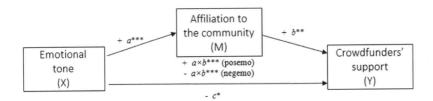

Note:    The variable is significant at the level of 5% (*), 1% (**) and 0,1% (***)
        $a$, $b$ and $c$ are non standardized coefficients of a linear regression
        $a \times b$ estimated with *bootstrap test* (Hayes 2013, PROCESS)

*Figure 10.2    Mediation of the emotional tone on the number of funders through the sense of affiliation to the community*

representation is provided in Figure 10.2. This schema presents the level of significance (*) and the direction (+/-) for each relationship.

In addition, hypothesis 4 suggested a moderation relationship between the emotional tone and the number of crowdfunders via the authenticity of the emotional tone. This interaction effect has been tested through model 1 of mediation with moderation and is significant under certain conditions. In order to further explore interactions between variables, we tested the conditional interaction effect between the emotional tone and the number of funders for different levels of authenticity (Hayes, 2013). This hypothesis is supported for level of authenticity below the average only.

Collectively, results indicate that the emotional tone has a direct and positive effect on the social dimension of the narrative. Then, the emotional tone has also a direct but negative effect on the number of crowfunders when social dimension does not mediate this relationship. In other words, alone, the expression of emotions on the crowdfunders' support is negative. However, when the emotional tone is mediated by the social dimension, the effect of the emotional dimension on crowdfunders' support becomes positive (model 2). Specifically, this mediated effect is positive for positive emotions (model 3) but negative for negative emotions (model 4). In addition, affiliation has a direct effect on crowdfunders' support (model 1). Finally, authenticity moderates the relationship between emotional tone and crowdfunders' support for low level only (model 1). Considering control variables, even when included in our models, the impact of the variables of interest stays significant.

Since these first tests provided results for projects on donation- and reward-based platforms (Ulule), we then looked at the influence of the emotional tone, the cognitive tone, the community dimension and the authenticity on the funding success on the MyMicroInvest database and conducted comparisons.

We observed that the means for emotional tone, community dimension and authenticity are significantly higher for narratives on Ulule than for the ones on MyMicroInvest. Conversely, the mean for cognitive tone is higher for narratives on MyMicroInvest than for the ones on Ulule.

Moreover, because MyMicroInvest is visited by two different types of funders, crowdfunders and professional investors, we further investigated the influence of each variable for both groups. It clearly appears that the level of cognitive tone is higher for the projects that have successfully acquired funds from professional investors compared to the ones that have not. In addition, results show that funds committed by professionals are higher when the emotional tone is lower than average. Then, results indicate that the mean of emotional tone is higher in the group of projects that failed to acquire money from professionals. Finally, the funds committed by professionals are higher when the community level is below average.

## DISCUSSION

In this chapter, we explore the extent to which the tone of narratives influences funders' decision to pledge on, or to invest in, a crowdfunding project. The research question emerges from both the paucity of research regarding the influence of emotional narratives and the emerging context that crowdfunding provides.

The popular assumption is that money providers are driven by economic motives (Martens et al., 2007). However, based on some preliminary works conducted in crowdfunding (Schwienbacher and Larralde, 2010; Davis et al., 2017; Fisher et al. (2017), we suggested that in donation- and reward-based crowdfunding, motivations to pledge a project primarily come from the emotions the campaign generates for the backers. Then, we suggested that the emotional tone should serve to strengthen the social dimension of the narrative that, in turn, should influence crowdfunders' support. Finally, we argued that in equity- and lending-based crowdfunding platforms, funders' motivations to fund a project should primarily come from cognitive dimensions.

We investigated our research questions by first examining a database of projects from a donation and reward-based crowdfunding platform. We found that emotional narratives indeed attract more funders compared to more neutral ones. Our findings further support the hypothesis that the social dimension mediates the relationship between emotional tone and crowdfunders' participation. We also expected the emotional tone to have a direct positive influence on crowdfunders' support. Surprisingly, the direct effect of the emotional tone on crowdfunders' support is negative. However, as hypothesized, the expression of emotions strengthens the social dimension (Rimé, 2009), and it is through this mediating relationship only that emotions positively influence crowdfunders' support. Therefore, we suggest that, first and foremost, narratives should create a social dimension to make funders feel engaged. The funders then can be touched and influenced by the emotional narrative. Without the development of a social connection, expression of emotions can be counterproductive.

Then, we further observe that only positive emotions positively influence funders through the mediation of the social dimension, not negative ones. A negative emotional content rather leads to the decrease of crowdfunders' support. This is surprising since some research indicates that the negative emotion of sadness may lead people to receive a supportive treatment (van Kleef et al., 2010; Gerber and Hui, 2013) (i.e. compassion venturing [Shepherd and Williams, 2014]). A more fine-grained approach of negative emotions is needed to better understand their effect on funders.

Furthermore, we suggested that authenticity would strengthen the positive influence of the emotional tone on crowdfunders' support. The effect is rather negative and only for low level of authenticity. One possible explanation is that authenticity is strongly correlated with negative emotions (anxiety, depression, self-doubt, lower status, etc.[8]). Therefore, being authentic can also mean expressing negative emotions. Since only positive emotions predict funding success, being authentic might damage the positive influence of the positive emotional tone. Future research should carefully examine the impact of authenticity and the inherent negative emotions (anxiety, depression, self-doubt, lower status, etc.) that might, counter-intuitively, damage crowd-funding performance.

Finally, we looked at the lending and equity-based database and compared results with the ones obtained from the donation and reward platform data-base. Our findings suggest that cognitive tone is a better predictor of success on lending and equity based-platforms. Then, since MyMicroInvest brings together two types of funders (nonprofessional and professional ones), we further examined and compared the influence of the emotional dimension for both types of funders. The narratives of the projects that received support from non-professional crowdfunders are more emotionally charged than the ones of the projects that did not succeed with non-professionals. Conversely, the emotional tone observed in the narratives of the projects successfully funded by professional funders is lower. This suggests that, on the same platform, if the audience is heterogeneous, the effectiveness of the same narrative differs according to the targeted audience's profile. This is consistent with the financial literature suggesting that the less/more individual investors are sophisticated, the more/less they rely on affect to evaluate an investment opportunity (Tetlock, 2007; Tetlock et al., 2008).

## IMPLICATIONS FOR RESEARCH

### Theoretical Contributions

We address and extend the literature on entrepreneurship and crowdfunding more specifically by showing that the influence of narratives has to be understood in light of the platform's context. Our findings make a set of contributions to the crowdfunding literature since our study provides support for the varying effect of emotions according to the type of platform underlying funders' motivations.

First of all, early research indicates that our understanding of crowdfunding should be enhanced by using theory from other literatures (McKenny et al., 2017). As we looked at the influence of emotions as key information for funders through the lens of the EASI theory borrowed from psychology (van

Kleef et al., 2009, 2010), we strengthen the idea that an understanding of the drivers of crowdfunding success requires a deeper emphasis on the influence of emotions. Our study provides evidence that emotions influence funders' participation in a campaign. This confirms that emotions have the power to be influential in entrepreneurial context in general (Shepherd, 2015) and in crowdfunding more specifically (Allison et al., 2013). If our results show that emotions expressed can be "hot" in crowdfunding as well (Shepherd, 2015), specifically for donation- and reward-based platforms, these also nuance emotions' effect since they are only beneficial when expressed in addition to a social dimension (engaging funders).

Another avenue for understanding crowdfunding provided by McKenny et al. (2017) was to look at the role of narratives. While previous works in entrepreneurial financing have mainly focused on the ability of narratives to shape the economic potential of the project in the eyes of the funders, we specifically highlight the strategic role of narratives via the emotional route (Baron, 2008). Looking at the influence of entrepreneurs' narratives in crowdfunding, our results provide some answers to the call of Allison et al. (2013) to understand how the language used in entrepreneurial narratives influences the founding of new venture (Allison et al., 2013).

Finally, by exploring and comparing the influence of narratives on different platform mechanisms, we provide a first attempt to deepen our understanding of the crowd by the "recognition of the different objectives and expertise of the finance providers through different types of crowdfunding platforms" (Bruton et al., 2015, p. 17). By addressing the use of narratives in crowdfunding in accordance with funders' objectives and expertise, we attempt to enrich knowledge in this emerging field of research. By studying if the emotional content is more or less influential according to the platforms' mechanism, we look beyond the simplistic assumption of a single venture audience composed of individuals all making decisions about resource allocation in the same way (Überbacher, 2014; van Werven et al., 2015; Fisher et al., 2017).

**Managerial Contributions**

Turning to the managerial implications of our findings, entrepreneurs should be aware that the content of their narrative influences their ability to be financed but also that the effectiveness of these narratives depend on the funders' interests (Lounsbury and Glynn, 2001). Our results suggest that funders differ in their motivational drivers, and accordingly, visit the type of platform mechanism that best fits their motivations. Therefore, narratives have to be adapted to the type of platform mechanism, revealing funders' underlying motivations. Accordingly, entrepreneurs should develop a strong emotional content to address funders on donation- and reward-based platforms, but be less emotional and spend more time on factual elements in the construction of their narratives for lending and equity-based platforms.

Additionally, even if we did not study other communicational elements which can be used by entrepreneurs on the platform such as video or audio clips and pictures, we suggest that these elements, such as narratives, have to be developed in accordance with the platforms and underlying funders' motivations.

The remaining managerial questions concern the practical and effective manner of speaking more "emotionally" or more "cognitively" with potential funders' in order to increase their willingness to support an entrepreneurial project. Emotions arise from the use of emotion words (such as *love, nice* or *sweet*) (Tausczik and Pennebaker, 2010). However, emotionality goes beyond the simple expression of emotions, it also relates to other key language elements. The use of pronouns, auxiliary verbs and negation (Tausczik and Pennebaker, 2010) expresses some emotionality. Conversely, key language elements such as articles, prepositions and relativity words (ex: *area, bend, go*) (Tausczik and Pennebaker, 2010) are rather found in a more cognitive language.

## LIMITATIONS AND FUTURE RESEARCH

Our results suffer from several limitations but also open potential avenues for research. First, we extracted "raw data" from crowdfunding platforms and did not measure direct attitudinal measures. Even if we found that there is a relationship between the tone of the narrative and funders' support, we cannot conclude that this effect is mediated by the funders' attitude toward the project/the entrepreneur. Additional research is needed to examine the impact of tone on the attitude of money providers and their subsequent decision to pledge for or invest in a project. Experimental research could be particularly relevant for that.

Then, all the collected texts were written in English (the LIWC dictionary is in English) while Ulule and MyMicroInvest are platforms attended by French-speaking people to a large extent. However, if the language used in the narratives might be of lower quality than if it was written in their mother tongue, we are confident that the entrepreneurs who have chosen to develop their narratives in English are fluent enough in English. However, additional research could be carried on English-speaking platforms (on which narratives are written by English-speaking project owners) to confirm the results.

Moreover, our results concerning the interaction between emotional tone, community dimension and authenticity are only statistically significant for a low level of authenticity, which might seem surprising. However, it should be noted that authenticity is also associated with anxiety, depression, self-doubt, lower status, and so on. These dimensions might be detrimental to the funding success. Future research should be conducted distinguishing the impact of authenticity from the one of anxiety, depression, self-doubt, lower status.

Furthermore, our study demonstrates that "emotion" is a too broad term that encompasses a range of positive and negative emotions. This shows the limit of studying such a dimension that incorporates elements that can have different influences. Accordingly, it is critical that future research examines specific emotions with a more fine-grained approach. In particular, it would be interesting to investigate the influence of anger and happiness, known to have an impact on people's willingness to donate (van Kleef et al., 2010; Liu, 2011; Gerber and Hui, 2013).

Finally, our research was limited to the analysis of written narratives provided by entrepreneurs on crowdfunding platforms. This narrows the range of emotional dimensions that we were able to analyze. We did not, for instance, capture the tone that may be communicated through multimedia data such as video clip, audio clips and pictures available on the platform. Studying verbal and nonverbal communication in video and audio clips and pictures may form an important opportunity for future research. In a similar way, we did not analyze the entrepreneurs' communication outside the platform (through social media, press ...). Future studies could focus on the emotional dimension of narratives developed by entrepreneurs both inside and outside the platform and its influence on resource acquisition.

## CONCLUSION

Through the social influence of emotions theory lens (van Kleef et al., 2009), we investigated how narratives affect crowdfunding success. For this purpose, we used a unique dataset that combines data from two crowdfunding platforms. Our findings suggest that, in donation- and reward-based crowdfunding campaigns, funders tend to participate more to emotionally-charged projects. Our results also suggest that emotions along with social dimension and authenticity are components of an effective narrative. Yet emotions expressed have a positive impact only if the narrative already creates a sense of community affiliation. Our study also indicates that the emotional influence is less salient in successful narratives on lending and equity-based crowdfunding platforms where the cognitive dimension is more important. For scholars, our research advances understanding of the crowdfunding context—introducing the influence of emotions in line with platforms' type of mechanism. For entrepreneurs, our results suggest that it is critical for them to be aware of the funders' differences in the extent to which they rely on emotion and cognition and, therefore, develop their narratives in accordance.

## NOTES

1. https://fr.ulule.com/.
2. https://www.mymicroinvest.com/.
3. Conversely to information-based narratives composed of neutral terms and phrases (Pollak and Gilligan, 1983) conveyed in a relatively impersonal and factual manner (Fischer and Reuber, 2014), emotionally-toned narratives employ a language relating to emotions (positive or negative, intense or not) (Wolfe and Shepherd, 2015).
4. Now called Spreds.
5. Called "contributors" on Ulule.
6. Called "investors" on MyMicroInvest.
7. See Tausczik and Pennebaker (2010) for a review of literature about this operationalization.
8. Further discussion with PhD. Pennebaker in December 2016.

## REFERENCES

Agrawal, A., C. Catalini and A. Goldfarb (2015), 'Crowdfunding: Geography, social networks, and the timing of investment decisions', *Journal of Economics and Management Strategy*, **41**(2): 253–274.

Ahlers, G., D. Cumming, C. Günther and D. Schweizer (2015), 'Signaling in equity crowdfunding', *Entrepreneurship, Theory and Practice*, **39**(4): 955–980.

Allison, T.H., A.F. McKenny and J.C. Short (2013), 'The effect of entrepreneurial rhetoric on microlending investment: An examination of the warm-glow effect', *Journal of Business Venturing*, **28**(6): 690–707.

Allison, T.H., B.C. Davis, J.C. Short and J.W. Webb (2015), 'Crowdfunding in a prosocial microlending environment: Examining the role of intrinsic versus extrinsic cues', *Entrepreneurship', Theory and Practice*, **39**(1): 53–73.

Baron, R.A. (2008), 'The role of affect in the entrepreneurial process', *The Academy of Management Review*, **33**(2): 328–340.

Belleflamme, P., T. Lambert and A. Schwienbacher (2014), 'Crowdfunding: Tapping the right crowd', *Journal of Business Venturing*, **29**(5): 585–609.

Bi., S., Z. Liu and K. Usman (2017), 'The influence of online information on investing decisions of reward-based crowdfunding', *Journal of Business Research*, **71**(1): 10–18.

Boje, David M. (1991), 'The storytelling organization: A study of story performance in an office-supply firm', *Administrative Science Quarterly*, **36**(1): 106–126.

Bruton, G., S. Khavul, D. Siegel and M. Wright (2015), 'New financial alternatives in seeding entrepreneurship: Microfinance, crowdfunding, and peer-to-peer innovations', *Entrepreneurship, Theory and Practice*, **39**(1): 9–26.

Cardon, M.S., M.D. Foo, D. Shepherd and J. Wiklund (2012), 'Exploring the heart: Entrepreneurial emotion is a hot topic', *Entrepreneurship, Theory and Practice*, **36**(1): 1–10.

Chen, X.-P., X. Yao and S. Kotha (2009), 'Passion and preparedness in entrepreneurs' business plan presentations: A persuasion analysis of venture capitalists' funding decisions', *Academy of Management Journal*, **52**(1): 199–214.

Cholakova, M. and B. Clarysse (2015), 'Does the possibility to make equity investments in crowdfunding projects crowd out reward-based investments?', *Entrepreneurship, Theory and Practice*, **39**(1): 145–172.

Cohn, M.A., B.L. Fredrickson, S.L. Brown, J.A. Mikels and A.M. Conway (2009), 'Happiness unpacked: Positive emotions increase life satisfaction by building resilience', *Emotion*, **9**(3): 361–368.

Collins, L. and Y. Pierrakis (2012), 'The venture crowd: Crowdfunding equity investment into business', Nesta Report.

Côté, S., I. Hideg and G.A. van Kleef (2013), 'The consequences of faking anger in negotiations', *Journal of Experimental Social Psychology*, **49**(3): 453–463.

Dalpiaz, E., P. Tracey and N. Phillips (2014), 'Succession narratives in family business: The case of Alessi', *Entrepreneurship, Theory and Practice*, **38**(6): 1375–1394.

Davis, B.C., K.M. Hmieleski, J.W. Webb and J.E. Coombs (2017), 'Funders' positive affective reaction to entrepreneurs' crowdfunding pitches: The influence of perceived product creativity and entrepreneurial passion', *Journal of Business Venturing*, **32**(1): 90–109.

Drover, W., M.S. Wood and A. Zacharakis (2017), 'Attributes of angel and crowdfunded investments as determinants of VC screening decisions', *Entrepreneurship Theory and Practice*, **41**(3): 323–347.

Fischer, E. and A.R. Reuber (2014), 'Online entrepreneurial communication: Mitigating uncertainty and increasing differentiation via Twitter', *Journal of Business Venturing*, **29**(4): 565–583.

Fisher, G., D.F. Kuratko, J.M. Bloodgood and J.S. Hornsby (2017), 'Legitimate to whom? The challenge of audience diversity and new venture legitimacy', *Journal of Business Venturing*, **32**(1): 52–71.

Galak, J., D. Small and A.T. Stephen (2011), 'Microfinance decision making: A field study of prosocial lending', *Journal of Marketing Research*, **48**(SPL): 130–137.

Gerber, E.M. and J.S. Hui (2013), 'Crowdfunding: Motivations and deterrents for participation', *ACM Transactions on Computer-Human Interaction*, **20**(6): 1–32.

Hayes, A.F. (2013), *Introduction to Mediation, Moderation, and Conditional Process Analysis: A Regression-Based Approach*, London: Guilford Press.

Herzenstein, M., S. Sonenshein and U.M. Dholakia (2011), 'Tell me a good story and I may lend you money: The role of narratives in peer-to-peer lending decisions', *Journal of Marketing Research*, **48**: 138–149.

Huskinson, T.L.H. and G. Haddock (2004), 'Individual differences in attitude structure: Variance in the chronic reliance on affective and cognitive information', *Journal of Experimental Social Psychology*, **40**(1): 82–90.

Jennings, J.E., T. Edwards, P. Jennings and R. Delbridge (2015), 'Emotional arousal and entrepreneurial outcomes: Combining qualitative methods to elaborate theory', *Entrepreneurship: Theory and Practice*, **30**(1): 113–130.

Josefy, M., T.J. Dean, L.S Albert and M.A. Fitza (2017), 'The role of community in crowdfunding success: Evidence on cultural attributes in funding campaigns to "save the local theater"', *Entrepreneurship Theory and Practice*, **41**(2): 161–182.

Jung, E.J., A. Susarla and V. Sambamurthy (2015), 'Evolutionary fundraising patterns and entrepreneurial performance in crowdfunding platforms', in *35th International Conference on Information Systems 'Building a Better World Through Information Systems', ICIS 2014*. Association for Information Systems.

Kuppuswamy, V. and B.L. Bayus (2017), 'Does my contribution to your crowdfunding project matter?', *Journal of Business Venturing*, **32**(1): 72–89.

Liu, W. (2011), 'The benefit of asking for time', in M. Oppenheimer and C.Y. Olivela (eds), *The Science of Giving. Experimental Approaches to the Study of Charity*, Hove, UK and New York: Psychology Press, 201–214.

Lounsbury, M. and M.A. Glynn (2001), 'Cultural entrepreneurship: stories, legitimacy, and the acquisition of resources', *Strategic Management Journal*, **22**: 545–564.

Lurtz, K. and K. Kreutzer (2014), 'What does your audience expect from you? How entrepreneurs acquire resources through storytelling', Academy of Management Annual Meeting Proceedings, 1400–1405.

Martens, M.L., J. Jennings and P.D. Jennings (2007), 'Do the stories they tell get them the money they need? The impact of strategy narratives on resource acquisition', *Academy of Management Journal*, **50**(5): 1107–1132.

McKenny, A.F., T.H. Allison, D.J. Ketchen Jr., J.C. Short and R. Duane Ireland (2017), 'How should crowdfunding research evolve?', A survey of the Entrepreneurship Theory and Practice editorial board. *Entrepreneurship Theory and Practice*, 291–304.

Mikolajczak, M., J. Quoidbach, I. Kotsou and D. Nelis (2014), *Les compétences émotionnelles*, Paris, France: Dunod.

Mollick, E. (2014), 'The dynamics of crowdfunding: An exploratory study', *Journal of Business Venturing*, **29**(1): 1–16.

Moss, T.W., D.O. Neubaum and M. Meyskens (2015), 'The effect of virtuous and entrepreneurial orientations on microfinance lending and repayment: a signaling theory perspective', *Entrepreneurship: Theory and Practice*, **39**: 27–52.

O'Connor, E. (2002), 'Storied business: typology, intertextuality, and traffic in entrepreneurial narrative', *International Journal of Business Communication*, **39**(1): 36–54.

Pennebaker, J.W., R.L. Boyd, K. Jordan and K. Blackburn (2015), *The Development and Psychometric Properties of LIWC2015*, Austin, TX: University of Texas at Austin.

Pollak, S. and C. Gilligan (1983), 'Differing about differences: The incidence and interpretation of violent fantasies in women and men', *Journal of Personality and Social Psychology*, **45**(5): 1172–1175.

Pollack, J.M., M.W. Rutherford and B.G. Nagy (2012), 'Preparedness and cognitive legitimacy as antecedents of new venture funding in televised business pitches', *Entrepreneurship Theory and Practice*, **36**(5): 1042–2587.

Preacher, K.J. and A.F. Hayes (2008), 'Contemporary approaches to assessing mediation in communication research', in A.F. Hayes, M.D. Slater and L.B. Snyder (eds), *The Sage Sourcebook of Advanced Data Analysis Methods for Communication Research*, Thousand Oaks, CA: Sage, 13–54.

Preacher, K.J., D.D. Rucker and A.F. Hayes (2007), 'Addressing moderated mediation hypotheses: Theory, methods, and prescriptions', *Multivariate Behavioral Research*, **42**(1): 185–227.

Rawhouser, H., J. Villanueva and S.L. Newbert (2016), 'Strategies and tools for entrepreneurial resource access: a cross-disciplinary review and typology', *International Journal of Management Reviews*, **19**: 473–491.

Rimé, B. (2009), *Le partage social des émotions*, Presses Universitaires de France.

Roberts, L.M. (2005), 'Changing faces: Professional image construction in diverse organizational settings', *Academy of Management Review*, **20**(4): 685–711.

Schwienbacher, A. and B. Larralde (2010), *Crowdfunding of Small Entrepreneurial Ventures*, Oxford: Oxford University Press.

See, Y.H.M., R.E. Petty and L.R. Fabrigar (2008), 'Affective and cognitive meta-bases of attitudes: Unique effects on information interest and persuasion', *Journal of Personality and Social Psychology*, **94**(6): 938–955.

Shepherd, D.A. (2015), 'Party on! A call for entrepreneurship research that is more interactive, activity based, cognitively hot, compassionate and prosocial', *Journal of Business Venturing*, **30**(4): 489–507.

Shepherd, D.A. and T.A. Williams (2014), 'Local venturing as compassion organizing in the aftermath of a natural disaster: The role of localness and community in reducing suffering', *Journal of Management Studies*, **51**: 952–994.

Skirnevskiy, V., D. Bendig and M. Brettel (2017), 'The influence of internal social capital on serial creators' success in crowdfunding', *Entrepreneurship Theory and Practice*, **41**(2): 209–236.

Smith, R. and A.R. Anderson (2004), 'The devil is in the e-tale: Forms and structures in the entrepreneurial narratives', in D. Hjorth and C. Steyaert (eds), *Narrative and Discursive Approaches in Entrepreneurship. A Second Movements in Entrepreneurship Book*, Cheltenham, UK and Northampton, MA, USA: Edward Elgar Publishing, 125–143.

Spiller, S. (2013), 'Mediation practicum—on using Hayes (2003) Process Macro, Indirect Effects, & Bootstrapping', in Simona Botti and Aparna Labroo (eds), *Advances in Consumer Research*, 41.

Tausczik, Y.R. and J.W. Pennebaker (2010), The psychological meaning of words: LIWC and computerized text analysis methods', *Journal of Language and Social Psychology*, **29**(1): 24–54.

Tetlock, P.C. (2007), 'Giving content to investor sentiment: the role of media in the stock market', *The Journal of Finance*, **62**(3): 1139–1168.

Tetlock, P.C., M. Saar-Tsechansky and S. Macskassy (2008), 'More than words: Quantifying language to measure firms' fundamentals', *The Journal of Finance*, **63**(3): 1437–1467.

Überbacher, F. (2014), 'Legitimation of new ventures: A review and research programme', *Journal of Management Studies*, **51**(4): 667–698.

van Kleef, G.A., C.K. De Dreu and A.S. Manstead (2010), 'An interpersonal approach to emotion in social decision making: The emotions as social information model', in P. Devine and A. Plant (eds), *Advances in Experimental Social Psychology* (Vol. 42), London: Academic Press, 45–96.

van Kleef, G.A., L.W. Heerdink and H. van den Berg (2015), 'The persuasive power of emotions: Effects of emotional expressions on attitude formation and change', *Journal of Applied Psychology*, **100**(4): 1124–1142.

van Kleef, G.A., A.C. Homan, B. Beersma and D. Van Knippenberg (2009), 'Searing sentiment or cold calculation? The effects of leader emotional displays on team performance depend on follower epistemic motivation', *Academy of Management Journal*, **52**(3): 562–580.

van Kleef, G.A., E.A. Van Doorn, M.W. Heerdink and L.F. Koning (2011), 'Emotion is for influence', *European Review of Social Psychology*, **22**(1): 114–163.

van Werven, R., O. Bouwmeester and J.P. Cornelissen (2015), 'The power of arguments: How entrepreneurs convince stakeholders of the legitimate distinctiveness of their ventures', *Journal of Business Venturing*, **30**(4): 616–631.

Victoravich, L.M. (2010), 'Overly optimistic? Investor sophistication and the role of affective reactions to financial information in investors' stock price judgments', *The Journal of Behavioral Finance*, **11**(1): 1–10.

Wolfe, M.T. and D.A. Shepherd (2015), 'What do you have to say about that? Performance events and narratives' positive and negative emotional content', *Entrepreneurship Theory and Practice*, **39**(4): 895–925.

Zhao, X., J.G. Lynch Jr and Q. Chen (2010), 'Reconsidering Baron and Kenny: Myths and truths about mediation analysis', *Journal of Consumer Research*, **37**(2): 197–206.

# 11. Freelancing and the struggle for work-time control[1]

## John Kitching and Marfuga Iskandarova

## INTRODUCTION

Freelance workers, defined as independent own-account workers who provide goods and services alone (or with co-owning partners) but do not employ others, are the most common form of small business (Kitching and Smallbone, 2012). Freelancers have been major drivers of UK job growth in the years 2001–2016 (ONS, 2018a), much of it in 'privileged' rather than 'precarious' sectors (Tomlinson and Corlett, 2017). UK Labour Force Survey data suggest there were 4.06 million freelance workers in main jobs in Q4, 2017 (ONS, 2018b), an increase of more than one million since Q4, 2008, the period immediately prior to the start of the recession resulting from the global financial crisis. But despite their growing numbers, and a substantial presence in all sectors of the economy, freelancers have been a minority interest among small business researchers, because of their lower visibility, and policymaker and academic interest in business growth. A developing stream of research has, however, begun to investigate these *nano*businesses, their characteristics, activities and relationships (Fraser and Gold, 2001; Barley and Kunda, 2006; Burke, 2012; Armstrong, 2013), including studies of the so-called 'gig economy', where freelancers find and win projects using online platforms (CIPD, 2017; Broughton et al., 2018; Burtch et al., 2018). We seek to contribute to this research stream by exploring freelancers' experiences of operating the very smallest firms, in particular, the management of working time.

Freelance working reflects, in part, a desire to enjoy greater control over working life (Benz and Frey, 2008; Stephan et al., 2015; Taylor Review, 2017). Popular and media discourses often assume freelancers possess the autonomy to choose what work they do, who they work for, and how, where and when they work (Dellot, 2014; O'Leary, 2014; Lenton, 2017). Control over working time is one important dimension of freelancer autonomy (Evans et al., 2004; van Gelderen and Jansen, 2006) and a source of greater meaningfulness in work (Bailey and Madden, 2017). But because freelancers are responsible for generating their own work and income, they must contribute the labour time necessary to satisfy a portfolio of fee-paying clients sufficient to sustain a subjectively acceptable livelihood. This can give rise to an 'autonomy paradox' (Huws et al., 1996) whereby freelancers *choose* to work long or 'unsocial' hours to ensure market survival (Shevchuk et al., 2019).

We conceptualise freelancer-client relations in terms of a struggle for work-time control. Freelancers seek to valorise their labour time by taking on new projects, while also resisting 'client colonisation' of non-working time (Gold and Mustafa, 2013), as clients simultaneously seek to elicit freelancer effort to ensure prompt project completion. Unlike employees who negotiate the use of their time with a single employer, freelancers must choose how to allocate their time between *multiple* clients and projects. The outcome of work-time control struggles is uncertain; assumptions that freelance working *necessarily* leads to either a high degree of control over work-time, or conversely no control at all, therefore need to be investigated rather than assumed.

This study explores the struggle for work-time control in two professional sectors, architecture and publishing. Given the diversity of the freelance population (Kitching, 2016; Vermeylen et al., 2017; Williams et al., 2017; Bögenhold, 2019), we might hypothesise that freelancer control of work-time varies considerably. Occupations requiring the exercise of high levels of skills and judgement – those we might describe as 'privileged' rather than 'precarious' – might be expected to permit freelancers to exert substantial work-time control. If highly skilled, professional freelancers lack control of working time, those in less-skilled occupations might be expected to possess even less. Researching these two groups provides a strong test of arguments about freelancer autonomy and flexibility. We seek to answer the following two questions:

• What practices do freelancers engage in to control work-time?; and
• How do relations with clients influence freelancer capacity to control work-time?

The chapter is structured as follows. First, we review the literature on freelancing and identify a number of research gaps related to relations with clients that facilitate or frustrate freelancer attempts to control working time. Next, we develop an analytical framework linking client type and resources, client demand for freelancers' services, and two interdependent dimensions of working time which freelancers seek to control – work duration and work-time scheduling. We then set out our methodological approach and present the main findings before concluding and drawing out the implications for theory and research.

## FREELANCING, CONTROL OF WORKING TIME AND CLIENT RELATIONS

People work freelance for a variety of reasons, including to have greater control over working time (van Gelderen and Jansen, 2006; Sappleton and Lourenço, 2016; Kautonen et al., 2017; Lenton, 2017).[2] Cohen (2019) suggests that freelance work is characterised by temporal and spatial unboundedness, that is, work activities are *not* demarcated by formal time and space boundaries; work can be performed at different times and in different places. Cohen emphasises unboundedness as a structural component of freelance work, rather than an incidental by-product or a consequence of freelancer choice. Work activities that are temporally unbounded lend themselves to being organised on a freelance, rather than an employment, basis. Occupations vary in their temporal boundedness, contingent upon whether work needs to be performed where clients or co-workers are present, or where immobile plant and machinery must be used (Cohen, 2019). Hence freelancers in different occupations, varying in temporal unboundedness, might be expected to differ in their capacity to control working time. Home-based freelance working, for example, allows greater control over work scheduling than working at client premises (Osnowitz and Henson, 2016) and home-based freelancers enjoy high levels of time flexibility (Mason and Reuschke, 2015).

Research on working time is typically discussed in terms of work–life, work–family and work–retirement balance. This literature largely refers to employees but can easily be extended to freelance workers who are presumed to possess greater time flexibility than employees because they are not tied to employers' workplace routines (Baines and Gelder, 2003). Work–life balance issues vary across the life course for both men and women related to career stage, family stage and biological ageing (Darcy et al., 2012). Freelancing might be considered suitable for prime working-age men who can take on as many projects as they can manage to increase earnings to support a family, for working mothers who take primary responsibility for childcare (Bell and La Valle, 2003), for those seeking to combine paid work with caring for elderly relatives (Dellot, 2014), and for older workers seeking to enact a 'phased retirement' (Keohane, 2017) or a better 'work–retirement' balance (Wainwright and Kibler, 2014).

A dominant research theme has therefore been the contradiction between the prospect of freelancers' time sovereignty and the reality of demands on working time (Osnowitz and Henson, 2016). Possessing the legal right to determine one's working time cannot guarantee a satisfying work–life balance (Annink and den Dulk, 2012; FSB, 2016). Where freelancers perceive 'time as money' (Bailey and Madden, 2017), or as an 'expense' (Hilbrecht and Lero,

2014), their control of work-time may be limited because they feel a persistent pressure to take on more projects to generate income. Many freelancers experience an 'autonomy paradox', whereby they choose to work longer or 'unsocial' hours (Shevchuk et al., 2019) to meet project deadlines (Platman, 2003, 2004), or to comply with last-minute client demands (Shevchuk et al., 2019) or requests for information, with a view to winning future work (Gold and Mustafa, 2013). Where work flow is uncertain, freelancers might feel extra pressure to take on projects (Dex et al., 2000).

Freelancers report longer weekly hours on average than employees (e.g. Bell and La Valle, 2003; Hyytinen and Ruuskanen, 2007; European Commission, 2016). Freelance fathers work long, atypical hours and undertake more weekend working than employee parents (Bell and La Valle, 2003), and mothers often struggle to combine freelance work and childcare (e.g. Bell and La Valle, 2003; Kirkwood and Tootell, 2008; Annink and den Dulk, 2012; Hilbrecht and Lero, 2014; Johannsen Sevä and Öun, 2015). Studies of publishing freelancers have found that evening and weekend working is widespread (Baverstock et al., 2015). Freelancers must also devote time that cannot be charged to clients (Evans et al., 2004) to project search, skill development and other activities (Shevchuk et al., 2019). Yet, despite often working long hours, the capacity to exercise autonomy over work-time is a source of satisfaction (Smeaton, 2003; Croson and Minniti, 2012).

Paradoxically, freelancers can work too few as well as too many hours (Baumberg and Meager, 2015; CIPD, 2017). Freelancers are more prone than employees to short hours working (Field and Forsey, 2016) or irregular hours – and, therefore, to inadequate or volatile earnings (Hardy and Sanders, 2015; FSB, 2016; Lockey, 2018). Unlike employees who may be laid off when there is no work, freelance workers can simply adjust their hours downwards, however financially damaging this might be, but without abandoning being a freelancer (Hatfield, 2015). UK sources suggest some earn very little income from self-employment, which is probably an indicator of limited hours in many cases (HMRC, 2018).

This chapter contributes to the literature on freelancing and working time in two ways. First, freelance workers might be expected to possess variable powers to control work-time, partly due to occupational differences in temporal boundedness (Cohen, 2019) which depends, in part, on project characteristics such as the skills required or the need to work alongside others. Second, studies typically under-theorise the variability of client influence on freelancer capacity to control work-time. Gold and Mustafa's (2013) concept of client colonisation, referring to responding to client requests for information during 'unsocial' hours, is useful but if pressed too far ('work always wins') can easily overemphasise freelancer vulnerability to client pressure, allowing little room for freelancers to pursue their own work-time goals. Studies, however, do not always differentiate clients by type or resources, or, alternatively, they assume freelancers are dependent on large organisations in 'hierarchical sub-contracting' relations (Stanworth and Stanworth, 1997; Muehlberger, 2007; O'Leary, 2014; Morris et al., 2016). Client characteristics vary markedly and likely influence the parties' bargaining power and the struggle for work-time control in diverse ways.

## CONCEPTUALISING FREELANCER WORK-TIME CONTROL

We now present an analytical framework to address our two research questions and to help fill the research gaps identified above. The framework sets out the connections between client type and resources, the demand for freelance labour and freelancers' work-time goals, resources and practices. Only clients can *initiate* freelance projects, by designing work assignments and outsourcing them to freelance workers, although freelancers may be able to shape their precise content, scheduling and remuneration. Clients must stipulate the work to be done, start and end dates, whether work must be performed at client premises or elsewhere, what counts as satisfactory performance, payment terms and who will be offered the work. Freelancers' clients and projects vary substantially in terms of a number of dimensions that potentially influence freelancers' bargaining power and their capacity to control working time (Table 11.1).

Clients are individuals as well as organisations, and organisational clients may be small or large, with varying levels of resources such as knowledge and finance. Relations with clients may be high-trust and long-term, or low-trust and new. Projects vary with regard to content, timescale and the requirement for close synchronisation with co-workers' activities. Projects vary in terms of the skills they require for successful performance. They may consist of specific tasks of finite duration or comprise a 'retainer model' whereby clients engage freelancers for an indefinite period or with an intention of continuity (Camerani et al., 2015).[3] Moreover, projects might require freelancers to perform work alone or to coordinate their activities closely with co-workers (employees or other freelancers). Projects also vary with regard to client requirements to work at client premises or whether freelancers may work at home. Projects and client relations are likely to vary across occupational groups, with implications for struggles over work-time control.

Freelancers' work-time goals can be conceptualised along two dimensions: *work-time scheduling*, the choice of precisely when to work within a given time period (for example, across the day, week, month, year); and, second, *work duration*, referring to the total hours worked during the period (Evans et al., 2004; Hilbrecht and Lero, 2014). Freelancer capacity to control both sched-

*Table 11.1*   *Key client and project characteristics influencing the struggle for work-time control*

| | |
|---|---|
| Client type and resources | Individual clients and freelancers may be more equally balanced in bargaining power, particularly where freelancers possess specialist knowledge and have access to alternative projects and clients. Organisational clients, particularly large ones, are more likely to possess the resources (knowledge, finance) to define project content, scheduling and remuneration unilaterally. |
| Client demand | Freelance workers seek to balance competing pressures of generating a sufficient volume of projects to support a preferred lifestyle, while simultaneously seeking to limit long or 'unsocial' hours *and* to minimise involuntary non-working time. |
| Client relationship quality | Long-term/high-trust relations between freelancers and clients are likely to involve a greater degree of informal negotiation over project scheduling than new, or low-trust relations. |
| Project content | The higher the occupational skill requirements, the greater the likelihood that freelancers possess the resources (especially professional knowledge) to influence project scheduling and remuneration. |
| Project timescale | Short projects might prohibit deadline-shifting, unless clients are able to absorb delays within their own supply chains or extend them to their own customers. Long projects may facilitate deadline-shifting, particularly where risks to prompt completion can only be discovered after projects start (e.g. failure to obtain regulatory approval). |
| Project synchronisation | Projects requiring close synchronisation between freelancer and client, or between freelancer and co-workers, will likely constrain freelancer control of work-time scheduling. Projects *not* requiring close synchronisation permit greater freelancer control over scheduling. |
| Work location | Home-based freelance working, in principle, permits greater control over work-time scheduling. Working at client premises enables clients to determine attendance and timekeeping norms. |

uling and duration may vary over time (Cohen, 2019). Freelancers schedule work-time by organising activities on one or more projects; work duration is the aggregate outcome of scheduling choices. As a consequence, freelancers' scheduling and duration goals are often in tension. Taking on new projects increases duration while simultaneously reducing the flexibility to schedule work as one would prefer. Working a 70-hour week, for instance, provides less choice over which hours to work than a 10-hour week, other non-work commitments being equal.

Freelancer work-time control is largely a function of the interaction of client type and resources, and level of demand, with freelancer decisions to take on specific projects in order to support a particular lifestyle, combining work and non-work preferences. Market conditions shape project offers and the fees/

rates clients are prepared to pay. Project search and take-up are motivated by anticipated financial and non-financial rewards, enabled and constrained by personal, family and market circumstances; freelancers are therefore keen to avoid involuntary periods of non-work. Freelancers vary in their standard of living preferences, family responsibilities, household outgoings and reliance on freelance income to support a preferred lifestyle. Subject to there being sufficient client demand, freelancers may make an explicit trade-off between work duration and income by accepting or declining (or not seeking) project offers.

Our specific focus is on how freelancers seek to preserve or extend control over working time, even where this sacrifices financial rewards. Freelancers might engage in various practices to control working time, subject to the requirement to meet client expectations. Such practices will likely vary with the parties' relative bargaining power. Freelancers possess variable capacities to control work-time, conditional upon their positioning within wider social structures, including relationships with clients. Relations with clients both constrain *and* enable freelancers' pursuit of work-time scheduling and work duration goals.

## METHODOLOGICAL APPROACH

To answer the research questions, a qualitative research design was adopted. Qualitative strategies are well suited to capturing dynamic social processes, linking freelancers' perceptions and actions to the clients with whom they interact within the wider market and institutional setting that enables and constrains the parties' activities. The study draws on interview data from freelance workers in architecture and publishing (principally, copy-editors and proofreaders). Labour Force Survey data indicate that freelance working is a longstanding practice in both sectors (e.g. ONS, 1992). In Q4, 2017, freelancers comprised approximately 25,000 (15 per cent) of the 166,000-strong publishing workforce in main jobs (ONS, 2018a); a further 6,700 work freelance in publishing as a second job. In architecture, there were approximately 21,000 freelancers in main jobs (data are not available for second jobs).

The sample comprised 25 freelance workers, 13 in publishing and 12 architects (Table 11.2); we also consulted a number of professional and membership organisation representatives.[4] Publishing freelancers were identified using the Society for Editors and Proofreaders online directory; Architects were identified using the Architects Registration Board and Royal Institute of British Architects online members' directories. We confined our interest to freelancers in Greater London (and Oxford, for publishing freelancers only), in order to make it easier to interview clients and freelance workers for the study and because both groups have a strong presence in these locations. Approximately

*Table 11.2*     *Sample profile*

| Respondent code | Sex | Age | Year started freelance |
|---|---|---|---|
| *Publishing freelancers* | | | |
| 101 | Female | 74 | 1961* |
| 102 | Female | 67 | 1979 |
| 103 | Male | 74 | 1982* |
| 104 | Male | 59 | 1990* |
| 105 | Female | 66 | 1982 |
| 106 | Female | 48 | 2013 |
| 107 | Female | 50 | 1995* |
| 201 | Female | 61 | 1998 |
| 202 | Female | 50 | 2011 |
| 203 | Female | 65 | 2004 |
| 204 | Female | 79 | 1986 |
| 205 | Female | 56 | 2012 |
| 206 | Female | 50 | 1997 |
| | | | |
| *Architects* | | | |
| 301 | Male | 65 | 1969 |
| 302 | Female | 43 | 2010 |
| 303 | Male | 60 | 1989 |
| 304 | Male | 49 | 2000 |
| 305 | Female | 45 | 2010 |
| 306 | Male | 47 | 2009 |
| 307 | Female | 41 | 2010 |
| 308 | Female | 45 | 2006 |
| 309 | Male | 43 | 2011 |
| 401 | Male | 47 | 2014 |
| 402 | Male | 85 | 1961 |
| 403 | Male | 67 | 1986 |

*Note:* Respondent 205 holds a second freelance job. Starred (*) responses refer to an interrupted career, with freelance working interspersed with periods of employment, unemployment or labour market inactivity, for example, to raise a family.

36 per cent of publishing employment and 21 per cent of architects are based in London (ONS, 2018a). No sample sub-quotas were explicitly set for gender, age, place of work or other characteristic, although the online directories we used as our sampling frames were more likely to include established, experienced freelancers rather than younger practitioners.

Most respondents were female (15); and all were at least 40 years of age. All respondents had worked freelance for at least three years, some for several decades. Our findings are therefore relevant primarily to experienced freelancers. In publishing, we focused primarily on copy-editors and proofreaders. Copy-editing involves reviewing manuscripts for print and online publication to check spelling, grammar, punctuation, consistency, conformity to 'house style' and to verify factual claims; this often requires substantial academic, professional or practical knowledge of specific disciplines or fields. Proofreading involves reviewing copy-editors' work, text layout, and ensuring the typesetter has understood what the copy-editor intended. Projects vary in timescale depending on the length and complexity of manuscripts, for example, a couple of hours for a letter or a press release, through a couple of weeks for journal and magazine articles, and student theses, up to 1–2 months for a book. Publishing freelancers often provided other services, including developmental editing, project management, training and translation, partly because of a decline in copy-editing and proofreading projects. All publishing freelance respondents were educated to at least first degree level.

Architects are a more homogenous group in terms of job skills. To call oneself an architect in the UK requires completion of a three-part programme of study and practical experience, and requires registration with the Architects Registration Board. All respondents reported a degree qualification (or equivalent if non-UK educated). Architects provided a range of services: initial, outline sketches as possible ideas for development; detailed design drawings; submitting drawings to the planning regulator for approval (and resubmission, if necessary); finding construction professionals (surveyors, engineers) to provide specialist services direct to clients; and supervising construction work on-site. Projects involving all stages can take 1–2 years and possibly even longer where there are delays due to amendments to initial plans, changes in client circumstances (for instance, due to illness or financial concerns) or problems obtaining planning approval.

Face-to-face interviews were conducted with all respondents. Questions were asked regarding services provided, motivations for working freelance, methods of finding work, type of clients served, hours of work and reasons for variation, fee-setting processes, satisfaction with pay, hours and other aspects of work, and broader attitudes to freelancing as well as profile questions relating to education, work history and personal/family circumstances. Interviews were 64 minutes long on average.

All freelancer interviews were transcribed in full and coded using Nvivo, edition 11. Data were analysed guided by our conceptual framework, linking respondents' perceptions and actions to the wider market and personal/family contexts. Freelancer control over working time is connected causally to relations with clients, balancing pressures to meet multiple clients' expectations with the desire to preserve some degree of autonomy over hours of work. Respondents and their references to particular clients have been anonymised. The following sections present data on freelancers' struggles to control work duration and work-time scheduling.

## CONTROL OF WORK DURATION

Freelancers' powers to control work duration are circumscribed in practice by the need to generate a flow of fee-paying clients sufficient to support a preferred lifestyle. High levels of client demand increase freelancers' bargaining power, enhancing their capacity to choose more satisfying projects with regard to project content, scheduling and remuneration. Freelancers seek to balance the competing pressures of generating an adequate volume of work to support a preferred lifestyle with simultaneously seeking to avoid both excessively long or 'unsocial' hours *and* involuntary non-working time. This section presents data on how freelance workers manage these competing pressures.

Architects were better placed to control work duration for several reasons. First, architects were typically in a more powerful position vis-à-vis clients than publishing freelancers. Architects typically served *individual* clients, mostly homeowners, rather than organisational clients, and these clients were more dependent on the architect's professional expertise: 10 architects reported working mainly for individual clients at the time of interview; only two worked mainly for organisations (Architects 309, 401). Homeowners were heavily reliant on the architect's professional knowledge to determine project feasibility and timescales. All publishing freelancers, in contrast, served organisational clients, though a few had worked previously for individuals, for example, on student dissertations. Publishing clients, in particular, are extremely knowledgeable about the services they require freelancers to provide and capable of estimating project timescales, making it difficult for publishing freelancers to negotiate longer project deadlines or more generous fees or hourly rates. Where freelancers worked for *non*-publishing clients, they were better positioned to secure more favourable payment terms and timescales.

Second, architects reported high levels of client demand, enabling them to be selective in accepting project offers. South West London has a large affluent homeowner population that can support a buoyant freelance architect market. Architects attributed high client demand to the combined effect of limited house price rises, the costs of moving and Stamp Duty Land Tax, each perhaps encouraging homeowners to refurbish current homes rather than buy new properties – although a number noted a slowdown following the UK referendum to leave the EU in 2016. Publishing freelancers, in contrast, reported fewer lucrative projects, particularly from conventional publishers. Many freelancers, particularly those working full-time, had sought new, better-paying clients in the education, hospitality and media sectors, for example (Publishing freelancers 102, 106, 107, 201, 204, 205, 206), and most had added new services to their copy-editing and proofreading skillsets.

Third, architects have a wider range of labour market alternatives available to them. Architects can work freelance or as an employee in a small or large practice if freelancing proves to be financially unrewarding. In sharp contrast, copy-editing and proofreading jobs are today largely organised on a freelance basis, following restructuring of the publishing sector in the late 1980s and early-1990s (Stanworth and Stanworth, 1997; interviews with publishing industry respondents). Few employee jobs in these roles remain. Copy-editors and proofreaders must work freelance if they wish to continue in their chosen profession.

Architects' bargaining power was most obvious in their capacity to turn projects down. Respondents linked market demand, current workloads and the capacity to decline new work:

> There's so much work round here, I think I'll always be turning work down. (Architect 302: female, 43, part-time)

Being busy, and anticipating a secure stream of future work, encouraged architects to be selective in choosing projects, turning down those perceived as low-paid or uninteresting, or where clients were perceived as likely to be 'labour intensive' (Architect 306: male, 47, full-time).

Architects also reported subcontracting projects to other freelance workers, where respondents were too busy to undertake the work themselves (Architects 207, 307). Respondents also reported examples from their earlier freelancing days of being the recipient of such outsourcing practices. Subcontracting projects was not common, but illustrates the high levels of client demand reported by sample architects.

> I took a project on and then something else came on and I just didn't have the time to do everything. So I gave her – like that other person had done to me – a percentage of the fee and sort of said 'Run it how you like. Check in with me, but it has to be done in this time'. (Architect 307: female, 41, full-time)

Because of their greater bargaining power in relation to clients, architects were able to choose the most lucrative or interesting projects, while subcontracting or declining other work. This enables architects to retain a high level of control over work duration while also achieving acceptable earnings. Publishing freelancers were less likely to report turning work down while also reporting lower levels of satisfaction with project fees/rates.

Respondents in both sectors found it challenging to report 'usual' weekly hours. Most reported *daily* hours, accompanied by qualifications that these waxed and waned with planned and unplanned work and non-work contingencies (Table 11.3). Eighteen respondents worked as full-time freelancers (defined as 31 hours per week or more), six worked part-time, and one straddled the divide, depending on whether they worked a 3- or a 4-day week. At the high-end of the scale, two architects reported working 70 hours a week on occasion (Architects 301, 306) while, at the low end, one part-time architect reported working 16.5 hours a week (Architect 302) and a publishing freelancer reported working 4–5 hours per day three days a week (Publishing freelancer 103). All sample working-age males worked full-time, mostly adopting a 'family breadwinner' role. Working-age females' hours varied, depending on whether they were provisioning for a family and took primary responsibility for childcare. Semi-retired freelancers, male and female, tended to work part-time.

Freelancers may choose to work a conventional Monday to Friday, 9–5 pattern, or, alternatively, during what are often termed 'unsocial' hours – in the evening, during the night, at weekends, and in the early morning. All architects and almost all publishing freelancers reported evening and weekend working at least some of the time, even those working part-time; only publishing freelancers 103 and 204 reported no recent evening or weekend working. A number of the sample reported a willingness to trade-off weekend working occasionally for time off for leisure and other activities during the conventional working week.

Freelancers often experience an 'autonomy paradox' (Huws et al., 1996), where they take on additional projects to increase income and trade-off time for non-work activities – leisure and family/childcare. This paradox leads publishing freelancers and, to a lesser extent, architects, to occasionally take on projects that raise work duration beyond what freelancers would prefer.

> I didn't really understand how difficult that would be. I thought that because I was so stressed in that job and I worked really, really hard and long hours, I thought that … I would have more free time. And sometimes I do. But a lot of the time I don't, because depending on what clients want and juggling things around, I quite often don't have very much free time because … there'll be a period where I'm working six days a week and some days when I work quite long hours. I probably do have more time – but it doesn't feel like I have more free time because I feel like I need to fill it with work, basically, and spend a lot of my time working – or doing work to get more work or admin and stuff like that. (Publishing freelancer 107: female, 50, full-time)

Architects reported a long hours culture in the industry (Architects 308, 309, 401, 402, 403). These timekeeping norms were striking for one respondent

*Table 11.3     Hours of work*

| Interview code | Full/Part-time status; Hours of work | 'Unsocial Hours' working |
|---|---|---|
| *Publishing freelancers* | | |
| 101 | Full-time: 5 days x 9 hours (45 hours). | Only very early morning, from 7am. |
| 102 | Full-time: 8 hours per day, start at 12, work till 8 and sometimes later into the night (40 hours). | Occasional Sunday working, if absolutely necessary. |
| 103 | Part-time: although can work up to 7 hours a day, combined with (mostly) voluntary periods of no work at all. | None recently. |
| 104 | Full-time: 9.5–10.5 hours, sometimes longer, when working at client premises; at home 10 hours, sometimes longer. | Occasional evening working until 8.30/9.30 when based in client's office. |
| 105 | Full-time: highly variable, 10–12 hours some days, then no work for 2–3 weeks. | Occasionally works 12 hours days and often at weekends to meet a deadline. |
| 106 | Full-time: 5 days x 7.5-8 hours (37.5-40 hours). | Occasionally works Sundays for 3 hours. |
| 107 | Full-time: 30–35 hours weekly average, but varying from 20–50. | Occasionally works at weekends before taking time off. |
| 201 | Part-time: 20 hours per week. | Works at weekends if necessary, reluctantly, mainly to avoid work backlog when taking time off, though less often than previously. |
| 202 | Full-time: 5 days x 6.5 hours (32.5 hours). | Occasionally works evenings, and very occasionally at weekends, to meet a deadline. |
| 203 | Part-time: 20 hours weekly average. | Sometimes works until 8.30pm having taken time off for leisure activities earlier in the day; occasionally until 2am, and in the very early morning from 5am. |
| 204 | Part-time: works full-time hours when working, interspersed with non-work periods. | None reported. |
| 205 | Part-time: no more than 5 hours a day. (Respondent holds a second job and therefore works full-time overall). | Has worked evenings and weekends when necessary. |
| 206 | Full-time: 5 days x 9–9.5 hours (45–47.5 hours). | Quite often works 4–5 hours at weekends and occasional evenings to meet deadlines. |

| Interview code | Full/Part-time status; Hours of work | 'Unsocial Hours' working |
|---|---|---|
| *Architects* | | |
| 301 | Full-time; 6 days, up to 12 hours per day (72 hours). | Frequently works a 12-hour day and at least one day at weekends. |
| 302 | Part-time: 3 days x 5.5 hours (16.5 hours). | Often works in the late evening beyond 9pm and occasionally at weekends to meet deadlines. |
| 303 | Full-time: 5 days x 7–8 hours (35–40 hours). | Very occasional evening or Saturday morning work to meet a client. |
| 304 | Full-time: 5 days x 10–12 hours (50–60 hours). | Works 6am to 6pm, plus occasional evening work; occasional client visits at weekends. |
| 305 | Full-time: 35–40 hour week. | Works occasional Saturday or Sunday morning to visit clients; occasional evening work if work cannot be completed during the day. |
| 306 | Full-time: variable, up to 70 hours some weeks. | Occasional weekend working (up to 6 hours) and in the evening. |
| 307 | Full-time: 4 days, variable hours each day due to childcare (approx. 35–40 hours). | Wednesday is a planned 12-hour working day because husband has childcare responsibilities; very occasional weekend working to meet a deadline. |
| 308 | Full-time: 5 days x 7 hours (35 hours). | Very occasional client meetings in the evenings and at weekends. |
| 309 | Full-time: 3 days x 11 hours (when working at client premises), plus 1 day at home, variable hours | Works early evening to make up 11-hour days. |
| 401 | Full-time: 37.5–40 hours. | Works a 10-hour day, and into the evening, at major client's premises; some weekend working on own separate projects. |
| 402 | Full-time: 50 hours, weekly average. | Occasional few hours on a Sunday. |
| 403 | Full-time: 50 hours per week. | Frequently works until 9pm in the evening, with occasional weekend working. |

*Note:* 'Unsocial Hours' working defined as working time outside a 'conventional' Monday to Friday, 9–5 pattern.

working on client premises, although partly a consequence of his choice to compress four working days into three (Architect 309). But, arguably, such norms continue to influence architects who choose to become freelance. A long hours culture, combined with unpredictable client demands to 'juggle' multiple projects simultaneously, suggests that freelance architects may occasionally be prone to evening and weekend working:

> I seem to work more hours now than I did when I wasn't [a freelancer], and more kind of weekends and evenings – which is ironic! The way work always is … you'll have two projects running simultaneously, and then both want what they need simultaneously … So that's fine, architectural practices are well known for working late … I find myself, there's no start and no end to my day really, unless I'm out doing something. So, it quite easily can slip into the evening. (Architect 401: male, 47, full-time)

Seven publishing freelancers (102, 103, 104, 105, 107, 204, 205) and one architect (307) reported experience of *involuntary* non-working time. This is a serious concern, particularly for full-time freelancers, as they are major contributors to household finances. Consequently, freelancers occasionally accepted low-paid projects where they perceived the alternative to be having no work at all. This practice was reported to be more common by publishing freelancers, partly because publishers' fees/hourly rates were widely perceived to be poor, having hardly increased at all in recent years. Accepting poorly-paid projects was more palatable where the client offered the prospect of a secure stream of future work, albeit modestly-rewarded.

> … sometimes there are some articles, quite honestly, I would work on an article and the hourly rate that it converts to is less than the minimum wage. Why would I do it? Well, it's regular work, you can plan your year; you can plan your budget. That's why I do it. (Publishing freelancer 203: female, 65, part-time)

Part-time freelance workers found it difficult to report involuntary temporary/shorter hours as they did not work fixed weekly hours. Freelancers working part-time hours were more likely to be older, semi-retired individuals generally satisfied with their hours of work, though not necessarily with their freelance incomes. Some received other sources of income such as from pensions and property (Publishing freelancers 103, 203). Part-time freelancers have tacitly learned to live with lower incomes because they do not have fixed weekly hours in mind, have narrow client bases, are not proactively seeking additional projects or clients and are not keen to extend work duration.

Summarising, freelancer capacity to control work duration depends heavily on their bargaining power which, in turn, is heavily shaped by client type and resources, level of demand and client dependency on their expertise. Architects possessed greater capacity to choose lucrative projects and to turn down work because clients were typically affluent homeowners heavily dependent on the architect's professional expertise in determining project feasibility and timetables. Publishing freelancers, in contrast, generally worked for publishers who were more knowledgeable with regard to project scheduling and setting fees.

## WORK-TIME SCHEDULING PRACTICES

This section presents data on how freelance workers seek to control work-time scheduling. Freelancers reported a range of practices intended to preserve or extend their control of scheduling, and to resist client colonisation of non-work time. These practices were diverse, but all related to the time-shifting of work obligations, so that freelancers were better able to schedule workloads as they wished, albeit explicitly or tacitly trading off the higher earnings that would result from greater project take-up. This supports Croson and Minniti's (2012) argument that autonomy over working time is often preferred to increased income. We now discuss some of the important practices freelance workers reported to control scheduling.

### Negotiating Attainable Project Timescales

Both architects and publishing freelancers sought to build in 'slack' when negotiating project timescales with clients prior to starting work. Clients may, of course, resist setting longer deadlines where this might cause problems meeting their own customers' deadlines. Book publishers, for instance, organise copy-editing and proofreading functions as distinct phases in production cycles that connect complex supply chains linking authors (who submit manuscripts), jacket designers, layout specialists, illustrators, photographers and indexers, marketing activities and book launch as well as copy-editing and proofreading functions. There may be scope for some flexibility with book publishers although academic journals and magazines publishing monthly or quarterly may operate according to very strict deadlines that allow no flexibility to shift deadlines. Negotiating attainable timescales was common in both publishing and architecture:

> I will just give myself plenty of time – and then I always meet the date. With some people, I deliver things early. So, for example, this book that I'm working on now, even though I want to finish it, they wanted it by next Wednesday. I said 'I'm just worried about getting it in the post in time. How about if it came on Friday, would it be a disaster?' And she said 'No, you can have it until then'. So I probably won't need it, and I'll probably deliver it by the Wednesday, but I just know that I've got that flexibility. Then it also means that when I deliver it early, she'll be like 'Oh! It's come early' – which is quite good … (Publishing freelancer 107: female, 45, full-time)

> I make sure that I always promise things, hopefully, much further away than I need the time to do it because I always think it's better to promise it in two weeks and do

it in a week and a half ... Whereas if you promise it in a week, and do it in a week and a half, there's a different mind-set from the client straight away ... I know that, actually, there are limited hours that I can work and so, as I say, I try not to over-promise. I try to stagger the start of projects, so I'm at different parts on different projects. For example, at the moment ... I'm not taking on any more projects till next year because I've already got so many on ... (Architect 305: female, 45, full-time)

Freelancers are better positioned to secure better project deadlines where clients are heavily dependent on the freelancer's expertise (as in architecture) or where they have long-term or high-trust relations with a client (common in publishing). Where clients can trust freelancers to meet deadlines *and* their own supply chains are not likely to be compromised, they may be willing to negotiate long deadlines. Because architects mostly serve homeowners, there is usually no wider supply chain to consider.

**Working for Local Clients**

Time spent travelling is 'dead time' for freelancers unless they can charge it to clients. Architects working at home emphasised the time savings arising from working for local clients. Architect 306 reported a preference for clients 'within cycling distance' from his home and several others reported a strong preference for working for local clients (Architects 302, 303, 305, 307, 308, 402, 403). Close proximity enabled freelancers to visit clients at their homes several times during the lifetime of a project, both planned and unplanned, and to absorb their cost within the budget. Architects reported meeting clients and their spouses/partners, to be important in assessing whether clients are genuine, likely to be 'labour intensive' and in building a rapport for a relationship that might last up to two years:

It's all house extensions and my furthest away client is about a 5 minute walk. It's crazy. It's just there's so much work around here; it's great. And the fact that my time is very limited, it just saves so many hours in travelling. (Architect 302: female, 43, part-time)

Architects were able to be selective in choosing local clients because of the level of demand for their services. In contrast, publishing freelancers typically work remotely for organisational clients whom they never meet, conducting business and communicating by email and telephone. Client location was therefore less important to publishing freelancers.

## Renegotiating Deadlines

Requesting deadline extensions was reasonably common in publishing. Publishing freelancers reported publishers often delivered manuscripts or draft copy late while retaining the original deadline, compressing the time available to complete copy-editing and proofreading work. Respondents reported that clients varied in their willingness to grant extensions, partly contingent upon the parties' prior relations:

> But if you've kind of developed a good relationship with them and they know that you've delivered, even if you've only done two projects for them before and you delivered them both on time, then they kind of know they can trust you … I think that's the most important thing really is having that trust that people know you're reliable and then if you do say 'Can I have an extra day?' Usually they've already written that in. (Publishing freelancer 107: female, 50, full-time)

For architects, project timescales were typically much longer and deadlines tended to be less rigid than in publishing. Delays arising from external contingencies that could not be anticipated at the planning stage were common. The discovery of on-site problems when supervising construction work such as hidden, natural obstacles or the legal rights of third parties often led to delays.

## Declining Unplanned (and Uncosted) Client Requests

Another common practice, particularly in architecture, was to decline client requests for additional, unplanned – and therefore uncosted – project meetings or site visits (Architecture 301, 304, 305, 306, 307). One architect described a subset of clients as 'labour intensive' (Architect 306), those making, or anticipated to make, substantial demands on their time, for example, by requesting additional meetings, or requesting additional information outside 'normal' work hours – at night, at weekends and even while on holiday having notified clients they would be taking time off. Publishing freelancers referred to similar types of client (103, 107).

## Home-based Freelancing

In principle, home-based working allows freelancers to schedule work as they wish, free from close client supervision. Freelancers are able to choose when to work and when to take breaks for leisure, childcare/family time, caring for elderly relatives, household chores and medical appointments. Working at home also eliminates commuting time (Publishing freelancer 102, 106, 203; Architect 302, 305, 308). Nearly all sample respondents, 22 of the 25, were home-based; only three reported working at clients' premises at the time of interview (Publishing freelancer 104; Architects 309, 401). The power to control work-time scheduling was highly valued by all home-based respondents:

> I think the most important is the times of day that I can work, because I'm not really a morning person. Well, I think, on average, I start work at 10.30 in the morning and finish at around 7 o'clock at night, and have a little break every now and then. And, also, I'm in control of when I work. So that is a big positive for being freelance. (Publishing freelancer 202: female, 50, full-time)

> If I want to take some hours off during the day to go and see an exhibition or do something like that, because it's easier to travel up to town, you don't have the rush, then I'll do that and I'll add those hours at the end of the day and work late in the evening. (Architect 402: male, 85, full-time)

Summarising freelancers in both sectors reported a range of practices to control work-time scheduling, although architects possessed greater power to negotiate attainable deadlines, renegotiate deadline extensions, particularly on long projects, where external contingencies such as regulatory approval were unpredictable, and resist client requests for additional, unbudgeted meetings and site visits. This superior power rested on relations with homeowners dependent on their expertise and the high levels of client demand which enabled architects to be selective about projects. Publishing freelancers typically worked to shorter deadlines and often worked for clients knowledgeable about how long projects should take. Each of these factors enabled architects to schedule work-time in ways that enabled them to control work-time better than publishing freelancers.

## CONCLUSIONS AND IMPLICATIONS

Freelance working reflects, in part, a desire to enjoy greater control over working life decisions. Using qualitative data from interviews with 25 skilled freelance workers in two professional sectors, publishing and architecture, this study has investigated the extent to which freelancers are able to control working time. We present two contributions to the literature on freelance working as a form of small business activity and working time. First, freelance workers vary in their capacity to control work-time, conditional upon the parties' relative bargaining power. This rests, in turn, on a range of client and project characteristics. Freelancers serve different types of clients, form different kinds of relations with them, and take on variable levels of project work. Projects vary with regard to skill demands, timescale and spatio-temporal boundedness. Architects enjoyed high levels of client demand, and tended to work alone on long projects for individual homeowners, all of which enabled them to exercise a high level of influence over work scheduling and duration. Publishing freelancers, in contrast, tended to work for organisational clients on shorter projects where clients were able to estimate timescales, but with lower levels of client demand. Both architects and publishing freelancers typically worked on projects permitting home-based working that did not require close synchronisation with co-workers or clients.

Second, freelance workers engage in a variety of practices to preserve and extend control of work-time scheduling and duration, and to resist client colonisation of non-working time. These practices include winning new, better-paying clients that enable greater discretion over project selection and a range of deadline-shifting activities that trade off a more equitable distribution of working time in place of higher financial rewards. Freelancers are better positioned to control work-time where they stand in an equal bargaining relationship with clients. Architects serving homeowners are in a stronger position to shape project content and scheduling than publishing freelancers serving organisational clients because they possess greater knowledge relative to clients to influence the struggle for work-time control.

The principal implication of our work for theorising and research is to recognise the occupational heterogeneity of freelance work and its variable impact on struggles for work-time control. Working freelance does not necessarily facilitate greater control of working time. Freelancer capacity to control work-time varies across occupations, conditional upon client demand and a range of project and client characteristics, for example, client type, resources and relationship quality. Clients influence the struggle for work-time control through their project design, scheduling and allocation decisions. Temporal unboundedness may be a structural feature of freelance work (Cohen, 2019) but there is variety in the *extent* of unboundedness, and the capacity of freelancers to manage it, even in skilled, professional occupations. Differences between professional and non-professional occupations are likely to be more marked. Freelance workers in non-professional occupations may have more limited powers to control working time.

## NOTES

1.  We are grateful to the British Academy for funding the research upon which the chapter is based.
2.  We substitute the term 'freelance' for 'self-employed' when discussing prior research. This is not ideal because studies do not always distinguish the self-employed without employees – freelancers, as we define them here – from the self-employed *with employees* when presenting findings.
3.  Retainer arrangements might be scrutinised by national tax authorities where they believe freelancer/client relations are really relations between employer and employee.

4. The data are taken from a larger study which also explored the views of freelancers' clients; these data are not reported here. We also conducted Skype/telephone interviews with representatives from three professional and membership organisations to build our knowledge of the publishing industry prior to interviewing freelancers. Respondents were asked about recent changes in the industry, drivers of change and their implications for the use of freelance workers. We also obtained information from an architecture association representative.

## REFERENCES

Annink, A. and L. den Dulk (2012), 'Autonomy: The panacea for self-employed women's work–life balance?', *Community, Work & Family*, **15** (4), 383–402.

Armstrong, V. (2013), 'Women's musical lives: Self-managing a freelance career', *Women: A Cultural Review*, **24** (4), 298–314.

Bailey, O. and A. Madden (2017), 'Time reclaimed: temporality and the experience of meaningful work', *Work, Employment and Society*, **31** (1), 3–18.

Baines, S. and U. Gelder (2003), 'What is family friendly about the workplace in the home? The case of self-employed parents and their children, *New Technology, Work and Employment*, **18** (3), 223–234.

Barley, S. and G. Kunda (2006), 'Contracting: A new form of professional practice', *Academy of Management Perspectives*, **20** (1), 45–66.

Baumberg, B. and N. Meager (2015), 'Job quality and the self-employed: Is it still better to work for yourself?, in Felstead, A., Gallie, D. and Green, F. (eds), *Unequal Britain at Work*, Oxford: Oxford University Press, 105–129.

Baverstock, A., R. Blackburn and M. Iskandarova (2015), 'Who are the independent editors, how did they reach their role and what are their associated job satisfactions?', *Learned Publishing*, **28** (1), 43–53.

Bell, A. and I. La Valle (2003), *Combining Self-Employment and Family Life*, Bristol: Policy Press.

Benz, M. and B. Frey (2008), 'The value of doing what you like: Evidence from the self-employed in 23 countries', *Journal of Economic Behavior & Organization*, **68** (3–4), 445–455.

Bögenhold, D. (2019), 'From hybrid entrepreneurs to entrepreneurial billionaires: observations on the socioeconomic heterogeneity of self-employment', *American Behavioral Scientist*, **63** (2), 129–146.

Broughton, A., R. Gloster, R. Marvell, M. Green, J. Langley and A. Martin (2018), *The Experiences of Individuals in the Gig Economy*, BEIS, https://www.employment-studies.co.uk/resource/experiences-individuals-gig-economy (accessed 14 May 2019).

Burke, A. (2012), 'The entrepreneurship enabling role of freelancers: theory with evidence from the construction industry', *International Review of Entrepreneurship*, **9** (3), 1–28.

Burtch, G.S. Carnahan and B. Greenwood (2018), 'Can you gig it? An empirical examination of the gig economy and entrepreneurial activity', *Management Science*, **64** (12), 5497–5520.

Camerani, R., M. Masucci and J. Sapsed (2015), *Brighton Fuse 2: The Brighton CDIT Cluster Three Years Later, Second Wave Firms Survey*, http://www .brightonfuse.com/brighton-fuse-reports-and-findings/ (accessed 14 May 2019).

CIPD (2017), *To Gig or Not to Gig? Stories from the Modern Economy*, https:// www.cipd.co.uk/knowledge/work/trends/gig-economy-report (accessed 14 May 2019).

Cohen, R.L. (2019), 'Spatio-temporal un-boundedness: A feature, not a bug, of self-employment', *American Behavioral Scientist*, **63** (2), 262–284.

Croson, D. and M. Minniti (2012), 'Slipping the surly bonds: the value of autonomy in self-employment', *Journal of Economic Psychology*, **3** (2), 355–365.

Darcy, C., A. McCarthy, J. Hill and G. Grady (2012), 'Work–life balance: One size fits all? An exploratory analysis of the differential effects of career stage', *European Management Journal*, **30** (2), 111–120.

Dellot, B. (2014), *Salvation in a Start-up? The Origins and Nature of the Self-Employment Boom*, RSA report, https://www.thersa.org/globalassets/ pdfs/blogs/salvation-in-a-start-up-report-180714.pdf (accessed 14 May 2019).

Dex, S., J. Willis, R. Paterson and E. Sheppard (2000), 'Freelance workers and contract uncertainty: The effects of contractual changes in the television industry', *Work, Employment and Society*, **14** (2), 283–305.

European Commission (2016), *Employment and Social Developments in Europe 2015*, Brussels: Directorate-General for Employment, Social Affairs and Inclusion, http://ec.europa.eu/social/main.jsp?catId=738&langId=en& pubId=7859&furtherPubs=yes (accessed 14 May 2019).

Evans, J., G. Kunda and S. Barley (2004), 'Beach time, bridge time, and billable hours: the temporal structure of technical contracting', *Administrative Science Quarterly*, **49** (1), 1–38.

Federation of Small Businesses (FSB) (2016), *Going It Alone, Moving On Up: Supporting Self-employment in the UK*, http://www.fsb.org.uk/ docs/default-source/fsb-org-uk/fsb-supporting-self-employment-uk f15f3abb4fa86562a286ff0000dc48fe.pdf?sfvrsn=0 (accessed 14 May 2019).

Field, F. and A. Forsey (2016), *Wild West Workforce: Self-employment in Britain's 'Gig Economy'*, http://www.frankfield.co.uk/upload/docs/Wild %20West%20Workplace.pdf (accessed 14 May 2019).

Fraser, J. and M. Gold (2001), '"Portfolio workers": Autonomy and control amongst freelance translators', *Work, Employment & Society*, **15** (4), 679–697.

Gold, M. and M. Mustafa (2013), '"Work always wins": client colonisation, time management and the anxieties of connected freelancers', *New Technology, Work and Employment*, **28** (3), 197–211.

Hardy, K. and T. Sanders (2015), 'The political economy of "lap dancing": contested careers and women's work in the stripping industry', *Work, Employment & Society*, **29** (1), 119–136.

Hatfield, I. (2015), *Self-Employment in Europe*, http://www.ippr.org/files/publications/pdf/self-employment-Europe_Jan2015.pdf?noredirect=1 (accessed 14 May 2019).

Hilbrecht, M. and D. Lero (2014), 'Self-employment and family life: Constructing work–life balance when you're "always on"', *Community, Work & Family*, **17** (1), 20–42.

HM Revenue & Customs (HMRC) (2018), *Personal Incomes Statistics 2015 16*, https://www.gov.uk/government/collections/personal incomes -statistics (accessed 14 May 2019).

Huws, U. and others (1996), *Teleworking and Gender*, Brighton: Institute of Employment.

Hyytinen, A. and O.P. Ruuskanen (2007), 'Time use of the self-employed', *Kyklos*, **60** (1): 105–122.

Johannsen Sevä, I. and I. Öun (2015), 'Self-employment as a strategy for dealing with the competing demands of work and family? The importance of family/lifestyle motives', *Gender, Work and Organisation*, **22** (3), 256–272.

Kautonen, T., E. Kibler and M. Minniti (2017), 'Late-career entrepreneurship, income and quality of life', *Journal of Business Venturing*, **32** (3), 318–333.

Keohane, N. (2017), *Rules of Engagement: Reviewing Self-employment and Employment in the UK*, Social Market Foundation, http://www.smf .co.uk/wp-content/uploads/2017/06/5600-SMF-PRISM-Report-WEB-AW -FINAL.pdf (accessed 14 May 2019).

Kirkwood, J. and B. Tootell (2008), 'Is entrepreneurship the answer to achieving work–family balance?', *Journal of Management & Organization*, **14** (3), 285–302.

Kitching, J. (2016), *Exploring the UK Freelance Workforce in 2015*, report for IPSE, https://www.ipse.co.uk/resource/exploring_the_uk_freelance _workforce_in_2016.html (accessed 14 May 2019).

Kitching, J. and D. Smallbone (2012), 'Are freelancers a neglected form of small business?', *Journal of Small Business and Enterprise Development*, **19** (1), 74–91.

Lenton, P. (2017), *Being your own boss: the many faces of self-employment*, Sheffield Economic Research Paper Series, https://www.sheffield.ac.uk/economics/research/serps/articles/2017_003 (accessed 14 May 2019).

Lockey, A. (2018), *Free Radicals*, DEMOS, https://www.demos.co.uk/project/free-radicals/ (accessed 14 May 2019).

Mason, C. and D. Reuschke (2015), *Home Truths: The True Value of Home-Based Businesses*, a report for FSB Scotland, https://www.fsb.org .uk/docs/default-source/fsb-org-uk/policy/rpu/scotland/assets/home-truths ---final.pdf?sfvrsn=1 (accessed 14 May 2019).

Morris, J., C. Farrell and M. Reed (2016), 'How the role of the independent editor is changing in relation to traditional and self-publishing', *Human Relations*, **69** (12), 2274–2297.

Muehlberger, U. (2007), 'Hierarchical forms of outsourcing and the creation of dependency', *Organization Studies*, **28** (5), 709–727.

Office for National Statistics (ONS) (1992), *Quarterly Labour Force Survey, April–June 1992*, ONS, London, data made available from the UK Data Archive.

Office for National Statistics (ONS) (2018a), *Trends in Self-employment in the UK: Analysing the Characteristics, Income and Wealth of the Self-employed*, https://www.ons.gov.uk/employmentandlabourmarket/peopleinwork/ employmentandemployeetypes/articles/trendsinselfemploymentintheuk/ 2018-02-07 (accessed 14 May 2019).

Office for National Statistics (ONS) (2018b), *Quarterly Labour Force Survey, October-December, 2017* [data collection], 3rd edition, UK Data Service. SN: 8326, http://doi.org/10.5255/UKDA-SN-8326-1 (accessed 14 May 2019).

O'Leary, D. (2014), *Going it Alone*, DEMOS, https://www.demos.co.uk/files/ DEMOS_GoingitAlone_web.pdf?1409503024 (accessed 14 May 2019).

Osnowitz, D. and K. Henson (2016), 'Leveraging limits for contract professionals: Boundary work and control of working time', *Work and Occupations*, **43** (3), 326–360.

Platman, K. (2003), 'The self-designed career in later life: A study of older portfolio workers in the United Kingdom', *Ageing & Society*, **23** (3), 281–302.

Platman, K. (2004), 'Portfolio careers' and the search for flexibility in later life', *Work, Employment and Society*, **18** (3), 573–599.

Sappleton, N. and F. Lourenço (2016), 'Work satisfaction of the self-employed: The roles of work autonomy, working hours, gender and sector of self-employment', *International Journal of Entrepreneurship and Innovation*, **17** (2), 89–99.

Shevchuk, A., D. Strebkov and S. Davis (2019), 'The autonomy paradox: how night work undermines subjective well-being of internet-based freelancers', *ILR Review*, **72** (1), 75–100.

Smeaton, D. (2003), 'Self-employed workers: calling the shots or hesitant independents? A consideration of the trends', *Work, Employment and Society*, **17** (2), 379–391.

Stanworth, C. and J. Stanworth (1997), 'Reluctant entrepreneurs and their clients – the case of self-employed freelance workers in the British book publishing industry', *International Small Business Journal*, **16** (1), 58–73.

Stephan, U., M. Hart and C.C. Drews (2015), *Understanding Motivations for Entrepreneurship: A Review of Recent Research Evidence*, https://research.aston.ac.uk/portal/files/15972188/Understanding_motivations_for_entrepreneurship.pdf (accessed 14 May 2019).

Taylor Review (2017), *Good Work: The Taylor Review of Modern Working Practices*, https://www.gov.uk/government/uploads/system/uploads/attachment_data/file/626772/good-work-taylor-review-modern-working-practices.pdf (accessed 14 May 2019).

Tomlinson, D. and A. Corlett (2017), *A Tough Gig? The Nature of Self-Employment in 21st Century Britain and Policy Implications*, Resolution Foundation, http://www.resolutionfoundation.org/publications/a-tough-gig-the-nature-of-self-employment-in-21st-century-britain-and-policy-implications/ (accessed 14 May 2019).

van Gelderen, M. and P. Jansen (2006), 'Autonomy as a start-up motive', *Journal of Small Business and Enterprise Development*, **13** (1), 23–32.

Vermeylen, G., M. Wilkens, A. Fromm and I. Biletta (2017), *Exploring Self-Employment in Europe*, Dublin: European Foundation for the Improvement of Living and Working Conditions.

Wainwright, T. and E. Kibler (2014), 'Beyond financialization: older entrepreneurship and retirement planning', *Journal of Economic Geography*, **14** (4), 849–864.

Williams, M., A. Broughton, N. Meager, K. Spiegelhalter, S. Johal and K. Jenkins (2017), *The True Diversity of Self-Employment: Uncovering the Different Segments of the UK's Self-employed Workforce*, http://www.crse.co.uk/research/true-diversity-self-employment (accessed 14 May 2019).

# Index

Entrepreneurial Personality Test 74
entrepreneurial-skilled employees 92
entrepreneurship
    corporate 93
    emergence of 18–19
    institutionalization of 19
    professorships in 10
Entrepreneurship as Practice (EaP) 3, 29,
    32–4
Entrepreneurship Education (EE) 107,
    108
entrepreneurship policies 12
entrepreneurship scholarship 11, 12
Enumeration Areas (EAs) 79
environmental process 154
EO *see* entrepreneurial orientation (EO)
Essers, C. 30
ethnographic interviewing techniques
    147
European Council for Small Business
    and Entrepreneurship (ECSB) 1
European Union's 2020 Growth Strategy
    141
EU's 2020 Growth Strategy 156
exploratory factor analysis (EFA) 75
external stakeholders 18, 22–4, 26

family-affiliated women 57
family firms (FFs) 48, 54
    analyse effects on 58
    women in 50–52, 56–9
    women-owned 59–60
female entrepreneurs 59
female entrepreneurship 59–60
FFs *see* family firms (FFs)
firms
    entrepreneurial-oriented 93
    with risk-taking behaviour 120
Fiske, D.W. 73
Fletcher, D.E. 145, 146, 156
Frakes, M.H. 74
Frank, H. 20

freelancer-client relations 191
freelancers 190, 192–3, 201, 204, 206
    hours of work 202–3
    in occupations 192
    renegotiating deadlines 207
    working for local clients 206
    work-time control 194–6
    work-time goals 194
Frese, M. 72, 94–5, 99

Gabrielsson, J. 142
Gaia Biomaterials (case study) 149–50
Gartner, W.B. 72
GEM *see* Global Entrepreneurship
    Monitor (GEM)
General Enterprising Tendency (GET)
    scale 75
Ghoshal, S. 9, 21
'gig' economy 11, 20, 190
Gimeno, J. 120
Global Entrepreneurship Monitor (GEM)
    70
Global Warning System (case study)
    152–5
Gnan, L. 48
Gold, M. 193
Gonin, M. 146
Goss, D. 33
Gras, D. 146
Grilli, L. 121
growth orientation, business experience
    and 120–22
Gruber, M. 142
GUESSS (Global University
    Entrepreneurial Spirit Students'
    Survey) 92, 95, 102
Gupta, V. 48, 50

Hall, C.M. 61
Hallward-Driemeier, M. 60
Hamilton, E. 57
Harrison, T.L. 74